The Failure of Sex Education in the Church:

Mistaken Identity, Compromised Purity

*Questions & Answers
for Christian Dialogue*

By Linda D. Bartlett

Published 2014 by Titus 2 for Life
3031 River Road, Iowa Falls, IA 50126

Copyright © 2014 Linda D. Bartlett

ISBN: 149497231X
ISBN 13: 9781494972318

Scripture quotations are from the ESV Bible® (The Holy Bible, English Standard Version®), copyright © 2001 by Crossway Bibles, a publishing ministry of Good News Publishers. Used by permission. All rights reserved.

❖ ❖ ❖

Bartlett has written a "catechism"—an exhaustive and completely honest one at that—outlining a half-century of what she rightly calls "sexual social engineering" in the culture and in the Church. She demonstrates that sex education is a tragically failed experiment in which the Church can no longer participate. She also exposes the dirtiest secret of the sexual revolution, that for many, the end of the sex education path has been the abortion clinic. But, Bartlett does more than diagnose; she proposes a hopeful, radical and thoroughly Scriptural remedy: Parents and grandparents teaching and mentoring children in biblical manhood and womanhood. Her message throughout is, despite all the damage done by sex education, it's not too late.

Todd Wilken,
Host of Issues, Etc.

The breakdown of traditional sexual ethics in society and church is an alarming symptom of a deep-seated malady. Linda Bartlett has the courage to identify some of the root causes of this malady, and to say what has been ailing the Church since the "sexual revolution" of the 20th century. Her wise words deserve to be heard.

Rev. Dr. Benjamin T.G. Mayes
St. Louis, MO., USA

Seduced by the promise that we were helping our children understand them-selves, countless Christian parents have subjected our children to the dangers of living under a false identity. In this groundbreaking book Linda Bartlett, a consummate voice for life, reveals the lie that "sex education" is built upon, and warns us that self-identifying as "sexual beings" is a dead end. Bartlett's call to teach our children purity and to help them live as children of God is a healing word that every Christian parent should hear. I know I want my kids to read it for the sake of their children.

Terry Forke
President Montana District LCMS
Pastor of Trinity Lutheran Church—Harlowton, MT.

We live in a highly sexually centered culture. The world continues to entice the Church with Satan's age old question, "Did God really say...?" The Church must answer with Christ by saying that we are much more than just creatures of sensuality, we are temples of the Holy Spirit and redeemed children of God in Jesus. Linda Bartlett's book nicely lays out a clear way to engage in dialogue for the importance of a thoughtful and God-centered understanding of our identity before God in a sinful world. She affirms how important our ongoing work is to catechize and teach our youth about the faith so that we can articulate our redeemed station before God and its importance over and against the world's sexually defined one.

Rev. Steven Cholak
LCMS Youth Ministry

Linda Bartlett shows great courage as she confronts the sex education enterprise in society, churches and church schools. With careful, well documented research and thorough and prayerful analysis, she traces the history of so-called sex education in schools, universities and society in general. Exposing the misconceptions, false premises and depravity of Alfred Kinsey and his team, some of whom themselves were deviants, she illustrates how it has been embraced by our culture and the Church. She explains how acceptance of these false notions has produced a painful harvest of moral decay, disease and depression. The narrative of this book is built around a solid Christ-centered core of justification by grace through faith, the Bible and historic Christian theology. It constitutes a call to wake up, put aside our fear and indifference, and take action while there is still time. I strongly recommend this book for serious study by parents, pastors, teachers and any concerned Christian.

Pastor Don Richman
Founding Director of the East European Missions Network

In her latest book, Linda Bartlett asks the same question St. Paul did to the Church at Colosse. In Colossians 2:20, Paul asks, "Since you died with Christ to the basic principles of this world, why, as though you still belonged to it, do you submit to its rules?" Linda's research on this topic is second to none. She uncovers the perversity of the Kinsey Report, Margaret Sanger of Planned Parenthood, and Mary Calderone of SIECUS which have become the standard authorities on sexuality in America today. Linda points out how the Christian Church has adopted and accepted some of the basic tenets of these worldly voices when it comes to sex education. This book challenges the Church to return to instruction concerning purity, order of creation, family, and faith. She beckons the Church back to a biblical understanding of humanity and the limits of the young mind to understand sexual content. Her critique is not without recommendations to correct this downward trend in our society. I find her insights to be compelling and her use of biblical narrative to be in accord with the Lutheran Confessions. This is a must read, and I do mean a must read for parents, pastors, and teachers of the Church.

Rev. Brian Saunders, Ph.D.
President of Iowa District East, LCMS

The devil's plan is to desensitize us to what should shock our socks off. If you are a Christian who knows that you ought to be embarrassed about the sexually saturated culture but don't know exactly how to voice your concern, this book will help you put a confession to your thoughts. If you are a Christian who has never placed his views of sexuality under the scrutiny of Scripture, this book will make you think about how much you yourself have been influenced by contemporary sex education. Linda Bartlett exposes the lie about our identity as "sexual beings" and brings to light the truth of our identity as God's children, washed clean of our sins by the blood of Jesus, holy and precious in His sight. "The Failure of Sex Education in the Church" is a wake-up call to parents, pastors, and Christian educators, and a sobering study on a topic (very) often neglected in the Church.

Rev. Stephen K. Preus
Pastor of Trinity Lutheran Church, Vinton, IA

FOREWORD

For decades our churches have operated with the assumption that a Christianized version of sex education would have positive effects on our members, affirming the goodness of sexuality while avoiding the pitfalls of secular approaches. What has resulted instead is a Trojan Horse. Perhaps unwittingly, perhaps not, the language and ideas of sexologists like Alfred Kinsey and John Money—language and ideas which do not have support in God's Word—have made their way into the Church. Now, it is not uncommon to hear Christians describe themselves and their children as "sexual from birth", and identifying themselves by their sexuality.

In *The Failure of Sex Education in the Church: Mistaken Identity, Compromised Purity*, Linda Bartlett puts her finger on the real issue: identity. Through a series of questions and answers, Mrs. Bartlett documents the infiltration of secular ideas regarding sexuality into the Church and the damage it has caused. Decades of sex education in the Church have not resulted in less promiscuity as was hoped. Instruction in purity, she asserts, is a more biblical and holistic approach. Even abstinence education, though well-intended, focuses predominately on sexual intercourse and sexuality rather than addressing biblical manhood and womanhood. The result, according to Mrs. Bartlett, is that children are shown what a great and wonderful thing sex is, but told that they can't do it until they are married. Talking more about sex, in her opinion, is not the answer.

Mrs. Bartlett has done her research. She has taken painstaking care to reveal the origin of sex education. Then she explains how bringing it into Christian classrooms and homes bestows a false identity and compromises purity. Mrs. Bartlett takes no delight in pointing out flaws and failures, but is motivated by love for her own children and grandchildren and by a love for God's Word and Truth. Sometimes it is difficult to admit that we have erred in our thinking or actions. But as Christians, when we recognize our errors, it behooves us to repent, confess those errors, and seek God's grace in Christ. It is Mrs. Bartlett's hope, and mine, that this book will help us all to do this.

Rev. Paul L. Beisel, S.T.M.
Pastor of Immanuel Lutheran Church, Iowa Falls, IA

ACKNOWLEDGMENTS

Confession, they say, is good for the soul. I must confess that I found no joy in writing this book. There was, instead, a great deal of frustration and grief. There were distractions, too, and weariness. When I procrastinated, others affirmed the need to continue. If this book were all about the woes of sex education, I would not have pressed forward to the finish line. This book, however, is about identity. Our identity influences our faith and behavior. This book is also a firm, but gentle reminder: "All Scripture is breathed out by God and profitable for teaching, for reproof, for correction, and for training in righteousness" (2 Tm. 3:16).

When I became a grandmother, I started the mentoring outreach of Titus 2 for Life. Passing on Truth in an ever-changing culture took on new meaning. I dedicate this book to my grandchildren Jaden, Ethan, Andrew, Max, Kate, Leah, Sam, and Lane.

Surely, two are better than one. I thank my husband, Paul, not just for his patient support, but for asking hard questions and bringing clarity to my thought. I thank my accountability group: Dale and Mary, Mark, Karen, Liz, Judy, and Ed. I thank Janet for her professionalism, Mary for her evaluation as an educator, Bob for his thoughtful analysis and historic perspective, Miriam Grossman, M.D., for the "science of sex" that affirms instruction in purity, and Judith A. Reisman, Ph.D., for pursuing truth in the face of evil. I am humbled by Rebecca's encouragement to persevere on this journey and grateful for her discernment, eagle-eye, and many contributions. My pastor, Rev. Paul Beisel, kept me faithful to Scripture and his understanding of the need for this book renewed my zeal.

Above all, I am grateful to my Lord Jesus Christ. He did not come into the world to be like the world but to redeem us from our sin and set us apart from the world. In Baptism, He makes us sons and daughters of God who are called to great purpose. We are holy, not common—made for a life of purity, not bound to sensuality.

Our identity matters.

"[P]resent your bodies as a living sacrifice, holy and acceptable to God, which is your spiritual worship.

Do not be conformed to this world, but be transformed by the renewal of your mind,

that by testing you may discern what is the will of God, what is good and acceptable and perfect."

ROMANS 12:1-2

TABLE OF CONTENTS

Chapter 8   Mature Manhood & Womanhood is Not Sensually Driven · · · 99

Chapter 9   Parents Teach Children God's Design for Love, Sex and Marriage · 111

Chapter 12 The Learning Environment Influences Boys and Girls · · · · 155

INTRODUCTION

Language matters. The words we use matter. What we call something matters. When a woman decides to abort her baby, we ask, "What is it?" We ask the woman, "What is it that you want to abort?" How something is identified determines the value and purpose of that something. It affects what we do with that something.

Together with other pro-life Christians, I reject the language of Planned Parenthood, feminists and evolutionists because it opposes the language of God. When it comes to the unborn child, we cling to the Word of God that creates and identifies human life. But when it comes to the born child, I'm afraid that too many of us have doubted God's Word and accepted the language of others. This language changed the way we view children. It changes the way boys and girls view each other. Thinking ourselves wise, we embraced foolishness. We believed the lie.

What is that lie? It's the one that we've been told and the one that we've repeated for 50 some years. The lie is this: Children are sexual from birth. Have you heard children identified this way? Have you believed it? Do you identify yourself as a "sexual being"?

Years ago, I wrote a little booklet entitled *The Failure of Sex Education*. To my knowledge, no one protested. But when I began writing and speaking about the failure of Christian sex education, there was strong protest. Christian sex education, I was told, was distinctively different from the secular, Planned Parenthood-style education. Besides, I was told, good sex education beginning at an early age would strengthen marriages and help reduce teen pregnancy, abortion, and sexually-transmitted diseases. Good sex education would help boys and girls become "comfortable with their sexuality." Do you ever wonder:

- Why so many Christian parents assume their children will be sexually active?

- Why Christian women dress as provocatively as non-Christian women?

- Why (considering their years of abstinence education) so many Christian girls become pregnant outside of marriage and choose abortion?

- Why so many Christian couples move in together before the wedding?

- Why so many Christian husbands and wives express discontent in their marriage and go looking for "something better"?

- Why a pro-life woman has five children but is not married to any of those children's fathers?

- Why a growing number of Lutheran youth speak against abortion but defend the practice of homosexuality and same-sex "marriage"?

- Why girls from Christian colleges experiment with the lesbian lifestyle?

- Why so many children are sexually abused by a trusted Christian adult?

I believe the answer is the same for all of these questions. *We have been deceived about our identity.* We have believed the lie that "children are sexual from birth."

This lie changes the way we see, hear and obey God.

This lie takes us dangerously close to idolatry. It speaks what God does not and turns our eyes to the created rather than the Creator.

This lie changes the way we view children, what we teach them and what we expect from them. It changes the way we view ourselves.

Many parents, pastors and teachers are worried about the sexualization of boys and girls. The faithful ask, "How could this happen?" I am convinced that it happens when we are mistaken about our identity and purpose. This was brought home to me by 24 women of faith in my relational circle who have confessed their abortions to me. None of them wanted to end the life of their child, yet all accepted abortion as a "necessary evil." Why? It was the "sacrifice" that had to be made "for myself," after all, "I am a sexual being . . . it's who I am." Under the guise of mistaken identity, we compromise purity and faith. We may even position ourselves above our littlest neighbor.

Many Christians want to teach children about "God's gift of sexuality." But is this biblical language? Where does such language encourage us to focus? Where do our eyes turn when we, instead, speak about God's *design* for sexuality? God's design for sexuality is within the boundaries of one man/one woman marriage, but His design for manhood and womanhood is not bound by marriage. To be labeled a "sexual being" shadows our vocations of manhood and womanhood. The girls and women I listen to seem quite familiar with their "sexual identity" but express confusion about their identity as a woman. "I've had years and years of abstinence education," confided a 20-something woman. "It was just more talking about sex on top of all the other sex talk from TV, movies and magazines . . . [W]hy can't we learn about the rest of ourselves?"

God does not call us by our sexuality. God calls us by name (Isa. 43:1). We are not supposed to be captive to desires of the flesh but are to be free in Jesus

Christ to reflect the characteristics of God. We are a "people for his own possession." From that identity flows our purpose, which is to "proclaim the excellencies of him who called you" (1 Pet. 2:9). God tells us to abstain from sensuality, but He does not tell us to abstain from living our lives in different but complementary ways as male and female. Redeemed in Christ, we are set apart from the world, yet needed by the world as models of biblical manhood and womanhood. A man is called to be the steward of creation and defender of life. A woman is called to be man's helper and ally but also to bear and nurture life. Through divinely established roles (or vocations, if you will), men and women bring order out of chaos for generations to come.

God calls us to be holy, not "sexy." Sexuality is not our entire selves nor does it encompass everything. We are fully human—male or female— whether we are a child or an adult, whether we are married or single. Boys can be mentored by men to work, build, protect and engage in life without sensual implications. Girls can be mentored to help, encourage, counsel and build relationships without sensual suggestions.

Every so often a book like this needs to be written, if only to ask: *Who does God say that I am and what does this mean?*

Friends and family can attest to the fact that I did not want to write this book. I did not want to see what I have seen or know what I've discovered. I did not care to write about the woes of sex education. I did not want to point out errors and failures within my church. But life is at risk when God's people doubt His Word or interpret Scripture in light of new information. Sex education, as the social scientists intended, tampers with our identity. And that matters. It matters for eternity.

The silence that shrouds this false identity and takes men, women and children further from God must be broken no matter how odd I might appear. I cannot be silent. To accept that children are human beings and therefore sexual beings is to accept wrong teaching that leads to wrong practice. It bestows a mistaken identity that compromises faith and purity.

The aim of this book is not to malign or speak ill of those teaching sex education. This book is not written to accuse any parent, pastor or teacher of ill-intent but to sound an alarm within the Church. We have not been on guard, carefully discerning between human opinion and God's Word. We have flirted with humanism and embraced skewed social science. This book is written to encourage God's people to repentance, forgiveness and renewed faithfulness in teaching a God-given identity. For the sake of children, we must ask:

- Is how and what Christians teach distinctively different from the world?

- Are we bringing the language of unbelievers into congregations, schools and homes?

- Do we see how the science of neurobiology counters the notion of childhood sexuality but explains why we should not "stir up or awaken love" before its time (Sg. 2:7)?

We are more than sexual beings. We are spiritual beings; body, mind and soul. Therefore, more important than educating in all knowledge of sexuality is the teaching of identity and salvation in Jesus Christ.

It is never too late to repent of our wrong choices and, for the sake of generations, trust God's design for men, women, marriage, family and society. Our Father tenderly calls us from error to new beginnings in Christ. With that in mind, I offer this historical background and set of questions and answers to the Christian community for patient and kind dialogue.

Linda Bartlett

"See to it that no one takes you captive by philosophy and empty deceit, according to human tradition, according to the elemental spirits of the world, and not according to Christ."

COLOSSIANS 2:8

CHAPTER ONE

Worldviews in Conflict

"In the beginning, God created the heavens and the earth" (Gen. 1:1). God created—not by any kind of sexual behavior, but purely by His Word. The Creator of all life set in place proper worship and the Law to keep our lives aligned with His will. The law of marriage is a particular example of God's order found in all cultures. But many religions deviated from Jewish and Christian practice. For example, the gods of Greek, Roman, Egyptian and Hindu religions engaged in all manner of sex with other gods and humans. Men and women were tempted away from lives of purity to follow after sensuality. Sex dominated religion and social life. Alvin J. Schmidt writes,

> [W]hen the early Christians came to Rome, they encountered an extremely low regard for human life. But that was not the only moral depravity that confronted them. Depraved sexual relations were everywhere; they were an integral part of the pagan culture. Christians stepped into a culture that had indeed 'exchanged the truth of God for a lie, and worshiped and served created things rather than the Creator,' and because of this, 'God gave them over to shameful lusts' (Rm. 1:25-26). That is how St. Paul described the Greco-Roman rejection of the natural/moral law.[1]

---

1 Alvin J. Schmidt, *How Christianity Changed the World*, (Zondervan, Grand Rapids, MI., 2004), 79.

Children were not shielded from sexual images. In fact, sex and sexuality were glorified and nothing was considered a disgrace. Into this sexualized culture came the believers in Jesus Christ. Judeo-Christian ethics and morality called for modesty, self-discipline, and the dignity of God's institution of marriage. The marital boundaries of sex between one man and one woman enabled Western civilization to flourish. Men were called to be accountable to wives, children, and generational faithfulness. Women gained new respect. The innocence of children was to be guarded.

God wants His people to be different from the world; however, Christians who live in the world too easily mimic the ways of the world. Western civilization—our American culture, in particular—is crumbling in large part because the Church has failed to be distinctively different from the world. The Church has accepted the help of unbelievers rather than trusting God's Word and using it to shape society. Satan takes care to hide most of his work, but looking closely, one will see a subtle but relentless attempt to destroy the building blocks of society: marriage and family.

Holiness, modesty, and purity—all to God's glory and for the sake of each human life—are in stark contrast to the contemporary invention of sex education. To encourage kind and patient dialogue among parents and Christian leaders, we must first recognize the origin of sex education.

It has been said that Alfred Kinsey is the father of modern sex education. That he may be, but he did not stand alone. Author Timothy Matthews helped me see how deep the gnarly roots of sex education go. I knew that the purposeful sexualization of boys and girls and the changing of their values was weakening society, but who would set out to do such a thing? And why would Christian congregations and educators adopt their own form of sex education?

To better understand the history of sex education, I gathered together all the notes, books and articles I had collected over the years. One particular essay, "The Frankfurt School: Conspiracy to Corrupt"[2] by Timothy Matthews, was especially helpful. What follows are paraphrased portions of Matthews' essay.

The Frankfurt School was a group of Marxist thinkers and writers associated, in part, with the Institute for Social Research at the University of Frankfurt. These theorists, although sometimes loosely affiliated, shared common concerns about the conditions that allow for social change. As a group, these men developed perspectives on contemporary society that diametrically opposed Western civilization shaped by Judaism and Christianity.

In 1922, Vladimir Lenin called a meeting of these men at the Marx-Engels Institute in Moscow. By this time, the Communist International (an organization of communist parties) understood that a political rebellion like that of the Bolshevik Revolution in Russia would never sweep the United States. A social or cultural upheaval with sexual liberation at its core would be far more successful in establishing their desired socialist utopia. Among those present at the meeting were Georg Lukacs and Willi Munzenberg. Lukacs was a Marxist theoretician who had developed the idea of using sexual instinct as an instrument of destruction ("Revolution and Eros"). Munzenberg believed that intellectuals could be used to "make the West so corrupt that it stinks." Other ideas were drawn from Friedrich Nietzsche, Georg Hegel, and Karl Marx.

The philosophical tradition referred to as the Frankfurt School is commonly associated with philosopher, sociologist and social psychologist Max Horkeimer who, in 1930, took over as director. In 1933, when Hitler came to power, the School disbanded and members of the association fled to American institutions of higher learning: Horkheimer to Columbia University, Theodor Adorno to Princeton University, writer Eric Fromm to Michigan State and

---

2 Timothy Matthews, "The Frankfurt School: Conspiracy to Corrupt," *Catholic Insight*, 2009, Accessed on-line publication November 20, 2011 from www.CatholicInsight.com, Accessed Scribd publication August 5, 2013 from www.scribd.com/doc/28282102/The-Frankfurt-School-Conspiracy-to-Corrupt-by-T-Matthews.

Washington School of Psychiatry, Leo Lowenthal to UCLA- Berkeley, Jurgen Habermas to Northwestern University in Illinois, and Herbert Marcuse to Columbia, Harvard and Brandeis Universities. Marcuse, the 1960s guru of the New Left, is the author of *Eros and Civilization,* which argues for a greater tolerance of eroticism than permitted by the status quo. Marcuse believed that a tolerant attitude toward sexuality would lead toward a more satisfying life. He is remembered as a philosopher of America's sexual revolution.

The Frankfurt School knew that a social or cultural revolution required two important elements:

- *The rights of parents as primary educators and protectors of their children had to be removed.* One way for this to be achieved was Lukacs' idea of "Revolution and Eros." Raising children to focus on their "sexual instincts" would, in time, corrupt society's values, order and decency. The purpose of human life would come into question. In sexual chaos, a completely different worldview and form of government could assume control.

- *The Judeo-Christian legacy that had shaped Western civilization had to be undermined.* The Frankfurt School was well aware that as long as an individual believed and hoped that his or her divine gift of reason could solve problems facing society, then hopeless-ness that generally provokes a social revolution would never occur. The Frankfurt School and its followers had to steadily assault Christianity and, thus, remove hope.

Some may believe that Matthews' use of the words "conspiracy" and "cor-rupt" in the title of his essay are sensational. Perhaps they are. But it is for that reason that I read more about some of the members of the Frankfurt School, so that I could discern for myself what they taught and what they opposed. Each of us has a worldview, a belief in something that causes us to think what we think and do what we do. Christianity is a worldview based on Creation, The Fall, and Redemption. Atheism, socialism, or any other worldview is based on a different foundation. To remove one foundation and replace it with another, one must begin chipping away. This is not "conspiracy talk." This is an illustration of two worldviews at odds. The consequences of each are very different. God creates and sustains human life. All who oppose God corrupt and weaken what He has made.

Those who oppose God are always busy. But they show their shrewdness when they know where to attack and how to affect change. To establish their vision of a socialist utopia, the Frankfurt School and other humanists had to weaken the foundation of society, which is marriage and family. This could be accomplished with the devaluation of fatherhood, diminished differences between men and women, dependency on the state rather than God, and a focus on pleasure. Expedient to their cause would be control of the media, altered identity, changed moral and legal codes, and children saturated in sex and sexuality. In his book *Brave New World*, Aldous Huxley writes about sexualizing children as a way for the State to control the people. Chapter four of George Orwell's book *1984* explains how people are controlled by giving them pornography. Thomas Sowell is Senior Fellow on Public Policy at the Hoover Institution, Stanford University. In his article "Indoctrinating the Children," he explains that effective techniques for conditioning children "include emotional shock and desensitization . . . stripping away defenses . . . and inducing acceptance of alternative values."[3]

THE UTOPIAN LIE

Utopian thinking concludes that humans are untainted by sin, capable of obtaining perfection, and set free of social constraint and old ways. In contrast, the biblical worldview of Christianity affirms that humans are corrupted by sin, in need of a Savior, and the most free within God's boundaries for life.

---

3   Thomas Sowell, "Indoctrinating the Children," *Forbes*, February 1, 1993, 65.

Christians, too, sometimes operate with a utopian worldview. In their desire to return to the beautifully perfect sexual union of the first husband and wife, some Christian educators believe in teaching about the beauty of human sexuality beginning young and continuing to older age. But this is an adaptation of the secular or worldly model and does not take into account the role of desire and lust in human decision-making. Christians may claim to be different by using God's Word as they give knowledge about sex and sexuality. I do not question the best of intentions. We may desire to teach children an appreciation of God's gift of sexuality but, for the sake of these children, we dare not disregard sin. We must be faithful to help children daily battle Satan, the world, and their own sinful nature. What was declared "good" by God in the Garden of Eden suffered from the consequence of the Fall. In this world, we will never enjoy the perfect beauty of the Garden because we are inclined to pride and the self-centered ways of sin.

Those who oppose the biblical worldview of life, marriage, and family are always ready to challenge God's Word. Followers of the Frankfurt School believed that a socialist utopia could be established by way of cultural change. That change required sexual liberation which would weaken the family and, in time, erode American vitality and strength. What was the sexual revolution of the 1960s if not a social movement that challenged traditional codes of behavior related to sexuality and relationships? Americans increasingly accepted sex outside of traditional heterosexual, monogamous marriage. The Pill, undressing of American women, normalization of premarital sex and homosexuality, pornography, and the legalization of abortion all followed. What do you see in America today? Is human life of greater or lesser value since the 1960s and early 1970s? What is the state of the family? Is there evidence that sexual freedom trumps religious freedom in education and health care?

For more than thirty years, I have watched the subtle but determined revolution against God's Word with regard to what God says about men, women, and children. The breakdown of the family, legalized abortion, euthanasia, and same-sex "marriage" happens when we are deceived about our identity.

When we identify ourselves not as God does but as we so desire, then we and our neighbors are at risk. When we determine for ourselves what is right or wrong in any given circumstance, then we and our neighbors are at risk. Satan uses every deceptive tool against the humans God so loves.

> The breakdown of the family, legalized abortion, euthanasia, and same-sex "marriage" happens when we are deceived about our identity.

THE REALITY OF EVIL

In 1991, during my earliest leadership days with Lutherans For Life (LFL), we brought Dr. William Coulson to Iowa as a presenter.[4] Some of us in the pro-life community had concerns about sex education. We questioned the source and methodology as well as the behaviors and lifestyles of young men and women who had experienced classroom sex education in either public or parochial schools. We knew that Dr. Coulson left a lucrative practice in humanist psychology and behavioral sciences because he began to see destructive effects in the Church and society. Would Dr. Coulson's experience shed some light on sex education? We needed to hear what he had to say.

Dr. Coulson was a disciple of the influential psychologist Carl Rogers. He was intrigued by Rogers' use of non-directive psychotherapy or the theory that people can appeal to their conscience as an authority. "[A]s a practicing Catholic layman, I thought that was pretty holy: that God was available to every person who had a decent upbringing, that he could self-consult, as it were, and hear God speaking to him . . . that the conscience can provide access to the Holy Spirit." [5] Common to humanistic psychotherapy was the use of

---

4 Dr. William Coulson, "Values in the Classroom," a series of presentations in Ames, Waterloo and Grinnell, IA., April 1991.

5 Dr. William Coulson, interview by Dr. William Marra, "We Overcame Their Traditions, We Overcame Their Faith," *The Latin Mass*, Vol. 3, No. 1, January-February 1994, accessed August 15, 2012, www.scribd.com/doc/3983186/Coulson.

encounter groups. The encounter session (sometimes called training groups, sensitivity training or human relations) was first conceived as a behavioral research technique with a goal to change the standards, attitudes and behavior of individuals. In a classroom setting, students are encouraged to learn about themselves as they focus on a particular topic and interact with one another using problem-solving and role-playing. Coulson notes that this became a recommended practice of the National Educational Association (NEA).

Coulson was a man of faith who believed that every person is precious. He wanted to help the people he worked with to be better, but his use of encounter groups was a dangerous blend of humanism and Christianity. For example, Rogers and Coulson would speak of "glorious" human potential because "we are the children of a loving Creator who has something marvelous in mind for every one of us." However, Coulson confessed, "We failed to understand the reality of evil in the human life."

> "We failed to understand the reality of evil in the human life.
>
>

Coulson said, "When we implied to people that they could trust their impulses, they also understood us to mean that they could trust their evil impulses, that they weren't really evil. But they were evil."[6]

Coulson continued, "Humanistic psychology, the kind that has virtually taken over the Church in America, and dominates so many forms of aberrant education like sex education and drug education, holds that the most important source of authority is within you, that you must listen to yourself. . . . [W]e created a miniature utopian society: the encounter group." What was the result? In the words of Coulson: "A disaster."[7]

---

6 Quotes are from this author's personal notes taken during Dr. William Coulson's presentation, "Values in the Classroom," on April 13, 1991 at St. Paul Lutheran Church in Ames, IA.

7 Personal notes of this author.

Coulson became chief of staff at Rogers' Western Behavioral Sciences Institute in California. He was entrusted with the task of conducting a pilot study using humanistic psychotherapy in encounter groups with the faculty and students of The Order of the Sisters of the Immaculate Heart of Mary (I.H.M.). If Coulson's work at this college for women was a success, he knew he would have a positive influence on the ways the sisters lived and governed themselves as well as the development of so-called normal Catholic family life. Less than two years into the experiment, however, Coulson recognized his work in Catholic education to be a failure.

On an April day in 1967, Coulson met with 600 nuns gathered in the school's gymnasium. "I showed them a film about the encounter group. . . . It looked pretty holy. People in the film seemed to be better people at the end of the session than they were when they began. . . . They were open with one another, less deceitful."[8] The women went along with the encounter sessions and self-exploration because they trusted Coulson. He wouldn't hurt them because, after all, he was a Catholic, too.

Coulson's work with the faculty and students of I.H.M. had life-changing and destructive effects. He referred to a sad little book that documents the tragedy entitled *Lesbian Nuns, Breaking Silence.* [9] Sister Mary Benjamin, involved in the I.H.M. encounter group, was seduced by an older nun desiring to be more expressive of her true self. Benjamin was stricken with guilt. She talked to a priest but, already under the influence of humanistic psychology, that priest consulted himself and decided that the young woman's decision was personal. He chose not to judge Sister Mary Benjamin and, instead, let her decide for herself what was right or wrong. The I.H.M. ran some 60 schools before the pilot study with the encounter group began. At the end, they had one. There were some 600 nuns initially, but within a

---

8 Coulson, "We Overcame Their Traditions, We Overcame Their Faith," (interview), *The Latin Mass.*

9 Rosemary Curb, Nancy Manaham, *Lesbian Nuns, Breaking Silence,* (Naiad Press, 1985).

year of Coulson's first intervention, 300 of them were petitioning Rome to get out of their vows because they did not want to be under any authority but their own.

Coulson wanted to help, to make a positive difference. But the I.H.M. school closed. It ceased to exist. "We wanted to help make the nuns of I.H.M. better than they were," Coulson said, but "we destroyed them— and their faith." Coulson remembered one mother "who pulled her daughter out before it closed, saying, 'Listen, she can lose her faith for free at the state college.'"[10]

Coulson's testimony strikes at the heart of modern sex education in Christian schools. The I.H.M. community allowed the use of humanist psychology in its schools with faculty and students because it wanted to be progressive but, explained Coulson, "we provoked an epidemic of sexual misconduct among clergy and therapists." [11] Although Rogers, for example, "didn't get people involved in sex games, he couldn't prevent his followers from doing it, because all he could say was, 'Well, I don't do that.' Then his followers would say, 'Well, of course you don't do that, because you grew up in an earlier era; but we do, and it's marvelous: you have set us free to be ourselves and not carbon copies of you.'"[12]

The sex education classroom, intentionally or not, can too easily become an encounter group. We should take special note that Coulson and his wife pulled their children out of Catholic schools when sex education was introduced. He knows firsthand how Catholic education has been influenced by humanistic psychology. Coulson's warning to concerned Christian parents and grandparents is chilling: "The net

---

10 Coulson, "We Overcame Their Traditions, We Overcame Their Faith." (Author's Note: To hear Dr. Coulson tell his story, you may order Tape #2-001 from *Issues, Etc.*, entitled "A Dangerous Trip: The Encounter Dynamic," *www.issuesetc.org*)

11 Coulson, "We Overcame Their Traditions, We Overcame Their Faith"

12 Coulson, "We Overcame Their Traditions, We Overcame Their Faith"

outcome of sex education, styled as Rogerian encountering, is more sexual experience."[13]

In the best interest of our children and grandchildren, there are important questions to be asked. What are the consequences of putting boys and girls in a classroom where, together, they can encounter new emotions, perspectives and celebrations of sexuality? In trying to help boys and girls—beginning at a young age—to appreciate what some Christians call "God's gift of sexuality," what interpretation of God's Word is given? What is the effect on each individual child's learning process and decision-making? Every educator should have objective and measureable goals for their students. What are the goals of Christian sex education and how are they measured? Have students who have been through Christian sex education been evaluated? If so, what do those evaluations reveal?

> "The net outcome of sex education, styled as Rogerian encountering, is more sexual experience."
>
>

THE SEXUAL NETWORK

In 2002, I stepped down from the role of Lutherans For Life president to start Titus 2 for Life. So many Lutheran women had confessed their abortion choices to me. They detailed the physical, emotional, and spiritual suffering. But they also gave me reason to dig beneath the symptom of abortion to learn why so many Christian women become sexually intimate and pregnant outside of marriage. Abortion, I was convinced, becomes thinkable only after men and women are deceived about their identity and purpose. Women who have had an abortion tend to see themselves (and, thus, their babies) not as God sees them, but as the world sees them. They find identity in their sexuality or sensuousness. They measure their value

---

13 Coulson, "We Overcame Their Traditions, We Overcame Their Faith"

by words of love or the attention of others. In so many words, they have told me, "God made me sexual; it's who I am." But is it?

Emphasis on human sexuality can change the way we view ourselves and others. It should not be surprising, then, that some people would utilize sex education as a powerful tool for social engineering or cultural change. I am but one of many parents who has watched the network of evolution, sex education, values clarification, and moral relativism assault the sanctity of human life, the institutions of marriage and family, and the culture in which our sons and daughters-in-law are raising our grandchildren.

The ideology and subtle efforts of the Frankfurt School paved the way for acceptance of Alfred Kinsey's description of children as "sexual from birth." Few people have done more to assault the family by encouraging focus on "sexual instincts" than Kinsey. In the decades following World War II, Kinsey ushered in sexual anarchy in the name of "liberation." But this so-called liberation would actually separate men and women from their God-given identity and true freedom.

Kinsey, a professor of zoology at Indiana University, began his formal sex research when asked by the Association of Women Students to create a course on human sexuality. "Surprised by the alleged dearth of source materials," writes Dr. Judith A. Reisman, "he set out to fill the void with his own research." [14] Dr. Reisman spent over 30 years researching the work of Kinsey and those who adopted his horrifying theories of sexuality. She exposed the scientific fraud and criminally-derived data contained in the publicly-funded Kinsey Reports. Kinsey's work affected marriage, family, the Church, and institutions of higher learning before gutting the tough laws in America that kept pornography and predators at bay. Kinsey was not, according to Reisman, a gentleman. He defamed the values of one

---

14 Judith A. Reisman, Ph.D., *Kinsey: Crimes and Consequences*, (Crestwood, KY: The Institute for Media Education, Inc., 2000), 17.

generation and gave sons and daughters license to uninhibited sexuality. His so-called science was abusive and broke the law; nevertheless, it turned the heads of Christians and non-Christians, teachers and parents, legal judges and ministers of the Gospel.

"Kinsey was our first and loudest sex educator," writes Reisman. "[O]ne man's psychopathic mission—and the eagerness of opinion-molders who could propagate it—repudiated the Greatest Generation and normalized decadence in the United States. What's more, Kinsey's work was translated into a dozen languages, seeding a new, Western international academic field: sexology."[15] In 1960, the Conference on Children and Youth advocated bringing Kinsey-style sex education into all educational institutions. [16] In 1967, the American Society for Sex Educators, Counselors, and Therapists (ASSECT) was formed and in 1968 the Institute for the Advanced Study of Human Sexuality (IASHS) opened its doors. Both entities trained in "Kinseyan sexuality," and shortly after, child sex abuse and incest were endorsed in pornography magazines by those trained sexologists.[17] "In 1970, Playboy Enterprises funded a University of Minnesota program to 'change the attitudes of men and women medical students' toward sexuality; using pornography to 'desensitize' future doctors to their patients' sexual peculiarities."[18] By 1968, homosexual activists Deryck Calderwood and Kenneth George were both giving Kinseyan sex education certificates to students. Wardell Pomeroy, one of Kinsey's intimate partners, was busy creating the Sex Information and Education Council of the United States (SIECUS) using funds from Hugh Hefner.[19] Although AIDS and HIV resulted from the code of

---

15 Judith A. Reisman, Ph.D., *Sexual Sabotage*, (Washington, D.C: WorldNetDaily, WND Books, 2010), 176.

16 Reisman, *Sexual Sabotage*, 178

17 Reisman, *Sexual Sabotage*, 178

18 Reisman, *Sexual Sabotage*, 179

19 Reisman, *Sexual Sabotage*, 53, 178. (Author's Note: SIECUS was first launched in 1964 under the name Sex Information and Education Council of the U.S. but later changed its name to Sexuality Information and Education Council of the U.S.)

Kinseyan promiscuity they, ironically, became the convincing argument to get AIDS awareness and human sexuality into both public and parochial schools.

There's something else quite ironic. Since the 1970s, promoters of sex education in both public and parochial schools have claimed that enlightening boys and girls about their sexuality would nurture a healthy openness in place of unnecessary modesty, sexual health instead of sexual "hang-ups," and a freedom from guilt. The programs have also been promoted as an appropriate societal and even religious response to the crisis of teenage pregnancy. Today, sex education, birth control and abortion are pillars of a powerful industry funded by massive federal grants. If we Christians do our homework, we will discover an unholy alliance between Planned Parenthood, SIECUS, and the population control or eugenics movement.

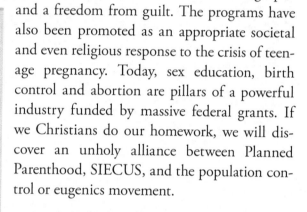

Today, sex education, birth control and abortion are pillars of a powerful industry funded by massive federal grants.

❖ ❖ ❖

A growing emphasis on sexuality has transformed secular and Christian education, the media, music, fashion, health care, and the military. Over the years, as I worked with youth and their parents, I could see how the dress, language, and behavior of many Christians were influenced by a growing comfort with anything sexual or sensuous. However, there was limited understanding of or appreciation for the vocations of biblical manhood and womanhood. Human life is placed more at risk when men and women, married or single, do not understand their valuable roles. If we are all just "sexual beings," might we be tempted to give ourselves more latitude in our thinking and behavior because, after all, "it's who I am"? How will this affect relationships? Will protective emotions of shame and guilt be diminished? When we make choices based on who we think we are rather than on who God calls us to be, might we be in danger of moving farther away from God?

The sexual social engineering already at play in my youth of the 1960s had life-altering consequences for my sons' generation. By the time my sons were in high school, I was well aware of SIECUS and Planned Parenthood. A book titled *The SIECUS Circle: A Humanist Revolution*[20] explains the philosophy and comprehensive goals of the humanist revolution and provides detailed information on 35 humanist organizations, including Planned Parenthood. Mary Calderone, the first director of SIECUS, had close ties to Planned Parenthood; in fact, in 1980, she received the Margaret Sanger award from Planned Parenthood. The goals of SIECUS and Planned Parenthood were strangely similar to those of the Frankfurt School. They included merging or reversing the roles of male and female, liberating children from their parents, and abolishing the family as we know it.[21] With all of this in mind, I volunteered to serve on the committee that would select the health and human development curricula at my sons' school. I had done my homework and knew that "health and human development" was synonymous with sex education. However, I was chosen to serve only as a token parent. The curriculum had already been selected.

Did anything good come from that experience? Yes. One of the members of the school committee was a pastor. He and I often stayed after meetings to discuss our perspectives on sex education, abortion, and family matters. He assumed that children were going to be sexually active. He told me that he had taken a young girl for an abortion because he didn't think the parents would be supportive of their daughter's pregnancy. We never agreed with one another, but our conversations were respectful. The most positive outcome of serving on that school committee was that I was motivated to organize a small parent group to dialogue on sex education. We informed ourselves about what was happening not just in our public school but nationwide. By 1997, I was not only sharing

---

20 Claire Chambers, *The SIECUS Circle: A Humanistic Revolution*, (Belmont, MA: Western Islands Press, 1977).

21 Chambers, *The SIECUS Circle*, 14.

what I'd learned as a pro-life and family speaker to teens and parents but, with two other moms, I co-founded the pregnancy center called Lighthouse Center of Hope in my hometown of Iowa Falls, Iowa. In 2005, I authored *The Failure of Sex Education*[22] with the hopes of helping other Christian parents recognize the origin and philosophy of sex education.

Valerie Riches is another wife and mother who was concerned enough about sex education to carefully research its origins and philosophical ideas. Neither of us speaks as academics but as moms who care. We ponder and investigate for the sake of generations of children and the well-being of society. Mrs. Riches, a member of Britain's Family and Youth Concern, writes, "[Sex education] is a vehicle to spread an amoralism that is destructive of the family and of society." Of greatest concern, she continues, "is the very fabric of society, the very future of the human race."[23]

Mrs. Riches began with careful scrutiny of the Family Planning Association (FPA), the British equivalent of America's Planned Parenthood. She writes:

> What we unearthed was a power structure with enormous influence. Deeper investigation revealed that the network in fact extended further afield, into eugenics, population control, birth control, sexual and family law reforms, sex and health education. Its tentacles reached out to publishing houses; medical, educational and research establishments, women's organizations and marriage guidance—anywhere where influence could be exerted. It appeared to have great influence over the media and over permanent officials in

---

22 Linda Bartlett, *The Failure of Sex Education* (Nevada, IA: Lutherans For Life, 2005), www.lutheransforlife.org or www.cph.org.

23 Valerie Riches, *Sex and Social Engineering*, Family and Youth Concern (The Responsible Society, 1986), 29, accessed May 20, 2012, www.amen.ie/downloads/SEXANDSOCIAL-ENGINEERING.pdf.

relevant government departments, out of all proportion to the numbers involved. During our investigations, a speaker at a Sex Education Symposium in Liverpool outlined tactics for sex education, saying: 'If we do not get into sex education, children will simply follow the mores of their parents.' The fact that sex education was to be the vehicle for peddlers of secular humanism soon became apparent.[24]

> "The fact that sex education was to be the vehicle for peddlers of secular humanism soon became apparent."
>
>

It is one thing to suggest that parents might be inadequate in teaching the truths of physics. But to undermine their God-given authority in the area of spiritual, moral and social behavior is a serious matter with a myriad of consequences for society.

IS SEX EDUCATION IN THE CHURCH DISTINCTIVELY DIFFERENT?

When my husband and I knew our sons were ready to learn more about their bodies, the created differences between male and female, and God's careful placement of sex in the faithful marriage between one man and one woman, we purchased books from the *Learning About Sex* series from Concordia Publishing House to help us with the task. We trusted the publisher; however, something troubled me as I began to read from the book for parents:

> It may be surprising to realize that our children are sexual beings from birth. For instance, a parent changing a male infant's diaper may accidentally stimulate the child and be

---

24 Riches, *Sex and Social Engineering*, 6.

shocked to realize the child is having an erection. Similarly, researchers tell us that baby girls have vaginal lubrication regularly. In fact, a little girl being bounced on her parent's knee may feel pleasant sensations and begin to make natural pelvic thrust movements.[25]

I had every confidence that the book for parents, together with the complete series (beginning with pre-kindergarten), was written with the intent of being faithful to God's Word. But on our sons' behalf, I had important questions:

- Who were the "researchers" being quoted?

- From where did the phrase *sexual beings from birth* originate?

- Does sex education promote instruction in purity or hinder it?

- Is sex education in the Church distinctively different from non-Christian?

- How does God identify us?

In recent years, the publishers of this book made some positive changes after listening to concerned parents. I am grateful to one editor in particular who met with me on several occasions over a period of years. He took care to listen and then asked me to share with him my written notes. He addressed some of my concerns. For example, my most simple but biblically sound request was this: Please don't follow the SIECUS model[26] by putting boys and girls together in the classroom as if "equal" means "being the same" and desensitizing them through intimate discussions of sexuality. In other words,

---

25 Lenore Buth, *How To Talk Confidently with Your Child about Sex*, Book 6 of the *Learning About Sex for the Christian Family* series (St. Louis, MO: Concordia Publishing House, 1982, 1988, 1995, 1998), 23.
26 Chambers, *The SIECUS Circle*, 12

please make the books specific to boy or girl so that parents and teachers can mentor boys to be biblical men and girls to be biblical women. Thankfully, *Sex and the New You* (ages 13-15) was rewritten as two separate books, one for boys and one for girls. The re-write of *Love, Sex and God* (ages 15 and up) allowed the girls' book to include an excellent discussion on modesty with respectful warnings against provocative dress and behavior that wasn't included in the previous book for boys and girls together.

However, concerns remain. The most recent edition of the parent book quoted above still contains reference to an infant boy's "stimulation" and a baby girl's "vaginal lubrication." After noting this, the author writes, "Yet somehow the thought of a child's sexual nature is vaguely disturbing to many adults."[27] What is meant by "a child's sexual nature"? Are Christians under the wrong influence?

I believe we are. In 1961, the National Council of Churches hosted a conference on church and family with Mary Calderone, co-founder of SIECUS, speaking on the role of the church and sex education. Five hundred delegates from 38 Protestant denominations attended.[28] That same year, Concordia Publishing House published *Sex and the Church* edited by Oscar E. Feucht. In the book, Kinsey is introduced as "presenting facts about sexual behavior."[29] Kinsey's book, *Sexual Behavior in the Human Male*, is referenced throughout the book as authoritative on sex practices in America.[30] "Table C" in Feucht's book is a sexual assessment of members of the Lutheran Church-Missouri Synod (LCMS) based on the Kinsey statistical model.[31] This book, co-authored by two professors from Concordia Seminary, St. Louis, Missouri, and endorsed by the president of Concordia

---

27 Buth, *How To Talk Confidently with Your Child about Sex*, (2008), 26.

28 Chambers, *The Siecus Circle*, 259.

29 Oscar E. Feucht, et al., *Sex and the Church* (St. Louis, MO: Concordia Publishing House, 1961), 7.

30 Feucht, et al., *Sex and the Church*, 7, 99, 187.

31 Feucht, et al., *Sex and the Church*, 248.

Seminary, Springfield, Illinois, notes that "the Church has some new things to learn from the social sciences with regard to sex education."[32] Many sexologists are referenced in the book, including humanists associated with SIECUS.[33]

My own church body re-interpreted Scripture in light of "new" information presented by "social scientists." Here are two examples:

> My own church body re-interpreted Scripture in light of "new" information presented by "social scientists."
>
>

... there is emerging a kind of thought and concern about sex in relation to the total person under God, a structure of thinking and teaching which *unites what modern knowledge and insight have given us* with the traditional concern and intent of Christian doctrine, which needs to be described forcefully and adequately enough so that the thinking of the church might be deepened and expanded[34] ... there are some old facts and *new facts* about which there should be an expanded openness of discussion, some deepening understanding of Christian points of view, and therefore something new to be said."[35] (Emphasis mine.)

How have these social scientists influenced marriage and family? It may seem a small thing, but in the section on marriage in the girl's book, *Love, Sex and God*, we read:

---

32 Feucht, et al., *Sex and the Church*, 210.

33 Author's note: Humanists and SIECUS-affiliated "social scientists" referenced in Feucht's book include William G. Cole, Evelyn Duvall, Seward Hiltner, Jerome Himelhoch and Sylvia F. Fava.

34 Feucht, et al., *Sex and the Church*, 9-10.

35 Feucht, et al., *Sex and the Church*, 10.

"Of course Christians, like anyone else, are affected by the times in which they live. Old-fashioned marriages were far less likely to end in divorce than marriages today. Each person had clearly spelled-out duties, and neither expected more than a reasonable amount of comfort and security.

"People today expect marriage to be a loving, deeply intimate joining of two equal partners. That's much more demanding than the old-style marriage. The partners must work together to set realistic goals for themselves . . ."[36]

Let's pause for a moment to remember an objective of the Frankfurt School and others whose worldview opposes Christianity. They sought to liberate children from parents and abolish the family. Without realizing it, are we contributing to the generation gap and breakdown of the family when we miss opportunities to mentor perseverance and encourage by way of lessons learned? Discussions with my grandmother helped me understand that relationships between men and women in a sinful world have always been difficult. Marriage, which unites two completely different sexes with different personalities and from different backgrounds, has been a challenge since the Fall. What were my parents' and grandparents' reasons for resisting divorce? I needed to know. Can we really infer that husbands and wives of previous generations didn't experience fears, doubts and emotions similar to ours when it comes to love and marriage? Is it fair to say that they really didn't expect any more than a "reasonable amount of comfort and security"? If we were to say to our great-grandparents, "Certainly, your marriage was less difficult and demanding than modern marriage," would they agree? What circumstances did husbands and wives of the past have to endure? Were they not also challenged to be partners who worked together and, if so, how did they accomplish that? Here, then, is an opportunity to do exactly what every Christian parent is called to do: Tell your children

---

36 *Love, Sex and God*, Book 5 of the *Learning About Sex for the Christian Family* series, (St. Louis, MO: Concordia Publishing House, 2008), 81.

and grandchildren about the things God has done in your life so that they, too, might set their hope in God. (See Psalm 78:2-8)

Today's parents, not unlike parents of previous generations, find themselves challenged to raise their children in a world corrupted by sin. They need the help of a Church that resists the social experiments of sex education, abortion, and same-sex "marriage" that tamper with God's creation. The Body of Christ should insist that Christian publishers provide books on manhood and womanhood, marriage, sex, and family distinctively different from the world. There is no reason to be bound to the social-science of secular humanists or our own error in accepting their "science" as fact. There is true, tested and ethical science available to the Church that bears witness to God's amazing creation of male and female; explains the influence of hormones such as oxytocin on decision-making; uses neurobiology to explain why too-much, too-soon information can't help a child whose prefrontal cortex is not yet developed; and supports the generational mentoring of patience, self-control, and a lifestyle of purity. I am optimistic.

> There is no reason to be bound to the social-science of secular humanists or our own error in accepting their "science" as fact.
>
>

A mature Christian does well to acknowledge mistakes and then set about correcting them and learning from them. However, two obstacles come to mind: the Enemy of life and our own pride. The Word of God overpowers them both. The Church can make a difference by faithfully contrasting the Word with the sensual world. This means continuing to dialogue and asking some hard questions:

- Is there evidence to prove that sex education introduced into Christian communities leans the wrong way because it is built on the wrong foundation?

- If we looked carefully, how much language of Kinsey, SIECUS, and secular humanism would we find in sex education materials published and promoted by the Church?

- Who told us that "children are sexual from birth"? Does this affect what we expect from them? Does it affect how they view themselves? Is this how God sees children?

- Is it a good thing to raise sexual awareness for boys and girls in the same classroom?

- Does the theory of "more information, the earlier the better" complement the science of neurobiology?

- Is lots of sex talk in Jesus' name good for children? Does it help them combat the media and sexual predators? In what ways do we give children a break from this topic?

- Has sex education in the Church produced the outcome desired by those who teach it?

- Considering the daily battle with Satan, the world and our own sinful flesh, is it a good idea to accentuate a young person's identity as being "sexual"?

Danger lurks when we let sexuality shape our identity.

The Church confessing Jesus Christ is called to be distinctively different from the world, but there is nothing different when:

> **Danger lurks when we let sexuality shape our identity.**
>
>

- parents are encouraged to let experts in human sexuality teach their children.

- children are taught in a "one-size fits all" classroom.

- natural childhood innocence is disregarded in favor of open discussions about intimate topics by boys and girls.

- modesty is considered a "thing indifferent" and offensive to feminists.

- fear becomes the driving impetus for teaching something God does not.

- parents rush to sex education rather than the patient study of biblical manhood and womanhood.

The questions bear repeating: Why are so many Christians sexually intimate outside of marriage?[37] Why do so many Christians have abortions or defend them as a woman's choice?[38] Do you think it possible that sex education plays a key factor? Even back in the early days of sex education, the numbers should have warned us of what was to come. A survey of 6,000 young women in 1984 revealed that fifteen-year-old girls who had had sex education were 40 percent more likely to begin sex activity than girls not having the instruction.[39] A Lou Harris poll, commissioned

---

37   Gene Edward Veith, "Sex and the Evangelical Teen," posted August 11, 2007, www.worldmag.com/2007/08/sex-and-the-evangelical-teen. Veith writes, "[T]here is evidence that evangelical teenagers on the whole may be more sexually immoral than non-Christians. Statistically, evangelical teens tend to have sex first at a younger age, 16.3, compared to liberal Protestants, who tend to lose their virginity at 16.7. And young evangelicals are far more likely to have had three or more sexual partners (13.7 percent) than non-evangelicals (8.9 percent)."

38   Author's Note: Twenty five of my Christian friends, relatives or acquaintances have confessed their abortion to me. Of these 25, 18 are Lutheran, four are wives of pastors, and at least three have had more than one abortion.

39   Jacqueline R. Kasun, "Sex Education: The Hidden Agenda, *The World and I* Vol. 4, No. 9 (Washington, D.C: *The Washington Times* Corporation, September 1989), 493.

by Planned Parenthood in 1986, showed that "64 percent of seventeen-year-olds who had had 'comprehensive' sex education (i.e. including information about contraception) had had intercourse. This was higher than the corresponding percentage for the group that had no sex education (57 percent) and also higher than the percentage for the group that had some but not 'comprehensive' sex education (51 percent)."[40]

Is sex education good enough? In a time when "rights" are raised above responsibilities, sodomy is celebrated, marriage is counterfeited, and abortion is viewed as a routine solution for psychological discomfort, don't we need something better?

SEX EDUCATION VERSUS INSTRUCTION IN PURITY

Two worldviews are at odds. Each is built upon a distinct foundation.

Cornerstones of sex education include:

- Children are sexual beings, too.[41]

- Sexuality is our entire selves, influences us in every way, and encompasses everything.[42]

> It is time for the Church to separate herself from the philosophies of sexologists, the population control and eugenics crowd, restless feminists, and utopian dreamers.

---

40 Kasun, "Sex Education: The Hidden Agenda," *The World and I*, 494

41 Lenore Buth, *How to Talk Confidently with Your Child about Sex*, 23.

42 Miriam Grossman, M.D. *You're Teaching My Child What? A Physician Exposes the Lies of Sex Education and How They Harm Your Child* (Washington, D.C., Regnery Publishing, 2009), 28.

- The more information the better, and the earlier your small children get it, the better.[43]

These are not the cornerstones of instruction in purity. It is time for the Church to separate herself from the philosophies of sexologists, the population control and eugenics crowd, restless feminists, and utopian dreamers. They may see the world and children one way, but followers of Jesus see the world and the children God created and redeemed in a different way. Consider some contrasts:

- Sex education teaches abstinence yet elevates curiosity about human desires, the sexual union, and things of the flesh. *Instruction in purity focuses on a holy identity and sets us free within God's merciful boundaries to live full and productive lives as male or female whether we are married or not.*

- Sex education brings the language of "social scientists" into the Church, adds to God's Word and puts its trust in man. *Instruction in purity begins in the home where parents unapologetically trust the Word of God for use in equipping sons and daughters for their vocations of manhood and womanhood*

- Sex education focuses on the joys and pleasures of sex/sexuality. *Instruction in purity refrains from provocative imagery, discusses a lifestyle for either the single or married person and connects the act of sex with procreation and God's design for family.*

Sex education sees teen pregnancy, STDs and abortion as consequences of a lack of information. *Instruction in purity understands that these sad consequences don't result from lack of information, but from wrong identity and lack of judgment.*

---

43 Miriam Grossman, M.D. *You're Teaching My Child What?*, 29.

Some Christians use the terminology of the Bible and Church to promote sex and sexuality education for young people. In the article entitled "Sexuality: What Congregations, Parents, Pastors and Teachers Need to Teach," we read,

> God gave to the church the Great Commission in Matthew 28:19-20a. [. . .] unfortunately we often miss out on the second directive of the Great Commission, 'teaching them to observe all things I have commanded you.' The 'teaching' all things includes the very thing he created within each of us – the gift of sexuality. [44]

But when Jesus says we are to "[G]o therefore and make disciples of all nations, baptizing them in the name of the Father and of the Son and of the Holy Spirit, teaching them to observe all that I have commanded you," is sex or sex education part of the "all"? *What does knowing our sexuality have to do with knowing our salvation?*

Scripture teaches sexual ethics and we should teach that, too. Nowhere in Scripture, however, does God call us "sexual beings" or infer our identity as primarily sexual. God in Jesus Christ came to earth to live fully as a man yet He could never be called a "sexual being." Nowhere in Scripture does it say that we should teach sex to children in the way proposed by contemporary sex educators. God bids us to flee from sensuality and desires of the flesh. "Temptations to sin are sure to come, but woe to the one through whom they come! It would be better for him if a millstone were hung around his neck and he were cast into the sea than that he should cause one of these little ones to sin. Pay attention to yourselves! If your brother sins, rebuke him, and if he repents, forgive him" (Luke 17:1-3).

---

44   Rev. Roger Sonnenberg, "Sexuality: What Congregations, Parents, Pastors and Teachers Need to Teach," *Issues in Christian Education* (An on-line publication of Concordia University, Seward, Nebraska), Spring 2013, Vol. 46, No.2: 19, accessed July 7, 2013, www.cune.edu/about/publications/issues-in-christian-education/issues-spring-2013.

Too often, we Christians react to the world around us in fear. We may fear that children won't correctly understand God's gift of sex within marriage and, thus, attempt to Christianize the best resources we can find on human sexuality. We may fear for the health and well-being of children and, thus, adapt a "cradle to grave" sex education in order to protect them. But we must not be deceived. Jesus does not embrace the things of this world.

THE CASE OF MISTAKEN IDENTITY

It matters how we identify ourselves. If we are mistaken about our identity, we will be mistaken about our purpose, behavior, and choices.

In all of the pro-life and purity discussions I've had with boys and their dads, or girls and their moms, or when I've listened to a parent admitting they'd put their daughter on birth control or a woman confessing her promiscuity and abortion, I have heard it too many times: "Well, after all, we *are* sexual beings!" Well, yes, if they mean that we are created male or female. But is that what they mean? Our current sinful lusts and desires are not part of God's good creation. Our current experience of sexuality and sexual desires is not in accord with how God created us. In truth, we are so much more than sexual beings.

We are, above all, spiritual beings who will live forever either with or apart from God. We are human beings—persons with body and soul that interact. We are male or female whose first parents, Adam and Eve, were created by God at different times, in different ways and for different purposes. Man and woman are the two eyes of the human race. Both are needed for better perspective on life. In marriage, male and female fit together in the most intimate of ways to become one. Such oneness is an expression of love, but it is also the way that humans procreate: sexually, not asexually. Married or single, we are fully human. Sexual activity is not an inherent part of being human.[45] As human beings, we are persons upon whom God bestows great dignity. This created dignity has continuing moral implications for how we treat one another. In Christ, male and female are neighbors. The way we identify our neighbor influences how we treat our neighbor.[46]

Instruction in purity ultimately benefits our neighbor, especially the littlest of neighbors, the unborn child. Is it even remotely possible that "Christian sex education" might, quite unintentionally, place our littlest neighbor at greater risk?

In Baptism, we become new persons in Christ. Is it possible that "Christian sex education" might unintentionally offend that new creation and compromise his or her purpose?

Is sex education in the Church more about sex and sexuality than the knowledge of "all things that pertain to life and godliness" (2 Pet. 1:3)? The knowledge of which God's Word speaks is the knowledge of salvation. Is it possible that a child's greater knowledge about all things sexual is not necessarily in the best interest of their spiritual well-being?

Identity matters. Through our Baptism, we became children of God in Christ Jesus, called to live as His sons and daughters. St. Paul exhorts us to be "a vessel for honorable use, set apart as holy, useful to the master of the house, ready for every good work" (2 Tim. 2:21). *Who is the "master"?*

> Identity matters. Through our Baptism, we became children of God in Christ Jesus, called to live as His sons and daughters.
>
> ❖ ❖ ❖

---

45 Author's Note: On this topic, see St. Paul's recommendation of a life of chaste virginity in 1 Corinthians 7. If sexual activity defined our humanity, it would be impossible for St. Paul to make this recommendation.

46 Author's Note: See Genesis 9:6 where our being created in the image of God is cited as the reason why murder is prohibited.

What is the "house"? What is our "good work"? How we identify ourselves influences this "work."

If we identify ourselves as sexual beings, does it follow that we might act like sexual beings? Might we grant ourselves special favor or excuse our passion? Does seeing ourselves as "sexual beings" change the way we see, hear and obey God?

Human sexuality and sex education—in or out of the Church—is defended by sexologists, feminists, educators, the politically-correct, and fearful parents. Christians have been told that contemporary sex education can be integrated with the Bible. But is such education really the same as biblical instruction in purity? Parents who teach their children about the "birds and the bees" and prepare them for marriage is one thing. Classroom sex education designed to help boys and girls celebrate their sexuality and break down inhibitions is quite another. It may sound like an exaggeration, but most sex education as we know it today leans the wrong way because it is built on the wrong foundation.

Martin Luther challenged the Church, asking only that it recognize and correct errors. That is the goal of this book as well. May the questions that follow promote kind and Christian dialogue.

May the brief answers lead to personal reflection and prayerful study.

May Christian parents be encouraged to reclaim their God-given responsibility to instruct and mentor sons and daughters.

May the Body of Christ resist reinterpretation of God's Word in light of "new information" and, instead, be encouraged to fear, love and trust God above all things.

May the Church distinguish itself from the world so that others will ask: Why do you teach what you teach and do what you do?

May we lead children away from mistaken identity that compromises their faith and purity.

It matters... for current generations and those yet to come.

CHAPTER TWO

Sex Education is a Social Movement

1. Why should Christians be concerned about sex education?

When we think of sex education, most of us probably think about the traditional "sex talk" moms and dads have with their child when he or she shows interest. The talk is about maturing bodies and roller coaster emotions, the differences between boys and girls, and from where babies come. Before the 1960s, that talk was never about childhood sexuality. It was never about sexual identity. Sexuality was not defined as our "whole being." It wasn't even a common term and did not have to be explained by trained sexologists or facilitators in a classroom "encounter" group.

"Up until 1920," said Charles Donovan of the Family Research Council, "there is no history of sex education. We managed as a race to 'replicate' ourselves quite well for centuries with nowhere near the level of family disruption we have today and we did it without ever there existing any classroom sex education." [47] Generally, the ethics texts of Protestants

---

47   Charles Donovan, "The History of Sex Education in the U.S.," presentation to the Human Life International's National Sex Education Conference in St. Louis, MO, October 21-23, 1994, accessed November 12, 2012, www.vidahumana.org/english/family/sexed-history.html. (Author's Note: Mr. Donovan gave this speech while serving as the Executive Director and Senior Policy Advisor for the Family Research Council in Washington, D.C. He has served as Deputy Director of Presidential Correspondents at the White House; appeared on ABC's Nightline, CNN, CBN, USA Radio Network; and has written for the *Wall Street Journal* and *The Washington Times*.)

and Catholics warned against classroom sex education. But determined forces were at work to change how, when, what, and why children were taught about sex.

> Sex education is built on a foundation that diametrically opposes God's design for parents to instruct their children in purity.
>
> ❖ ❖ ❖

Sex education is built on a foundation that diametrically opposes God's design for parents to instruct their children in purity. Sex education is not biblical; rather, it grows from the ideologies and humanist faith of sexologists like Alfred Kinsey and Wardell Pomeroy, birth control and eugenics advocate Margaret Sanger, social reformer and SIECUS co-founder Mary Calderone, and advocate of child sexual rehearsal play Dr. John Money. Sex and sexuality education, sometimes called family life education, is described by Miriam Grossman, M.D., as "a social movement, a vehicle for changing the world. It happens one child at a time, and it goes on right under your nose."[48]

2. What is the origin of sex education as we know it today?

In the early 1900s, a purity movement took place in America to stop the traffic of young girls and merchandising of sex; restore male chivalry; battle sexually-transmitted diseases; and protect marriage, women, and children. Society, as a whole, was family-oriented and church-going. Morality was shaped by the biblical worldview. But a man named Alfred Kinsey thought society much too prudish and sexually repressed. Kinsey believed that the legal codes of his day which governed sexual behavior were twisted by Christianity. If one takes the time to read about Kinsey, it becomes apparent that he chose to avoid those with a biblical worldview and, instead, adopt the ideology of men like Charles Darwin and Sir Thomas Huxley. Kinsey was a professor of zoology who worked with gall wasps before becoming a sexologist and the director of

---

48 Grossman, *You're Teaching My Child What?*, 15.

the Institute for Sex Research at Indiana University. In 1948, Kinsey authored *Sexual Behavior in the Human Male*[49] and claimed that "children are sexual from birth". Kinsey was perfectly clear. He did not mean that children are boy or girl from birth; rather, he meant that they have the capacity for sexual pleasure and response. He believed that children have the right to express themselves sexually and enjoy such expression with each other or with adults.

3. Did anyone question the so-called "science" of Kinsey? Did anyone doubt his research and data?

Yes, a great many happily married husbands and wives of the so-called Greatest Generation were very suspicious of Kinsey's claim that pre-marital sex, adultery and homosexuality were normal and prevalent. Some in government smelled fraud. Kinsey's estimate that 10 percent of the population is homosexual was discredited, but the child sexuality data was not given serious examination until Dr. Judith A. Reisman began her research. In 1990, Reisman and associates wrote *Kinsey, Sex and Fraud: The Indoctrination of a People.*[50] In 1994, *The Children of Table 34: The True Story Behind Alfred Kinsey's Infamous Sex Research* was produced by The Family Research Council.[51] Nevertheless, in 1998, the Kinsey Institute on the campus of Indiana University in Bloomington, IN., republished Kinsey's books [52] without apology or admission of crime. In 2003,

---

49   Alfred J. Kinsey, Wardell Pomeroy, and Clyde Martin, *Sexual Behavior in the Human Male* (Philadelphia, PA: W.B. Saunders Co., 1948).

50   Judith A. Reisman, Edward Eichel, *Kinsey, Sex and Fraud: The Indoctrination of a People*, John H. Court and J. Gordon Muir, eds. (Lafayette, LA: Huntington House, 1990).

51   *The Children of Table 34: the True Story Behind Alfred Kinsey's Infamous Sex Research* (Washington, D.C: The Family Research Council, 1994). (Author's note: The introduction of this documentary is narrated by actor Efrem Zimbalist, Jr. A companion booklet is authored by Robert H. Knight of the Family Research Council.)

52   Author's note: Kinsey's book *Sexual Behavior in the Human Male* was published in 1948 and *Sexual Behavior in the Human Female* was published in 1953. The statistics in both books were derived through unethical methodology which Reisman proves came from abusive experimentation on children, the intimidation of female subjects, and the behaviors of ungodly men. The sensational books, however, shook society's moral foundations and fueled the sexual revolution, no-fault divorce, legalized abortion, and homosexuality.

the Kinsey Institute published *Sexual Development in Childhood* [53] which promoted Kinsey's theory of "childhood sexuality."

4. Who is Judith Reisman?

Judith Reisman helped us discern a pre-Kinsey and post-Kinsey world. Reisman's thirty years of scholarly research and documentation reveals that Kinsey's theory about children was the first of its kind. Her work is documented in two books entitled *Kinsey: Crimes and Consequences*[54] and *Sexual Sabatoge.*[55] Reisman has served as a consultant to four U.S. Department of Justice administrations, the U.S. Department of Education, and the U.S. Department of Health and Human Services. She has lectured and testified worldwide in Media Forensics, scientific analysis of images, pornography, and sexual harassment of women and children. Reisman is Visiting Professor of Law at Liberty University and President of the Institute for Media Education.

5. Why did Reisman question Kinsey's research and data?

In the 1970s, Reisman was producing music videos for children. Her professional work with museum art and television had nurtured a concern for the way images impact the brain, mind and memory of a child. So, when advertisers began pressuring the producers of children's television shows to provide more fast action and visual stimulation, Reisman found herself unwilling to write for children that way. She returned to college for an advanced degree, studying mass media effects. In 1977, Reisman delivered a research paper on women, children and pornography to the

---

53 John Bancroft, MD., *Sexual Development in Childhood* (Bloomington: Indiana University Press, 2003).

54 Judith A. Reisman, Ph.D., *Kinsey: Crimes and Consequences* (Crestwood, KY: The Institute for Media Education, Inc., 2000). Author's note: The 2012 publication of *Crimes and Consequences* is re-titled *Stolen Honor, Stolen Innocence.*

55 Judith A. Reisman, Ph.D., *Sexual Sabotage* (Washington, D.C.: WND Books, WorldNetDaily, 2010).

British Psychological Association International Conference on "Love and Attraction" at Swansea University in Wales. She provided eighty slides as evidence to support her findings of child pornography in *Playboy* and *Penthouse*. Afterward, a Canadian psychologist took her aside. He agreed with her conclusion that sexual acting out on children would be a result of pornographic images either in magazines or on the screen. But if she was looking for the cause, he said, she should read about Kinsey in *The Sex Researchers* by Edward Brecher. When Reisman asked why, the psychologist replied that he worked with Kinsey and Pomeroy. "One is a pedophile," he said, "and the other a homosexual."[56]

Reisman did read Brecher's book. She was stunned both by "Kinsey's use of infants in sex experiments" and "Brecher's acceptance of their abuse as a research methodology."[57] Reisman had already heard from her own family members that "children are sexual from birth," but had no idea what the source might be for such thinking. She found that source while studying Kinsey's book, *Sexual Behavior in the Human Male*. Apparently, the child data on page 180 in Table 34 was the so-called proof that "children are sexual from birth." But had no scientist wondered about the children of Table 34?

Reisman wrote to the Kinsey Institute about that child data and, in March of 1981, received a letter from Kinsey's co-author Dr. Paul Gebhard. Reisman writes, "[He explained] to me that the children in Kinsey's tables were obtained from parents, school teachers and male homosexuals, and that some of Kinsey's men used 'manual and oral techniques' to catalog how many 'orgasms' infants and children could produce in a given amount of time."[58] Reisman notes that on pages 160 and 161 of his book, Kinsey

---

56 Reisman, Author's Preface to *Kinsey: Crimes and Consequences*, xxi.

57 Reisman, Author's Preface to *Kinsey: Crimes and Consequences*, xxi.

58 Reisman, Author's Preface to *Kinsey: Crimes and Consequences*, xxii.

Sex Education is a Social Movement

claimed his data came from "interviews." How could he say 196 little children—some as young as two months of age—enjoyed "fainting," "screaming," "weeping," and "convulsing"? How could he call these children's responses evidence of their sexual pleasure and "climax"? . . . One of us was very, very sexually mixed up.[59]

> Kinsey's theory about children placed the most innocent directly in harm's way.
>
>

Kinsey's theory about children placed the most innocent directly in harm's way. Kinsey had no regard for male and female as created by God, marriage and family as designed by God or the children that God calls by name. His own sexual lifestyle was uninhibited in every way. Reisman describes his far-reaching influence:

Kinsey's philosophy of early childhood sexual development became the standard for today's graphic sex instruction materials in many, if not most, American public, private and parochial schools, usually camouflaged by such euphemistic captions as sex education, AIDS prevention or awareness, family life, health, hygiene, home economics, physical education, even 'abstinence' education . . . Prior to Kinsey, no child development specialists suggested that children were either sexual from birth or that they benefited from early sexual activity.[60]

---

59 Reisman, Author's Preface to *Kinsey: Crimes and Consequences*, xxii.
60 Reisman, *Kinsey: Crimes and Consequences*, 7, 132-133.

6. Dr. Reisman tells us who coined the phrase "children are sexual from birth," but are there others who warn us against educating this way?

Yes. Dr. Miriam Grossman is a board-certified child, adolescent, and adult psychiatrist. She is the author of *Unprotected: A Campus Psychiatrist Reveals How Political Correctness Endangers Every Student* and *You're Teaching My Child What?* Dr. Reisman was the first to explain how Kinsey's sexual philosophy was institutionalized within modern sex education. From a unique vantage point, Dr. Grossman details the disastrous effect sex education has had on young people's behavior and health as well as their ideas about marriage and family. She speaks from her own experience on university campuses. Dr. Grossman has treated more than 2,000 students at one of Americas most prestigious universities. She has seen how political correctness and a world free of sexual taboos are making our sons and daughters sick. "The exaggerated place of sexuality is grotesque and destructive," writes Dr. Grossman. "We are not defined by our urges . . . we are defined by something more essential, uplifting, and transcendent."[61]

There are others who warn against sex education made popular since the 1960s. Two of them are Dr. William Coulson (mentioned in chapter one of this book) and Dr. Philip G. Ney, retired professor of psychiatry at five universities and the director of child and adolescent psychiatric units who will be referenced in the section entitled "No Particular Need for Sex Education."

7. Besides Kinsey, are there others who believe that humans are defined by our sexual urges and desires?

Yes, and among them are humanists. Humanism is a religious conviction that stands in opposition to God and His creation. Christians have the Bible which is God's Word. The biblical worldview explains

---

61 Miriam Grossman, M.D., *Unprotected* (New York, NY: Penguin Group, 2006), 149.

Creation (our origin and purpose), the Fall (why things in this world go wrong), and Redemption in Jesus Christ (why we have hope). Humanists have a Manifesto. The document denies God as Creator, accepts evolutionary theory of man's origin as fact, and promotes humanist control of all human institutions through scientific approach. Signers of the Humanist Manifesto include John Dewey, Betty Freidan, B.F. Skinner, Sir Julian Huxley, Alan F. Guttmacher, and Lester Kirkendall.[62]

Lester Kirkendall writes in the SIECUS Study Guide #1, saying, "Once and for all, adults must accept as fact that young people of all ages are sexual beings with sexual needs."[63] John Money, Deryck Calderwood, William Masters and Virginia Johnson, all associated with Kinsey, were SIECUS officials and humanists by faith.[64]

8. What were the reasons for institutionalizing sex education?

Mary Calderone, the former medical director of Planned Parenthood, did not like the way that sex was taught to children and young people. There was too much focus on waiting for sex until marriage and preventing diseases and pregnancy. Like Kinsey, Calderone believed it was time to replace the biblical warnings against sexual immorality and sensuality with an acceptance of more open, tolerant, and enjoyable expressions of sexuality. It was necessary to break from the traditional view of procreative sex and the mainstream of American manners and morals. This required a bold separation of children from what she considered to be negative and religiously repressed teaching of parents and grandparents. It required separating children from their God-given identity.

---

62 *The Humanist Manifesto I & II*, ed. Paul Kurtz (Amherst, N.Y: Prometheus Books, 1973). The Manifesto may be read in brief form at www.americanhumanist.org.)
63 Lester A. Kirkendall, *Sex Education*, SIECUS Study Guide No. 1, (New York: SIECUS Publications Office, January 1969), 15.
64 Chambers, *The SIECUS Circle*, 57.

Early in the 1960s, Mary Calderone founded SIECUS (Sexuality Information and Education Council of the U.S.) with the hopes of expanding the boundaries of sexuality. Funds for the organization that would set guidelines for all sex education were provided by Hugh Hefner, founder of Playboy. Calderone, who was awarded the Humanist of the Year in 1974, wanted children to celebrate their sexuality and see it as positive, natural, and healthy. Calderone wrote, "Children are sexual and think sexual thoughts and do sexual things" so parents must "accept and honor [their] child's erotic potential."[65] Dr. Miriam Grossman writes, "Together, Calderone and [Lester] Kirkendall set out, through SIECUS, to transform how American children were taught about sex. Openness, tolerance, and joy were in; church lady . . . [was] out."[66] Kirkendall's area of study was sexual intimacy. According to his 1976 "bill of sexual rights," Kirkendall believed that the "boundaries of human sexuality need to be expanded."[67] The thinking of American people needed to be changed and SIECUS, using the "children are sexual from birth" theory of Kinsey, set out to do it. Dr. Reisman explains, "Speaking before the 1980 annual meeting of the Association of Planned Parenthood Physicians, Calderone said the primary goal of SIECUS was teaching society 'the vital importance of infant and childhood sexuality.'"[68]

9. Why can sex education be called a social movement?

It can be called a social movement because, in the words of Dr. Grossman, it is a "vehicle for changing the world . . . one child at a time."[69] Dr. Grossman studied the history of sex education after realizing her profession had been "hijacked" and her "patients [were] suffering." She was "fed up."[70]

---

65 Dr. Mary S. Calderone, Dr. James Ramey, *Talking with your Child About Sex* (New York: Ballantine Books, 1982), XV.

66 Grossman, *You're Teaching My Child What?*, 27.

67 Grossman, *You're Teaching My Child What?*, 27.

68 Reisman, *Sexual Sabotage*, 302.

69 Grossman, *You're Teaching My Child What?*, 15.

70 Grossman, Introduction to *Unprotected*, xvi.

Dr. Reisman's well-documented evidence reveals that Kinsey and his associates wanted to effect social and moral change through human sexual behavior. But who were these agents of change? Kinsey was completely captive to his obsession with any kind of sex. He was a homosexual, masochist, and promoted adult-child sexual relations believing that all were perfectly normal. His staff of Clyde Martin, Wardell Pomeroy, and Paul Gebhard were sexually involved with one another. Women and children became subjects for films produced and sexual scientific data collected by Kinsey and his staff at Indiana University. [71] Three of Kinsey's biographies confirm that he maneuvered the teaching of a course on marriage in order to secure university support of "sex travels, 'surveys,' and experiments." [72] Kinsey was welcomed by officials of the Midwestern university, but who really knew the dangers of Kinsey's "science" and published works? After he authored *Sexual Behavior in the Human Male* (1948), he wrote *Sexual Behavior in the Human Female* (1953). The readers of *McCalls, Ladies' Home Journal, Redbook* and other women's magazines were encouraged to learn from Kinsey "how to rear their children sexually, how to please their husbands, and how to evaluate themselves as sexually healthy women." [73]

Pomeroy went on to become academic dean of the Institute for the Advanced Study of Human Sexuality (IASHS) in San Francisco where, together with Methodist minister Rev. Ted McIlvenna, he repeated Kinsey's "science" by filming sexual acts among staff members. Today, the IASHS is the leading institution in the sexology field and has trained more than 100,000 sex educators, doctors, and "safe sex" instructors. *Meditations on the Gift of Sexuality,* written by Rev. Ted McIlvenna, includes graphic homosexual and heterosexual acts.[74]

---

71 Reisman, *Kinsey: Crimes and Consequences*, 77-78.

72 Reisman, *Kinsey: Crimes and Consequences*, 25.

73 Reisman, *Kinsey: Crimes and Consequences*, 77.

74 Reisman, *Kinsey: Crimes and Consequences*, 81.

The laborious and detailed work of Dr. Reisman and others helped Americans learn that Kinsey's theory of children being sexual from birth relied on fraudulent research and the sexual abuse of infants and children by known pedophiles.[75] The facts are shameful and turn one's stomach. Some educators quickly wanted distance between themselves and Kinsey. A gentle public mourned for the children who endured the abuse. But it was too late. The sexual revolution of the 1960s had begun. Kinsey's theory of childhood sexuality had a powerful impact on how we think about children, innocence, relationships, marriage, the family, and behaviors that in years prior would have been considered abnormal, socially destructive, and even criminal.

> The laborious and detailed work of Dr. Reisman and others helped Americans learn that Kinsey's theory of children being sexual from birth relied on fraudulent research and the sexual abuse of infants and children by known pedophiles.
>
>

The social movement of sex education comes at a very high price. Misidentified, the lives of children are altered. Dr. Grossman notes that one of the cornerstones of modern sex education is this: "Sexuality is our entire selves, influences us in every way, and encompasses everything." However, observes Dr. Grossman,

> [O]nce kids believe that sexuality is "who they are," "their entire selves" from womb to tomb, the idea that it's an appetite in need of restraint makes little sense. And the notion of waiting years for the right time and person

---

75 *The Children of Table 34*, video presentation of Dr. Judith Reisman's discovery of the systematic sexual abuse of 317 boys, some as young as two months of age, in the 1948 sex study of Alfred Kinsey (Produced by Robert Knight and The Family Research Council, Washington, D.C.)

sounds irrational. Why restrain "who you are"? Why wait for "your entire self"? Couldn't that be unhealthy"?[76]

Here's something else to consider. Thriving societies have historically understood that boys and girls are profoundly different and weren't afraid to say so. Traditional marriage and parenthood were valued for religious reasons but also because such institutions strengthened the nation. Society, however, was thrown into chaos when feminism paired with sex education. It is "sexist" to treat girls differently than boys, educate them apart from the boys about their different and more vulnerable procreative organs, mentor modesty in dress or behavior, instruct them in any way that might threaten their "rights," or infer that marriage and motherhood are noble aspirations. But as Dr. Grossman's experience on campus reveals, the political correctness of feminism, psychology and sex education hurts the very ones they propose to liberate, enlighten, and make happy. "Infection with one of the sexually transmitted viruses is a rite of passage," writes Dr. Grossman. "Abortion is the removal of unwanted tissue, sort of like a tonsillectomy... [Y]oung women think motherhood can be delayed indefinitely...[T]raditional marriage and a mother and a father are just one option; there are other alternatives, all equally valid."[77]

---

76 Grossman, *You're Teaching My Child What?*, 29.
77 Grossman, Introduction to *Unprotected*, xv.

CHAPTER THREE

Sex Education

Re-Defines & Sexualizes Children

10. Is it fair to conclude that those who initiated formalized sex education had a very different view of children than God does?

Most certainly. Men and women such as Kinsey, Calderone, Kirkendall, Pomeroy, Money, Masters and Johnson, Southard, Guttmacher, Duvall and others who formalized sex education and worked it into both public and parochial schools are also confessing humanists. They are not believers in the Lord Jesus Christ and do not see children as He does. They do not see that "children are a heritage from the Lord" (Ps. 126:3). When God asks, "Will you command me concerning my children and the work of my hands?" (Is. 45:11), they haughtily respond, "Yes! We will!" God "does not willingly afflict or grieve the children of men" (Lm. 3:33). But men (and women) have afflicted and grieved children by sexualizing boys and girls, leaving them vulnerable to abuse, and forever changing their lives.

11. In order for childhood to include sexuality, what has to happen?

In order "for childhood to include sexuality [or much thought about sex]," writes Dr. Reisman, "someone has to intrude upon childhood innocence."[78]

---

78 Reisman, *Sexual Sabotage*, 317.

> In order "for childhood to include sexuality, someone has to intrude upon childhood innocence."
>
> ❖ ❖ ❖

But who would want to do this? Does this not offend the little ones and their Creator? Jesus says, "See that you do not despise one of these little ones. For I tell you that in heaven their angels always see the face of my Father who is in heaven" (Mt. 17:10). In 1972, the U.S. Surgeon General warned of television toxicity. Parents expressed concern about the effects of television violence on their young children, but the mass media was not listening and, instead, became bolder with sexual messages and images. Today, many of us are concerned about the sexualization of children. According to the American Psychological Association's Task Force on the Sexualization of Girls, sexualization occurs when:

- A person's value comes only from his or her sexual appeal or behavior

- A person is held to a standard that equates physical attractiveness with being sexy

- A person is sexually objectified and made into a thing for others' sexual use

- *Sexuality is inappropriately imposed upon a person* (emphasis mine).[79]

Sex education has a boldness of its own. Sex education, in both secular and Church schools, may begin in pre-school or kindergarten. But how does a young child process such information? Do the sexual images and discussion raise questions that the child never had? Are sex educators meddling in a child's life at a time when sensuality is naturally and protectively repressed?

---

79 "Sexy Babies: How Sexualization Hurts Girls", Trusted Answers from The Hospital for Sick Kids, accessed December 20, 2013, www.aboutkidshealth.ca (search: "Sexy Babies: How Sexualization Hurts Girls")

Reisman notes that the term "childhood sexuality" is "an oxymoron, a political ploy to lull the populace into believing that these two words belong in the same sentence, much less paired together … since absent [sic] sex hormones, child sexual behavior before puberty is entirely unnatural." [80]

But childhood sexual innocence is a fable according to associates of the Kinsey Institute such as John Money and his student Suzanne Frayser. Frayser, past president of the Society for the Scientific Study of Sexuality (SSSS), has stated that children are free to enjoy "masturbation, oral sex, and sexual desire or activity." [81] Frayser is a contributor to the book *Sexual Development in Childhood* [82] published by the Kinsey Institute in 2003. The book promotes the harmlessness of "childhood sexuality," as earlier defined by Kinsey, and terms a child's enjoyment of sex "natural." Editor John Bancroft (director of the Kinsey Institute) selected several pedophile activists to help produce the book. When Bancroft was interviewed for the television documentary, *Kinsey's Paedophiles*,[83] he argued

---

80   Reisman, *Sexual Sabotage*, 317.

81   Resiman, *Sexual Sabotage*, 319.

82   John Bancroft (editor), *Childhood Sexual Development* (Bloomington: Indiana University Press, 2003), 266. (Author's note: This book followed Kinsey's first two books *Sexual Behavior in the Male* and *Sexual Behavior in the Female* which slandered fatherhood, motherhood, marriage, and family. Even after Kinsey's bad methodology and fraudulent statistics were exposed, the book *Sexual Development in Children* was published with absolutely no acknowledgment of errors in Kinsey data. The book broke down the protective wall God places around children and left them vulnerable to pornography, pedophilia, and incest. In the post-Kinsey world, many laws that protected women, children, marriage and family have been gutted.)

83   *Kinsey's Paedophiles*, a British documentary, accessed October 11, 2013, www.youtube.com/watch?v=uvc-1d5ib50. (Author's note: This explains to the viewer how Kinsey and his associates Gebhard and Bancroft took "sex" out of the closet and cast negative light on repression of any kind of sexual behavior including premarital sex, adultery, homosexuality, incest or pedophilia. Kinsey became the expert on what was seen as honest, wholesome and good sexuality, but this turned people away from the sacredness of sex as God created it.)

that to avoid "ignorance," some child sexual abuse could be scientifically acceptable. [84]

12. Is there anyone at the Kinsey Institute or its associate schools of sexology that condemns childhood sexuality or forms of child sexual abuse?

Dr. Dennis Fortenberry, a professor of pediatrics and medicine, was at a conference where Bancroft and the other contributors to *Sexual Development in Childhood* were gathered. Somewhat nervous about arbitrating "normalcy" (including childhood sexuality), Fortenberry said, "Our history as professionals over the past 100 years has been to be wrong more often than we've been right." [85] But Bancroft persisted in covering up Kinsey's crimes and would allow no criticism of past errors by sex "experts." Today, sexologists, SIECUS and Planned Parenthood justify their promotion of open, wholesome, joyful sexuality for people of *all* ages based on the shameful research and data compiled by Kinsey. So, how should Christians process this? What should our response be? Christians live in this world, but we are not of this world. We can appreciate the joy of sexual expression but only within the faithfulness of marriage designed by God for one man and one woman and for the benefit of children and society. Christians are set apart, not primarily as sexual beings, but as "holy ones" with body, mind and soul. The Church must break free of human opinion and error to trust God and lead His children through the maze of this life to their eternal home.

13. Sex education material used in the Church has, for many years, referred to children as being sexual, too. But what does it mean when we identify children this way?

"Sexual" is ambiguous. Christians may use the term to describe our sex: male or female. We may use the term to describe our procreative nature.

84 Reisman, *Sexual Sabotage*, 317
85 Reisman, *Sexual Sabotage*, 317.

But Kinsey, SIECUS and others like them refer to children as being "sexual" which, to them, means "capable of sexual activity." Are young children truly capable of sexual activity as Kinsey claimed? Before Kinsey, people commonly understood that sexual maturation was nearly synonymous with adulthood; it happens when sex glands become functional; it is when a person is first capable of procreation of offspring. No one, least of all me, wants to read about Kinsey's documented abuse of children,[86] but when we do, we learn that his research was driven by his own sexual sins. He wanted the world to think that children are sexual, so he eroticized toddlers and young children to "prove" what he wanted the world to believe. Today we know the evil of Kinsey's "science," but America is deceived and demoralized by the lie and the men and women who wanted to believe it.

> "Sexual" is ambiguous. Christians may use the term to describe our sex: male or female. We may use the term to describe our procreative nature. But Kinsey, SIECUS and others like them refer to children as being "sexual" which, to them, means "capable of sexual activity."

Even God's people are deceived. Sex education materials developed for Christian schools have for many years identified children as being "sexual from birth." In the book *How To Talk Confidently with Your Child about Sex* (1998) and under the heading "Children Are Sexual Beings, Too," we read, "It may be surprising to realize that our children are sexual beings from birth." The author continues,

> For instance, a parent changing a male infant's diaper may accidentally stimulate the child and be shocked to realize

---

86 Reisman, Part II: Crimes in *Kinsey, Crimes and Consequences*, 49-180. Also, *The Children of Table 34*, a video documentary produced by The Family Research Council, Washington, D.C., www.frc.org.

the child is having an erection. Similarly, researchers tell us that baby girls have vaginal lubrication regularly. In fact, a little girl being bounced on her parent's knee may feel pleasant sensations and begin to make natural pelvic thrust movements. [87]

In chapter one, we learned that *How To Talk Confidently with Your Child about Sex* has been updated since 1998 and some material deleted. However, reference to a baby boy's "erection" during the change of his diaper and a baby girl's "vaginal lubrication" remain. The author writes, "Yet somehow the thought of a child's sexual nature is vaguely disturbing to many adults."[88] Some important information is missing. Who are the researchers that tell us such things? What is the author's source? What is meant by "a child's sexual nature"? Dr. Reisman explains that it is only sexologists who tell us about child sexuality. Floyd Martinson, a pedophile advocate, notes the little boy's erection and little girl's vaginal lubrication in his essay "Infant and Child Sexuality: Capacity and Experience".[89] "But," explains Dr. Reisman,

> In girls, all bodily passages are naturally lined with mucosa, including the nose and vagina. And in boys, the reflexive nervous and vascular reactions of the penis respond to many biological stimuli—such as urinary buildup, friction, infections, and especially fear and terror. These are biologically natural and non-sexual states. But sexology-trained people sexualize everything, at the same time that they deliberately ignore that frightening sex stimuli, such as sex abuse and pornography, can prematurely disturb, emotionally arouse,

---

87 Lenore Buth, *How to Talk Confidently with Your Child about Sex* (1998), 23.

88 Buth, *How to Talk Confidently* (2008), 26.

89 Reisman, *Kinsey: Crimes and Consequences,* 149. (Author's note: Floyd Martinson, a Minnesota sociologist, advocated pedophilia and the legalization of incest and child pornography.)

and physiologically traumatize children. Could these sociologists truly have been ignorant of such basic biological facts?[90]

We are disregarding God's created order when we say that "children are sexual." Children are not "sexual" in the sense of being capable of sexual activity nor do they benefit from early libido. God does not mock His little ones by creating them with tendencies that would be harmful both physically and spiritually.

14. If we believe as Kinsey did that children are sexual from birth, would it be easier to de-criminalize pedophilia?

Yes, as evidenced by the 2011 conference hosted by the pedophile group B4U-ACT in Baltimore. What is the goal of B4U-ACT?[91] It is to remove pedophilia as a mental disorder from the American Psychiatric Association's Diagnostic and Statistical Manual of Mental Disorders (DSM), in the same manner homosexuality was removed in 1973. Speakers at the conference noted shifting social attitudes on child sexuality and attraction between adults and minors. Browsing the B4U-ACT website one learns that we should have compassion toward pedophiles (or, "minor attracted people") and not let criminal laws come between the one who is attracted to children and healing because "minor attracted people" need help dealing with issues resulting from society's negative reactions to their sexual feelings. It would appear that emphasis is on legally re-classifying "minor-attracted people" so that they are not shunned rather than protecting children by keeping laws in place.

Kinsey wanted society to accept pedophilia as a natural act and believed that sex with children is a problem only because we have laws against

---

90 Reisman, *Sexual Sabotage*, 322-323.

91 B4U-ACT, accessed October 17, 2013, www.b4uact.org. (Author's note: Speakers at the conference included Dr. Fred Berlin of Johns Hopkins University and Jacob Breslow of London School of Economics and Political Science who is a self-described gay-activist. Other speakers are listed at www.bruact.org/news/2011081.htm.)

it.[92] Five chapters of Dr. Reisman's book document the crimes of Kinsey who gathered data for his research from the sexual abuse of 317 infants and young boys by known pedophiles.[93] He used his fraudulent statistics to convince the world that "children are sexual from birth." This opened a Pandora's box of illicit sexuality. Forms of sex education, based on Kinsey's fraudulent research, worked their way into state and parochial schools with the purpose of helping children learn about sex. Children began experimenting with sex at earlier ages with sure and certain consequences. By the 1980s, schools that didn't have sex education welcomed it out of fear of AIDS. More recently, pro-sodomy groups have gained entrance into classrooms to encourage fellow "sexual beings" to express all manner of "sexuality" without fear of bullying.[94] Slowly but steadily, attempts to break down the walls guarding children have been made since those with Kinsey's worldview settled onto university campuses.

Anne Hendershott is a distinguished visiting professor at The King's College in New York City. She writes,

> It was only a decade ago that a ... movement had begun on some college campuses to redefine pedophilia as the more innocuous "intergenerational sexual intimacy."

> The publication of *Harmful to Minors: The Perils of Protecting Children from Sex* promised readers a "radical, refreshing, and long overdue reassessment of how we think and act about children's and teens' sexuality." The book was published by University of Minnesota Press in 2003 (with a foreword by Joycelyn Elders, who had been

---

92 Reisman, *Kinsey: Crimes and Consequences*, 57.

93 Reisman, Part II: Crimes in *Kinsey: Crimes and Consequences*, 49-180.

94 Author's note: Kirby Anderson, writing for the American Family Association, explains the foothold of pro-homosexual groups in many schools in "The Gay Agenda in Schools" (June 15, 2010) accessed December 15, 2013, www.afa.net/Blogs/BlogPost. aspx?id=2147495553.

the U.S. Surgeon General in the Clinton administration), after which the author, Judith Levine, posted an interview on the university's website decrying the fact that "there are people pushing a conservative religious agenda that would deny minors access to sexual expression," and adding that "we do have to protect children from real dangers … but that doesn't mean protecting some fantasy of their sexual innocence."

This redefinition of childhood innocence as "fantasy" is key to the defining down of the deviance of pedophilia that permeated college campuses and beyond. Drawing upon the language of postmodern theory, those working to redefine pedophilia are first redefining childhood by claiming that "childhood" is not a biological given. Rather, it is socially constructed—an [sic] historically produced social object. Such deconstruction has resulted from the efforts of a powerful advocacy community supported by university-affiliated scholars and a large number of writers, researchers, and publishers who were willing to question what most of us view as taboo behavior. [95]

Public opinion that pedophilia is deviant behavior still remains. We should take note that even SIECUS does not currently promote pedophilia or incest even though its early officials did. However, as we see the barriers protecting childhood innocence removed in classrooms and society in general, groups such as NAMBLA (North American Man/Boy Love Association) will push for "boy love" in every community claiming that child/adult sex is acceptable intimacy among generations.

---

95 Anne Hendershott, "The Postmodern Pedophile," *Public Discourse* (A publication of The Witherspoon Institute), December 20, 2011, accessed July 26, 2013, www.thepublicdiscourse.com/2011/12/4440/.

15. Does sex education help protect children from sexual abuse and predators?

> "The increase in talking graphically about sex to children is essentially pedophilic in nature."
>
> ❖ ❖ ❖

"[T]he increase in talking graphically about sex to children is essentially pedophilic in nature," believes Lynette Burrows. She continues,

It is increasing the number of people who are allowed to "talk dirty" to children, and so to breach the protective armor of their innocence. Thus it is widening the scope for pedophiles to target children. Warning children with slimy disclaimers about "inappropriate touching" is simply token and meaningless to a child. How can they recognize the danger signals from those who wish to exploit them if such a large number of adults are implicated in the same "dirty talk"?[96]

Sex education in any classroom encourages children to talk about sex and sexually-related subjects in explicit terms with adults who are not their parents. This strips them of natural embarrassment and modesty which play an important role in protecting them from sexual abuse. Let's also bear in mind that many of those trained or certified to teach sex education or family living have themselves been stripped of embarrassment and modesty in postgraduate degree programs developed by Kinsey followers and using Kinsey methods. The Christian should remember that embarrassment was a new emotion for Adam and Eve after their sin, but it was for their protection in a sinful world.

---

96 Lynette Burrows, "Worst Sexualisation of Children is Happening in Schools," presentation to the Society for the Protection of Unborn Children (SPUC) Safe at School "Sex Education as Sexual Sabotage" meeting in Westminster, London, accessed January 9, 2012, www.spuc-director.blogspot.com, Archives: Saturday, 10 December 2011.

16. What do Christians need to know about the intentions of the founders of sex education?

The primary goal of those who constructed the foundation for sex education was teaching society the importance of infant and childhood sexuality. Mary Calderone, for example, said that parents should not "come between the child and his/her body" or suppress a "child's sexuality." In her continuing remarks to the Sixth World Congress of Sexology, she said that a baby's "sexual pleasure center . . . has already been identified, from then on to be enjoyed as much as the surrounding culture will allow." She concluded that the parental "role should relate only to teaching the child the appropriateness of privacy, place, and person—in a word, socialization."[97] It does not seem that Calderone, co-founder of SIECUS, approved of adult/child sex, but her peers on the SIECUS board included Wardell Pomeroy, Lester Kirkendall, Deryk Calderwood (all practicing homosexuals), and John Money. Money, a professor at Hopkins University, believed that "affectional pedophilia was about love and not sex" and that heterosexuality is an example of societal and, therefore, superficial,

> The primary goal of those who constructed the foundation for sex education was teaching society the importance of infant and childhood sexuality.

---

97 Mary Calderone, "Fetal Erection and Its Message to Us" (*SIECUS Report*, May-July 1983), 9-10. (Author's note: Calderone was Humanist of the Year in 1974. In the January 21, 1980 issue of People magazine, Calderone told journalist Mary Vespa that, in order to liberate her sexual thinking and prepare herself professionally, Calderone attended sessions facilitated by Sex Attitude Reassessment [SAR]. She said, "You are subjected to a barrage of images, all the way from bestiality to couplings of heterosexuals and homosexuals . . . you do this to desensitize yourself." Calderone was president of Planned Parenthood before co-founding SIECUS to help parents get over their "fear with sex" and teach "natural sexuality" which "is every child's birthright." Calderone believed children should freely celebrate sexuality through the private act of masturbation.)

ideological concept." [98] Reisman notes that Money "was a mentor for June Reinisch (the third Kinsey Institute director), and served on the advisory boards of the Kinsey Institute and Big Pornography's incest-pushing periodical, *Penthouse Forum*."[99]

17. Might the theories of men such as John Money create a dilemma for the Church?

Yes. Some theories of Money have been referenced by pastors and priests who struggle with sexual sin. If children really are "sexual from birth" (as Kinsey meant it), it becomes easier to defend a pedophile's desire for children. It also becomes easier for those who know about the sin to cover it up. This will create a dilemma for the Church. A 1985 paper written by Rev. Michael R. Peterson, M.D., who died from AIDS, warned Catholic clergy that they should avoid potential sexual abuse suits by following Money's sexual training and treatment program. But in interviews with PAIDIKA (the Journal of Paedophilia), Money said that his clinic (Johns Hopkins Sexual Disorders Clinic) was designed to offer "leeway to judges" to free convicted child molesters.[100] He said, "If I were to see the case of a boy aged ten or eleven who's intensely erotically attracted toward a man in his twenties or thirties, if the relationship is totally mutual, and the bonding is genuinely totally mutual . . . then I would not call it pathological in any way."[101] Reisman writes, "Money further offered that adult sex with children is normal and often beneficial and stated, 'regarding paedophilia that I would never report anybody.'"[102]

---

98   John Money, "Pedophilia Opinions," accessed June 20, 2013, www.wikipedia.org/wiki/John_Money.

99   Reisman, *Sexual Sabotoge*, 223.

100   John Money, *PAIDIKA: The Journal of Paedophilia*, Spring 1991, vol. 2, no. 3, 12.

101   John Money, *PAIDIKA*, 5.

102   Reisman, *Sexual Sabotage*, 223-224.

When the Church seeks the wisdom of the world, we invite an opposing worldview into our midst. To consult prevailing "sex experts" is to let their language and perspective influence our teaching. Soon, people use unholy language to justify their sinful behavior. This compromises faith and purity. It sets the Church up for trouble. Sexual abuse of children even within the supposed safety of a Christian school or church is not uncommon. In my own denomination, I am aware of men in leadership positions who have sexually abused children. Reisman notes that church advisors such as Peterson and Money as well as "their institutional sponsors such as Johns Hopkins University, the Kinsey Institute, and the Institute for the Advanced Study of Human Sexuality, etc., are highly vulnerable for medical malpractice, fraud, negligence, and other claims."[103]

> To consult prevailing "sex experts" is to let their language and perspective influence our teaching. Soon, people use unholy language to justify their sinful behavior.
>
>

What does God say? Does His Word tell us that children are sexual from birth and that child-adult sex is normal? No, it does not. The culture desperately needs the Church to stand on the solid ground of God's Word about children, the act of sex, and marriage. For the sake of precious souls, we must resist evil even as we shed light in dark places.

---

103 Reisman, *Sexual Sabotage*, 224

CHAPTER FOUR

Sex Education & Christianity

are Unequally Yoked

18. Is it fair to say that Christianity and contemporary sex education are unequally yoked?

Yes, if we acknowledge that modern sex education originated with unbelievers. Knowing the history of sex education since the 1960s, it behooves the Christian to ask:

> For what partnership has righteousness with lawlessness? Or what fellowship has light with darkness? What accord has Christ with Belial? Or what portion does a believer share with a non-believer? What agreement has the temple of God with idols? For we are the temple of the living God; as God said, "I will make my dwelling among them and walk among them, and I will be their God, and they shall be my people" (2 Cor. 6:14-16).

Sex education, true to its origin, celebrates human sexuality. It strips away natural modesty and protective embarrassment in order to do it. But is the Christian called to celebrate sexuality (the creation) or God (the Creator)? Celebrating sexuality may sound appealing in a utopian sort of way, but what is the promise? What is the fruit? As more children and adults celebrate sexuality, do we also see greater problems of promiscuity, cohabitation, homosexuality, abortion, divorce and fractured families? Biblical instruction in purity helps us remember that we are sons and daughters of God in Christ. It sees each human being as a person capable of thinking, feeling and acting in more than sexual ways. While being sexual here on earth may bring the blessing of procreation in marriage, it is not the part of us that stays with us in our eternal home.

> Biblical instruction in purity is mismatched with sex education rooted in humanism like a donkey is mismatched to an ox.
>
> ❖ ❖ ❖

Biblical instruction in purity is mismatched with sex education rooted in humanism like a donkey is mismatched to an ox. Yoked together to plow a field, the larger animal will walk at a different pace than the smaller one. Attempting to drive the two together will be erratic and potentially dangerous. Mixing the Word of the Lord together with false teaching may, in time, weaken or even destroy a believer's relationship with Jesus and others.

Christianity and modern sex education are unequally yoked because the founders of sex education did not see children as God sees them and had no respect for the complementary differences of men and women. Neither did they have a respect for natural, innate modesty nor parental authority. Those who developed sex education had little or no regard for the conception and birth of human life. In fact, great effort went into disconnecting sex and sexuality from marriage and procreation. All of this compromises the teaching of purity.

But what is a Christian to do? Our children live in the real world and, for their sake, don't they need to be educated about sex in the right way? After all, God created sex; therefore, it is good, isn't it? Most of us agree that parents should be the ones to have the sex talk with their children, but they need help, don't they? From where does this help come? Busy and overwhelmed parents in today's world can easily be discouraged. Discouraged, they may doubt that the Word of God is enough. They may rationalize a partnership with unbelievers or make use of resources that appear beneficial for the healthy growth of their children. But, history proves that compromised faith and practice can turn a culture upside down... one child, one family, one neighborhood at a time. Perhaps there is a lesson about the dangers of being unequally yoked in the books of Ezra and Nehemiah.

19. What lesson do we learn from the books of Ezra and Nehemiah that can be useful for a discussion on Christianity and sex education?

The remnant of Israel that had survived exile in Persia returned home to find the walls of Jerusalem broken down and city gates destroyed. To this small number of faithful people was given the arduous task of re-building the temple and walls of Jerusalem. God also wanted His people to grow faithful families. He wanted them to be holy and set apart in their worship and practice. When people in the neighboring land saw that Jerusalem was being restored, they offered their help. After all, those people explained, they worshiped God, too. (In reality, they were a people of blended religions.) Fearing that they would commit themselves to false worship, the people of God refused the offer of resources and help. They knew that God had entrusted the job of rebuilding the temple and walls only to them. So, "the people of the land discouraged the people of Judah and made them afraid to build and bribed counselors against them to frustrate their purpose" (Ezra 4:4-5).

The culture in which God's people found themselves made the building project very difficult, but the Word of the Lord consistently commanded the people to persevere. God also reminded His people that they were to be holy and set apart for His good purpose. But the people of Israel, following the example of some of their leaders, mixed themselves with the Canaanites, Ammonites, Moabites, Egyptians and others through marriage (9:1-2). The people were guilty of breaking faith with God and allowing impurity of worship, teaching, and practice. There was confession and absolution but, because the potential for continued corruption of worship was so great, illegal marriages were identified and ended (10:18-19). The re-building of the temple, restoration of the walls, and growing of faithful families began anew.

However, when the neighbors in the land saw that the Israelites were again doing the work of God in rebuilding Jerusalem, they were angry. "[T]hey all plotted together to come and fight against Jerusalem and to cause confusion in it" (Neh. 4:8). It was easy to cause confusion and discouragement among the Israelites because fathers, mothers, and grandparents were overwhelmed by the task that lay before them. "There is too much rubble. By ourselves we will not be able to rebuild the wall" (4:10). The enemies said, "They will not know or see till we come among them and kill them and stop the work" (4:11). Nehemiah encouraged the people, "Do not be afraid of them. Remember the Lord, who is great and awesome, and fight for your brothers, your sons, your daughters, your wives, and your homes" (4:14). When the walls were rebuilt and the gates restored, the law of God was read to the people who were both joyful and repentant (chapters 8 and 9).

Everything was coming back into order and Israel was prepared to live by the truth of God's Word. What could go wrong? What went wrong is incredibly significant. Eliashib, the priest appointed over the chambers of God, gave Tobiah the Ammonite a place in the temple (13:4-5). Under the guise of helping God's people, Tobiah was given a room formerly used to store the offering for God. There, within the temple, sat Tobiah and his possessions. Nehemiah was away when this happened, but when he returned, he "was very angry, and [he] threw all the household furniture of Tobiah out of the chamber. Then [he] gave orders, and they cleansed the chambers, and [he] brought back there the vessels of the house of God." (13:8-9).

God entrusted the re-building of His temple and the city walls to His people. He entrusted the growing of holy families to husbands and wives equipped with His Word. He does the same today. God wants His people to keep their worship, teaching, and practices pure and different from that of the sinful world. Certainly, there are resources in the world that can be practical and helpful to the Christian. But we must take care especially when it comes to instructing Jesus' little ones. "See that you do not despise one of these little ones. For I tell you that in heaven their angels always see the face of my Father who is in heaven" (Matt. 18:10). It is a frightening thing indeed to compromise one of the Father's children.

> God entrusted the re-building of His temple and the city walls to His people. He entrusted the growing of holy families to husbands and wives equipped with His Word. He does the same today.
>
> ❖ ❖ ❖

20. Why weren't the faithful of God standing guard?

It is often true that when God's people are weary and burdened, or prideful and above reproach, it is easier for an opposing foe to gain access by offering some kind of help or resource. So Nehemiah "stationed the people by their clans, with their swords, their spears, and their bows ... each of the builders had his sword strapped at his side while he built" (Neh. 4:13, 18). The men were on guard at night and labored by day (22).

When the Church grows comfortable with the world, it lets down its guard. With guard down, our heads are easily turned. This is true with sex and sexuality education. A Christian parent might be complacent or even intimidated by the thought of teaching their child about sex. Christian educators may pride themselves on years of higher learning. But from where did they receive their education on the topic of sexuality? Christian educators may believe they possess the skill of discerning good material from bad. But the humanist sex education that entered schools and churches in the 1960s is in no way similar to "the talk" parents gave their sons and daughters prior to that time. Nehemiah did not allow Tobiah the Ammonite to remain in the house of God because he would confuse the people of God. For the same reason, the Church should resist the temptation to allow humanistic teaching within its walls. This includes the teaching that "children are sexual from birth" and "sexuality is our whole selves."

CHAPTER FIVE

Sex Education is a Concern for

The Pro-Life & Baptized Christian

21. Why is sex education a life issue?

"Christian sex education" that unwittingly builds on humanistic ideology and secular principles wrongly identifies children. Wrongly identified, the life of a child takes on a very different meaning and purpose. "Sexual from birth" affects the way we see ourselves and others and also the way we treat ourselves and others. It becomes who we are and easily influences the choices we make. It might assume a "right" or a "need." It provides an excuse for a buffet of sexual preferences. "Reproductive rights" become necessary to enable people to live their lives as "sexual from birth." The humanist founders of modern sex education denied that God has absolute authority over what we do with our bodies. The pro-abortion mantra of "my body, my choice" takes the premise that "children are sexual from birth" to a natural but deadly conclusion. It sacrifices children in the name of "my sexuality." It demeans the vocations of fatherhood and motherhood. It assaults marriage and family, which God designed as the pillars of civilization.

There was a time when abortion was clearly not an option for someone who professed faith in Jesus Christ. But has sex education that continually refers to boys and girls as "sexual from birth" or "sexual beings" made abortion thinkable for young Christians who have become sexually intimate? Ultrasound technology—indeed, a "window to the womb"—has caused

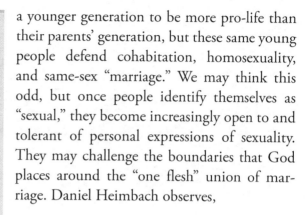

Once people identify themselves as "sexual," they become increasingly open to and tolerant of personal expressions of sexuality.

❖ ❖ ❖

a younger generation to be more pro-life than their parents' generation, but these same young people defend cohabitation, homosexuality, and same-sex "marriage." We may think this odd, but once people identify themselves as "sexual," they become increasingly open to and tolerant of personal expressions of sexuality. They may challenge the boundaries that God places around the "one flesh" union of marriage. Daniel Heimbach observes,

The gradual slide toward paganism starts when a person still committed to the Bible entertains dissatisfaction with something God says about sex, and a single logic connects a series of steps that extend from sliding ever so slightly from biblical teaching at one end to full-scale attack on biblical morality on the other. Letting dissatisfaction fester sparks interest in ways to soften or remove the offending biblical teaching. At first, this is done in ways that do not challenge the authority of Scripture but only try to change its meaning.

But shaping Christian morality to the culture destroys respect for the Bible, and as respect for biblical accuracy and authority collapses, biblical moral standards seem less and less relevant. Eventually the moral authority of the Bible is abandoned completely in favor of a culturally popular, indulgent approach. Sexual morality is defined by sexual desires, and the indulging of sexual desires is thought necessary to achieve higher levels of personal development. At this stage, biblical standards are ridiculed, sexual differences are maligned, and the boundaries God has set to keep sex pure and good are attacked as harmful or dangerous.[104]

If "sexuality is our whole selves" and "central to human life" as sexologists claim, then even Christians will be tempted to defend abortion as a "personal sacrifice." The number of surgical abortions appears to have decreased, but a sexualized generation is noticeably more dependent on pharmaceutical companies for chemical abortifacients and birth control, drugs to manage sexually transmitted and life-long diseases, and anti-depressants.

We want to grow a culture of life, but we cannot do so until we see that abortion is the consequence of an identity problem. Sexual intimacy outside of marriage, living together, pedophilia, the practice of homosexuality—these are all the consequences of an identity problem. Our behavior and choices say something about how we view ourselves. Even pro-life people stand on slippery ground when we default to labeling ourselves "sexual beings." Consider, for example, the woman with five children who says she will "never have an abortion" but is not married to any of her children's fathers. What is her behavior saying about her identity? Identifying first and foremost as a sexual being puts baptized children of God at odds with themselves.

22. Why is sex education a Baptism issue?

Sex education, as intended by its founders, assigns an identity contrary to the one God bestows at Baptism. At Baptism, the sign of the cross is made over us to indicate that we are redeemed by Christ the crucified.[105] We have His mark on us. We are baptized, not in the water of sexuality, but in the water of pure Word and through the work of the Holy Spirit. We are called not to ways of weak flesh, but to holy and noble purpose. We are encouraged not to

---

104 Daniel R. Heimbach, *True Sexual Morality: Recovering Biblical Standards for a Culture in Crisis* (Wheaton, Illinois, Crossway, 2004), 114.

105 "Holy Baptism", *Lutheran Service Book* (St. Louis, MO., Concordia Publishing House, 2006), 268-271.

glorify self, but to glorify Jesus Christ who makes us children of God. Baptism is "an appeal to God for a good conscience, through the resurrection of Jesus Christ" (1 Pet. 3:21). Even as Baptism cleans the sinner, it gives strength to be different from the world and restrain our own fickle desires. Baptism changes our perspective. Our Baptism is a daily reminder to see ourselves the way God sees us. We are so much more than sexual beings; we are heirs of God!

> Our Baptism is a daily reminder to see ourselves the way God sees us.
>
>

"He saved us through the washing of rebirth and renewal by the Holy Spirit, whom He poured out on us generously through Jesus Christ our Savior, so that, having been justified by His grace, we might become heirs having the hope of eternal life" (Ti. 3:5-8). Through daily contrition and repentance, the Old Adam in us is drowned and dies with all wrong thoughts and desires. A new person in Christ rises up to live before God in righteousness and purity (Rm. 6:4).

23. In what way might "cradle to grave" sex education create other identity problems?

Cradle to grave sex education is a phrase used by both secular and Christian educators. It means teaching about one's "sexual nature" or sexuality beginning at a very young age and continuing to emphasize it until death. But such teaching challenges our very being. Identified first and foremost as sexual beings, what becomes of us if we don't marry or are physically-challenged? It's not just the young who are sexualized. What becomes of us as our sexual desires and activities fade? Is there some product that restores that "sexual" identity? If not, are we less male? Less female? Are husband and wife less complete when they celebrate not so much the act of sex but the friendship, trust and companionship that comes with maturity and faithful marriage? What becomes of us as we grow older, don't feel so "sexy," develop health challenges, slow our pace, require more patience and care from others, and appear less productive but more costly to society? Are we less human?

24. What does "sexuality" mean?

There does not seem to be a definition that can be agreed upon. The term is ambiguous and has been in flux over the last 50 or more years. That is why it is so dangerous to use the term without further explanation of what one is trying to describe. I have been told that sexuality was not a word used in the pre-Kinsey world. I cannot find the word in my grandmother's books. Historically, male or female was descriptive of one's sex and intercourse was the act of sex. Hetero*sexual* is a biological term describing how the mammalian species reproduces. The only other means of natural reproduction is a*sexual* as with the lower invertebrates. The suffix *sexual* has always referred to reproduction or human procreation. (Thus, using the prefix *homo* which means "same throughout" with *sexual* is an oxymoron.)

Today, what does "sexuality" mean? *Random House Webster's College Dictionary* defines "sexuality" this way:

1. Sexual character; possession of the structural and functional traits of sex.

2. Recognition of or emphasis upon sexual matters.

3. Involvement in sexual activity.

4. An organism's preparedness for engaging in sexual activity."[106]

"Human sexuality," defined by *Wikipedia*, "is the capacity to have erotic experiences and responses. Human sexuality can also refer to the way someone is sexually attracted to another person—which is determined by their sexual orientation—whether it is to the opposite sex (heterosexuality), to

---

106 Sexuality: www.definitions.net/definition/sexuality, accessed July 9, 2013.

the same sex (homosexuality), having both these tendencies (bisexuality), to all gender identities (pansexuality or bisexuality), or not being attracted to anyone in a sexual manner (asexuality)."[107]

"Sexuality," as defined by *The Merriam-Webster Dictionary* is: "The quality or state of being sexual:

a. the condition of having sex,

b. sexual activity,

c. expression of sexual receptivity or interest especially when excessive."[108]

According to Planned Parenthood, sexuality "includes:"

your body, including your sexual and reproductive anatomy and body image— how you feel about your body,

your biological sex—male, female, or intersex,

your gender—being a girl, boy, woman, man, or transgender, or genderqueer,

your sexual identity—feelings about and how you express your gender,

your sexual orientation—who you're sexually and/or romantically attracted to,

your desires, thoughts, fantasies, and sexual preferences,

---

107 Sexuality: accessed July 9, 2013 www.wikipedia.org/wiki/Human_sexuality.
108 Sexuality: accessed July 9, 2013 www.merriam-webster.com/dictionary/sexuality.

your values, attitudes, beliefs, and ideals about life, love, and sexual relationships,

your sexual behaviors—including masturbation."[109]

Surprisingly, Planned Parenthood provides a resource for Christian parents and facilitators complete with many passages from Scripture. At quick glance, one finds credible information; however, it is fair to ask how Planned Parenthood and God's Word fit together. The resource, entitled "Christian Family Life Education," states, "Sexuality is the total expression of who we are as human beings. It includes our spirituality, emotions, physical development, gender, attitudes and values, personality, sexual orientations and sexual identity."[110]

In the post-Kinsey world, let us as Christians agree that:

- our sex is either male or female (Mt. 19:4);

- infants and children are either boy or girl, but not naturally sexual in thought, word or deed;

- sexual describes feelings, desires, thoughts, and the ability to join intimately with the opposite sex, but it is not the sum total of who we are as male or female persons;

- biologically, sexual describes the way male and female procreate; we are different from amoebas that produce asexually;

---

109 Sexuality: accessed July 9, 2013 www.plannedparenthood.org/health-topics/sexuality-4323.htm.

110 Shirley Miller, "Christian Family Life Education," Margaret Sanger Center International, 2001, 99, accessed July 9, 2013, www.plannedparenthood.org/nyc/files/NYC/CFL_Guide_web.pdf.

- male and female are made by God in such a way that they might "become one flesh" (Gn. 2:24) in marriage, which can include sexual intercourse as well as the intimacies of trusted companionship.

"Sexuality" is a modern word. Without definition, it is vague and unclear. For that reason, perhaps this is a good time for the Body of Christ to help bring some clarity. We can do that by speaking about "God's design for sexuality" rather than "God's gift of sexuality" (whatever that might mean to any individual).

> We bring some clarity ... by speaking about "God's design for sexuality" rather than "God's gift of sexuality (whatever that might mean to any individual).
>
> ❖ ❖ ❖

25. With such broad definitions of sexuality, is it any wonder that Christians have differing ideas about sex education?

Christians can become passionate—one way or another—about sex or sexuality education. Parents and pastors can be overwhelmed and even confused by the subject. Using the above definitions of "sexuality" and depending upon the instructor or mentor, the teaching and techniques can vary a great deal. In 1967, my own church body published a number of books with the goal of sharing God's perspective on sex and sexuality from kindergarten through adulthood. But:

- From where did the ideas about sexuality come?

- What guidelines and models were used?

- Who determined what terms and phrases children should learn and at what age?

- Upon whose recommendation did sex education shift to the Christian classroom?

- Where and by whom were the teachers trained?

- Who advocated for teaching boys and girls in the same classroom?

Parents, pastors, and educators unintentionally place children in harm's way when they bring false teachings and practices into the Christian home or classroom. Nehemiah was called upon by God to help the people of Israel discipline themselves as they worked to rebuild Jerusalem and stand against idolatry. He reminded the people not to enter into mixed marriages with neighbors in the land for this would violate the covenant and compromise the true faith. He was righteously angry with Eliashib the priest for giving Tobiah the Ammonite a place in the house of the Lord. Modern sex education, because it often blends together religious and humanistic ideas about human sexuality, should not hold a place in the Church's classrooms for the same reason that Tobiah was not tolerated in the house of the Lord. Like Tobiah, who did not see the people of Israel as God saw them, modern sex education should not be allowed to twist the identity of our sons and daughters and put believers at risk.

We do not want to sin against God by offending His little ones. "Sexual" does not describe an infant or child. If we say that "children are sexual from birth," we are saying what God does not. Let's remember who coined the phrase and why.

26. Do pro-life organizations identify the dangers of sex education?

Yes. The Society for the Protection of Unborn Children (SPUC) was the first pro-life organization in the world, established on January 11, 1967, in the United Kingdom. SPUC recognizes the connection between sexualizing our children, abortion, and life issues in general. Some of the worst sexualizing of children, observes the SPUC, happens in the class-room—secular or Christian. The SPUC's "Safe at School" program identifies sex education as "sexual sabotage." For this reason, the SPUC keeps close tabs on the Family Planning Association (FPA) and its work in the schools.

Here in the U.S., pro-life organizations monitor the efforts of Planned Parenthood which purposefully seeks to educate children at a young age. The key marketing demographic for the abortion industry is young people between the ages of 12 and 25. Planned Parenthood is the largest provider of abortions in the U.S. Sex education is the cornerstone of Planned Parenthood. Sexualized and desensitized children are the base of Planned Parenthood's pyramid. Within a short time after Planned Parenthood pushed for sex education in America's public and private schools, school-based health clinics were set up to provide birth control, treatment of sexually-transmitted diseases, and abortion.[111] Using the guidelines of SIECUS, Planned Parenthood worms its way into the sexuality, family life, and health education of many schools.

> Sex education is the cornerstone of Planned Parenthood. Sexualized and desensitized children are the base of Planned Parenthood's pyramid.
>
> ❖ ❖ ❖

27. Are you inferring that sex education offered by Christians is the same as that of Planned Parenthood?

No. Planned Parenthood has no regard for God's Word and, therefore, cannot treat children as the persons God created them to be. Christian

111 Author's Note: Some resources and statistics on Planned Parenthood and sex education are *Grand Illusions: the Legacy of Planned Parenthood* by George Grant; "Why Trust Planned Parenthood?" Prolife Action Ministries, St. Paul, MN; www.plam.org; www.abbyjohnson.org; www.stopp.org. If you want to know what Planned Parenthood tells boys and girls, visit their teen website at www.teenwire.org.

educators hold the children that God loves in high esteem, but may fear for them. Here, perhaps, is where the problem began. Sex education came into existence in the Church for three basic reasons: 1) fear of AIDS, sexually-transmitted diseases, and teen pregnancy; 2) fear that children would get the wrong information from peers and the media; and 3) fear that parents and the Church were silent on the topic of sex.

Most of our wrong choices in life are made in fear. Better choices are made when we trust and use the Word of God written for all people in all circumstances for all time. Better choices are made when we resist wrapping God's Word around worldly opinions and half-truths.

Christians who conduct sex education do what they do because they care about children, marriage and family. But with the goal of teaching healthy attitudes about sex and sexuality, well-meaning people can be deceived. We may all believe that we are capable of sorting the good from the bad, but we must pause on behalf of the children to ask: What has most influenced my thinking on topics such as sexuality? The world, or God's Word? Without meaning to, have I tried to blend the foolishness of the world with the wisdom of God?

There are several key phrases and principles of secular, modern sex education that are often repeated in Christian schools and homes. Here are a few:

- Children are sexual from birth. (Kinsey)

- Sexuality is central to being human. (SIECUS)

- Lack of knowledge is bad, more knowledge is good. (Humanist concept of "higher learning")

- Modern people have progressed from the puritanical ways of the past. (Humanism, atheism)

- Boys and girls should learn about sex/sexuality together in the same classroom. (Planned Parenthood, modern feminists)

- Sex education should be continuous from cradle to grave. (SIECUS)

Kinsey, SIECUS, and secular humanism are diametrically opposed to Christianity. "They are from the world; therefore they speak from the world, and the world listens to them. We are from God. Whoever knows God listens to us; whoever is not from God does not listen to us. By this we know the Spirit of truth and the spirit of error" (1 John 4:5-6). For the good of children, we must determine the origin and purpose of any kind of education. We must ask: Do the teachings and methodology honor the commands and instruction of God's Word? If modern sex education is built on a corrupt foundation, and if it purposefully saturates children in sex beginning at young ages and steals away their innocence, shouldn't the Christian want to build on something different?

28. There are some who say that sex has become such a mess because it was hushed up. There's truth in that statement, isn't there?

Let's allow C.S. Lewis to answer this one. The following is excerpted from *Mere Christianity* written by Lewis in 1952:

> We have been told, till one is sick of hearing it, that sexual desire is in the same state as any of our other natural desires and that if only we abandon the silly old Victorian idea of hushing it up, everything in the garden will be lovely. It is not true. The moment you look at the facts, and away from the propaganda, you see that it is not.
>
> They tell you sex has become a mess because it was all hushed up. But for the last twenty years it has not been hushed up.

It has been chattered about all day long. Yet it is still in a mess. If hushing up had been the cause of the trouble, ventilation would have set it right. But it has not. I think it is the other way round. I think the human race originally hushed it up because it had become such a mess. Modern people are always saying, "Sex is nothing to be ashamed of." They may mean two things. They may mean "There is nothing to be ashamed of in the fact that the human race reproduces itself in a certain way, nor in the fact that it gives pleasure." If they mean that, they are right. Christianity says the same.

But, of course, when people say, "Sex is nothing to be ashamed of," they may mean "the state into which this sexual instinct has now got is nothing to be ashamed of." If they mean that, I think they are wrong. I think it is everything to be ashamed of … There are people who want to keep our sex instinct inflamed in order to make money out of us. Because, of course, a man with an obsession is a man who has very little sales-resistance. God knows our situation; He will not judge us as if we had no difficulties to overcome. What matters is the sincerity and perseverance of our will to overcome them.[112]

29. Might it be correct to say that sex education has become a kind of religion?

At the very least, sex education is certainly defended as sacred ground. In spite of evidence that shows how sex education is founded on humanism and the work of Kinsey, many church leaders disavow any connection. Similarities between sex education used in the Church and that used

---

112 C.S. Lewis, *Mere Christianity* (New York, N.Y: Touchstone, Macmillan Publishing Company, 1952), Copyright renewed 1980 by Arthur Owen Barfield, 92-93.

elsewhere are commonly dismissed. Parents who question the appropriateness of boys and girls together in sex education are considered too parochial or naïve. There does not seem to be a willingness to discuss the possibility that sex education in the Church, though well-intentioned, might not have accomplished what it set out to do.

> There does not seem to be a willingness to discuss the possibility that sex education in the Church, though well-intentioned, might not have accomplished what it set out to do.
>
> ❖ ❖ ❖

Here are a few reasons why sex education founded on "children are sexual from birth" could be compared to a rival religion:

- Sex education that focuses on an identity that is sexual threatens to distract children from the holy identity given them by God.

- Sex education that focuses on "God's gift of sexuality" flirts with paganism because it turns eyes to the created rather than the Creator.

- Sex education that ignores the created differences of boys and girls to, instead, treat them the same goes against the order of God's creation.

- Sex education that focuses on the "yeses" of sexuality tempts young people to think that sex is impossible to corrupt when, indeed as Scripture tells us, sex is easily corrupted.

- Sex education from "cradle to grave" can shift thinking of sexuality in terms of Christian faith and doctrine to thinking of Christian faith and doctrine in terms of sexuality.

- Sex education that connects the "one flesh" of marriage with closeness to God crosses a very dangerous line in taking the goodness of sex and redefining it as the presence of God.

A focus on an identity that is sexual can lead to justification of abortion as "the sacrifice I had to make for myself." We do well to remember what happened whenever God's people mingled with those who worshiped gods of fertility and sexuality. Children usually paid the highest price, often with their lives. For example, archaeological excavations in the region of Canaan have uncovered a great many jars containing the remains of children. These children, found under the debris of temples to Baal and Ashtoreth, were sacrifices made by a pagan and sexualized people. There is a reason why God expressly commanded Joshua and the Israelites to destroy or drive out the Canaanites (Dt. 7:2, 3).[113] "And you shall consume all the peoples that the Lord your God will give over to you. Your eye shall not pity them, neither shall you serve their gods, for that would be a snare to you" (Dt. 7:16). Failure to completely destroy the Canaanites would lead to idolatry. Such idolatry later caused Israel's enslavement in Assyria and Babylon (cf 2 Ki. 17).

Sex education built on secular and humanist principles changes the way we see children, the way boys and girls see themselves, and the way men and women see each other. It removes boundaries set in place for our benefit and ultimately changes our behavior. It affects relationships, marriage, and family. It takes us perilously close to idolatry and places us in spiritual danger.

30. Why might sex education take us perilously close to idolatry and place us in spiritual danger?

Sex education is founded on the belief that "sexuality" is central to our being. But this is not God's language. Sexuality is not the sum total of who we are as male or female persons. *Focusing on ourselves as sexual beings bestows the wrong identity and purpose for life.* Bestowing the wrong identity, we put ourselves in God's

> Sexuality is not the sum total of who we are as male or female persons.
>
>

---

113 *Halley's Bible Handbook* (Grand Rapids, MI: Zondervan Publishing House, 1965), 166, 167, 198.

place. When we identify ourselves as "sexual beings," we may be tempted to give ourselves freedoms that God does not, to trust our own reason and desires, and to, in fact, worship and serve ourselves rather than God (Rom. 1:24-25). In time, sexual identity influences everything in society . . . even religion.

In America today, it appears that sex—sexual identity and sexual expression—is the one holy of holies. If, as children have been told for the last 50+ years, we are "sexual from birth," then that is who God made us to be. It is who we are and what we do. It is even our excuse for doing what we should not do. Identifying ourselves as "sexual" places little or no importance on self-restraint. After all, as sexual beings, why would we restrain what is natural to us? Focus on identity as a sexual being tempts us to think that human desires, which have been corrupted since the Fall into sin, are created by God. When current, post-Fall human desires are made the definition of how God created us, then it is difficult to resist approval of any and every desire that people have, whether it is toward unmarried sex, adultery, sodomy, same-sex marriage, or even sexual intimacy between a child and an adult.

There is spiritual danger in choosing to identify ourselves as sexual beings. We are male or female creations of God. As baptized believers in Jesus Christ, we are God's children. But when we call ourselves what He does not, when we focus on ourselves as "sexual beings" and not His children, then our wrong identity shapes our behavior. Wrong behavior changes our attitude toward God. A changed attitude toward God can dangerously tempt us to put ourselves in the place of God; to even become our own god, a god who defines "self" and "sexuality" as being supreme. Contemporary sex education (and Christian varieties that define human beings as fundamentally "sexual") raises the sensual and earthly nature to a level higher than our true and eternal identity in Jesus Christ.

What are the signs of sexuality becoming a false god? These signs are present when one begins to think: 1) It is who I am, 2) It is what I do, 3) It is my right, 4) It determines my preferences and lifestyle, 5) It gives me value, and 6) It is my glory. The essence of idolatry is worshiping something God made and not God Himself.

31. When we define ourselves as "sexual beings," what other trouble brews?

If we are "sexual from birth," then one may believe that his current lusts and desires were created that way by God, rather than being horribly corrupted by sin. If people believe their current desires are God-given, it would follow that no one has the right to tell them how to define or express their "sexuality." The consequences of life as a predominately "sexual being" have become evident in my lifetime. Here's what I see:

- Little girls allowed by their moms to wear thongs, play with sexy dolls, and dress up like little beauty queens complete with bikini or sequined, slinky gown.

- Three of the most common mental health problems of girls and women—eating disorders, low self-esteem and depression—have been linked to sexualization. Girls ages 10-19 are at higher risk of anorexia thinking they must be thin to be sexy. A sexual image is so important to some elementary-age girls that they feel shame if they don't conform to the look of the runway model. Teenage girls have breast implants and liposuction. [114]

- Contemporary heroines for little girls such as the Little Mermaid and Pocahontas, are "sexier" than previous heroines such as Cinderella and Snow White.

- Sexual harassment is a more common form of aggression by elementary-age boys taught by video games, the media and early sex education

---

114 "Sexy Babies: How Sexualization Hurts Girls," www.aboutkidshealth.ca.

to see girls as "touchable." Popularity of girls is measured, too often, by physical appearance and ability to capture a boy's attention.

- Pre-teen girls (and boys) are routinely taken for the Gardasil shot (a preventative measure against the human papilloma virus which can only be contracted through sexual intercourse with an infected person) and pre-teen girls are put on the Pill because, since "children are sexual from birth," they most likely "won't be able to stop from acting on those desires."

- The Pill, intended to "level the sexual playing field" of male and female, has divorced the act of sex from procreation and promoted "hook ups," "friends with benefits" and an unprecedented trend of cohabitation.

- Childhood sexual abuse by trusted, Christian adults is more prevalent, but the Christian community seems reluctant to address the life-changing implications.

- Tolerance of adolescents who experiment with homosexuality, lesbianism and bi-sexuality because, after all, if "sexual" is who we are, then "there are different ways to express that sexuality."

CHAPTER SIX

Our Identity is Defined by God
and Influences Our Behavior

32. How does God define us? What does His Word say about our identity?

God alone has the right to bestow our identity because "It is he who has made us and we are his" (Ps. 100:3). We are His creation (Gen. 1:27). All people were created in God's image, not the image of animals. God is holy, not sexual, sensual, or captive to instincts. God says, "You shall be holy, for I am holy" (1 Pet. 1:16). But the Fall into sin introduced horrible corruption to the human race, so that now the thoughts and desires of people are sinful and centered on serving the self (Gen. 6:5; Eph. 2:3). Christians, however, have been given the Holy Spirit who begins in them a "new creation" (2 Cor. 5:17; Gal. 6:15), and starts to re-form the image of God in them (Col. 3:10). We struggle with our sinful human nature because we are sons of Adam and daughters of Eve, but we are not bound to that human nature because of the washing and renewal of our Baptism (Tit. 3:5-8). In our Baptism, Jesus Christ restored our identity as "heirs" of eternal life. We are strengthened to "abstain from the passions of the flesh, which wage war against [our] soul" (1 Pet. 2:11). Re-creation in Christ makes us God's adopted children who are invited to cry "Abba! Father!" (Rom. 8:15).

> God says, "You shall be holy, for I am holy."
>
> ❖ ❖ ❖

Our bodies are "a temple of the Holy Spirit" bought at great price (1 Cor. 6:19). We are treasures of God for whom Jesus gave all He had. In Christ crucified, we reclaim our identity. Since Jesus is holy, God declares us holy through faith in Him. "I have called you by name," God says. "You are mine" (Isa. 43:1). "'I will be a father to you, and you shall be sons and daughters to me,' says the Lord Almighty" (2 Cor. 6:18). Jesus spoke to our full person and human identity when He said, "You shall love the Lord your God with all your heart and with all your soul and with all your mind and with all your strength" (Mk. 12:30).

We hold to a body-soul anthropology or understanding of the origin, nature and destiny of mankind as expressed in the Athanasian Creed.[115] We will be resurrected, not as disembodied spirits, but with perfect bodies joined with perfect souls. In heaven, we will not be angels but our resurrected bodies will be like angels (Matt. 22:30). We will neither marry nor be given in marriage. This is a sound argument against the idea that human beings are fundamentally "sexual." If that were true, in the resurrection we would be somehow less than human.

33. But isn't our identity inseparable from our sexuality?

That's what Christopher Yuan thought. As a young man, Christopher struggled with homosexual desires. He prayed that God would change him. When God did not, Christopher gave up the struggle, believing, "This is who I am." While serving time in prison for drug-dealing, Christopher confessed his sexual identity to a chaplain who told him that Scripture doesn't condemn homosexuality. Christopher was motivated to contrast the information given to him by the chaplain with God's Word of

---

115 "Therefore, it is the right faith that we believe and confess that our Lord Jesus Christ, the Son of God, is at the same time both God and man. He is God, begotten from the substance of the Father before all ages; and He is man, born from the substance of his mother in this age: perfect God and perfect man, *composed of a rational soul and human flesh;* equal to the Father with respect to His divinity, less than the Father with respect to His humanity." From the Athanasian Creed.

Scripture. In light of the Word, Christopher realized that "my identity shouldn't be defined by my sexuality." Christopher writes,

> Paul said in Acts 17:28, "For in him we live and move and have our being." Christ should be everything—my all in all. My sexual orientation didn't have to be the core of who I was. My primary identity didn't have to be defined by my feelings or sexual attractions. My identity was not "gay" or "homosexual," or even "heterosexual," for that matter. But my identity as a child of the living God must be in Jesus Christ alone.
>
> God says, "Be holy, for I am holy." I had always thought that the opposite of homosexuality was heterosexuality. But actually the opposite of homosexuality is holiness. God never said, "Be heterosexual, for I am heterosexual." He said, "Be holy, for I am holy."[116]

"My identity was not 'gay' or 'homosexual,' or even 'heterosexual,' for that matter. But my identity as a child of the living God must be in Jesus Christ alone."

❖ ❖ ❖

Christopher desired change. But, he writes, "change is not the absence of struggles; change is the freedom to choose holiness in the midst of our struggles."[117]

In *The Book of Man*, Bill Bennett tells about his friend who was recovering from life-threatening cancer. "His doctor told him that he could not work, exercise, or enjoy the other fruits of life," explains Bennett, "all things that men pride themselves on. I asked him what hurts the most to be without.

---

116   Christopher Yuan and Angela Yuan, *Out of a Far Country* (Colorado Springs, CO: Waterbrook Press, 2011), 187.

117   Yuan, *Out of a Far Country*, 188.

'Work,' he said. 'I don't feel like a man. Work has more to do with me being a man than sex or muscle.'"[118]

34. Will knowing who we are in heaven help us better understand who we are here on earth?

If we were fundamentally "sexual," then this would hold true not just before the resurrection but also after the resurrection. (Otherwise after the resurrection we would be less than human.) But what does Jesus say? "For in the resurrection they neither marry nor are given in marriage, but are like angels in heaven" (Matt. 22:30). Therefore being sexual, that is, capable of sexual activity, is not part of what it means to be human after the resurrection. And if it is not part of our divinely-created human identity in the resurrection where everything will be made perfect, then it is not the central part of our divinely-created identity now. In heaven there will be no act of marriage, no "one flesh" union. So, do we lose our identity in heaven? No! Our true identity will remain intact. We will be as He created us—fully human, but perfect in every way, sons and daughters at the Father's table. We will still be His treasures in Christ but, at last, able to truly reflect His magnificence. For now, we live on earth in human flesh. We do not have to obey the passions of our mortal bodies (Ro. 6:12) however, because holiness is all about God claiming us as His dear children in Christ through water and Word. Through Baptism, we are siblings—brothers and sisters in Christ who can anticipate His return. With the help of the Holy Spirit, we can encourage and care for one another in ways that will not bring shame on the Day of the Lord (1 Jn. 2:28).

> If we were fundamentally "sexual," then this would hold true not just before the resurrection but also after the resurrection ... But what does Jesus say?
>
> ❖ ❖ ❖

---

118 William J. Bennett, *The Book of Man: Readings on the Path to Manhood* (Nashville, TN: Thomas Nelson, 2011), 91.

35. What is the inevitable result of identifying ourselves as "sexual beings"?

It will affect the way we fear, love and trust God. It will affect the way we act in His presence and understand His purpose for our lives. It will also tempt us to see God in a way He is not. We fallen creatures have a troublesome habit of projecting onto the Creator God our ideas of Him based upon how we see ourselves. If we see ourselves as His son or daughter in Christ, we will be more inclined to recognize Him for who He is and acknowledge His authority. But if we see ourselves as "sexual beings," we will be more inclined to define God according to human perspective and on human terms and less inclined to acknowledge His authority. This corrupts the image of God. Why? Because God does not bear the image of man nor is He sexual or sensual. God is holy.

God mandates holiness and He reveals its source. It is nothing other than Himself, His very essence and character. God is holy and expects us to conform to Him. "As obedient children, do not be conformed to the passions of your former ignorance, but as he who called you is holy, you also be holy in all your conduct, since it is written, 'You shall be holy, for I am holy'" (1 Pet. 1:14-16). It is not absolutely necessary that we experience the joy of "one flesh" in biblical marriage, but it is absolutely necessary that we should be holy. That which is sexual should never be viewed as a way to become more intimate with God nor should it become the intrinsic identity of the male and female first made in the image of God. In Baptism, we put on the "new self" which is "the likeness of God in true righteousness and holiness" (Eph. 4:24).

> It is not absolutely necessary that we experience the joy of "one flesh" in biblical marriage, but it is absolutely necessary that we should be holy.

36. Does identity affect behavior? How should a child of God live?

Yes, identity affects behavior. It is important, for example, to ask the woman contemplating an abortion, "What is it? What is this that you want to abort?" Women have explained to me that when the doctor called their unborn child a "blob of tissue," it made the wrong thing that they knew they were doing much easier to do. When a woman identifies herself as a "sexual being" and her child as a "choice," then she may fail to guard the treasure for which Jesus died. She may fall into fear, then into idolatry. She—and all the rest of us—will find arguments for abortion, adultery, homosexuality and the counterfeiting or abolition of marriage.

The mistaken identity of "sexual from birth" tempts us to please ourselves. God did not have this in mind, so He does not identify us in this way because that phrase confuses our created maleness or femaleness with the corrupted state of our current sexual desires. A "sexual" identity is all about "me." It means being in debt to our own flesh and bound to live according to its fickle ways. But a "holy" identity is all about God claiming us as His dear children in Christ. In Christ, our fallen nature has no claim on us. Our flesh side may tempt us, saying, "This is who I am," or "I owe it to myself," but we aren't obligated to obey its impulses or satisfy its desires. Why? Because we "did not receive the spirit of slavery to fall back into fear" (Rom. 8:15). What a difference this makes in the way we live and who we worship.

In the biblical context, holy usually means "set apart for God."[119] It means being different from the sensual world. We are a people "for His own possession" (1 Pet. 2:9). As "temples of God," we have no agreement with idols (2 Cor. 6:16). This means no foolish or improper talk of sexual desire, no crude joking or teasing of the imagination. Our purpose in this world flows from our identity as God's holy ones. Our purpose is to "proclaim

---

119 Commentary: "Be Holy, for I Am Holy," *The Lutheran Study Bible* English Standard Version (St. Louis, MO: Concordia Publishing House, 2009), 2167.

the excellencies of Him who called [us]" (1 Pet. 2:9). Our behavior, just like our identity, is not common. Something that is common is useable by anyone. But we are useable by God. Our conduct as baptized children of God— indeed, "holy ones" or saints— should not reflect the ways of the sinful world, but reflect God's ways. Timothy exhorts us to be "a vessel for honorable use, set apart as holy, useful to the master of the house, ready for every good work" (2 Tim. 2:21). God is the master. The house is our body. Our good work is to turn the heads of others toward the master and away from ourselves. "[B]e holy in all your conduct" (1 Pet. 1:15). Why? Because we were created for God's glory, not our own. We are to "walk as children of light . . . and try to discern what is pleasing to the Lord" (Eph. 5:8-10).

CHAPTER SEVEN

Sexuality is Not a Central Part

of Being Human

37. Aren't we making too much out of this sexual identity thing? After all, humans are sexual and we do need sex, right?

We have stomachs and appetites, too. Some have even claimed, "You are what you eat." But, observes Bob Morrison,

> No one considers himself an alimentary being. Food—nourishment—is essential to human life. It's natural. But if we focus on that as the essence of our being, then, as St. Paul writes, our 'god is in our belly' (Phil. 3:19). Sex within marriage is right, but we should not forget that this gift is given so that the human race might continue and generations may know Christ."[120]

C.S. Lewis agrees with Morrison and St. Paul. "There is nothing to be ashamed of in enjoying your food: there would be everything to be ashamed of if half the world made food the main interest of their lives and

---

120 Author's note: Bob Morrison is Senior Fellow for Policy Studies at the Family Research Council www.frc.org and personal friend of mine. He is a pro-life advocate and served as the Director of the LC-MS Office of Government Information in Washington, D.C.

spent their time looking at pictures of food and dribbling and smacking their lips."[121]

38. It is true, isn't it, that sexuality is a central part of being human?

That's what SIECUS says. One of their core values is that "sexuality is a central part of being human."[122] But what does God say? Does He say that sexuality (understood as sexual desires and the ability to be sexually intimate) is a central part of being human? If so, where does He say that? And what does this mean, specifically when speaking about children?

Animals and humans bear similarity in the fact that both continue their species sexually, not asexually like amoebas. But should we be defined by the way we procreate? Central to being human is our distinction from animals. It is having the attributes of God. Unlike animals, humans have the ability to reason; to be kind, faithful, patient, and just. We derive knowledge of God's will for creation. In our vocations as male and female humans, we have opportunity to make use of our humanness in different yet compatible ways with glory to God. Even in the Garden of Eden, God did not clothe Adam and Eve with sexuality or sensuality. He clothed them with His glory. If sexuality is central to being human (as defined by Kinsey and company), what happens when we can't or don't express sexual desires and needs? Are we less human? The present culture seems to demand sexual rights. But is sexuality a right from God or a privilege and responsibility within the boundaries of marriage?

It would be cruel, don't you think, if God were to identify even children as "sexual beings" but then tell us we cannot freely be the very thing He created

---

121 Lewis, *Mere Christianity*, 92.

122 Sexuality Information and Education Council for the United States (SIECUS), Guidelines for Comprehensive Sexuality Education, 2004, 50, accessed June 22, 2013, http://www.siecus.org/pubs/guidelines/guidelines.pdf.

us to be? Quite the opposite is true. God wants us to be what He created us to be: holy people who live our daily lives as male or female not just in marriage, but in familial and social relationships, in school, at work, and in worship. He created us to be relational people but, because He did not make sexuality central to being human, we can relate to one another in non-sexual ways. We can be in all kinds of selfless relationships—parents and children, brothers and sisters, caring neighbors, coworkers—that draw attention to Jesus Christ. Jesus Christ was fully human, but only in error would we identify Him as a "sexual being."[123]

> He created us to be relational people but, because He did not make sexuality central to being human, we can relate to one another in non-sexual ways.
>
> ❖ ❖ ❖

Sin warped the image of God that we humans were created to bear. But the moment a person trusts Christ, he or she begins to receive a new nature (2 Cor. 5:17). Baptized, we are saints—or holy ones—set apart for God through the death and resurrection of Jesus. Holiness— whether it is reckoned to us freely (justification) or begins to characterize us (sanctification), whether we are receiving it as a free gift or cooperating with God to bring it about within us – is central to being human. We are "debtors, not to the flesh, to live according to the flesh" (Ro. 8:12), but to Christ in whom the fallen nature has no claim on us. We might want to say, "I am a sexual being. I can't help being who I am!" But in Christ, we are not obligated to obey impulses of the flesh or satisfy its desires. Why? Because Christians are sanctified. Sanctification is the process by which God develops our new nature, enabling us to grow into more holiness (not sexiness) through time. This is a continuous process with many victories and defeats as the new nature battles with the "old man" (Rom. 6:6) in which it presently resides. In heaven, the new nature will be set free, not as a sexual being (understood as sexually active), but as a holy being in the perfectly restored image of God.

---

123 Author's note: Authors and scriptwriters are playing fast and loose with Scripture today inferring, for example, that Jesus had a sexual relationship with Mary Magdelene.

39. When Christians use the phrases "sexual from birth" or "sexual beings," we're simply describing our maleness or femaleness, aren't we?

This is likely how many sincere Christians understand it. Remember, however, that male or female describes the kind of human we are. You may never have heard it explained this way before reading this book, so it bears repeating. Male or female has more than a sexual connotation; it is our divinely appointed vocation. It is a way to engage life. The vocation of male and female are God-given roles rooted in God's creation of each individual human, as opposed to the kinds of vocations that men and women choose or take up later in life (such as father, mother, teacher, or pastor). Those who oppose God don't care about this because, like Kinsey, they have no respect for male or female. God does. So, let's consider this in light of His Word.

God did not make male and female at the same time, in the same way or for the same purpose (Gn. 2: 7, 15, 18-22). Their differences did not conflict, but were complementary. As husband and wife, Adam and Eve were lovers, that is, they were sexually intimate. The human race came from their procreative sexual union; Eve became the "mother of all the living" (Gn. 3:20). But, not every complementary man or woman marries and, thus, becomes a lover or sexually active.

There is sexual love and there is *agape* love. Husbands and wives share sexual intimacy, but all males and females of any age can share (and practice) *agape* love. Scripture says it is the "will of God, your sanctification: that you abstain from sexual immorality; that each one of you know how to control his [or her] own body in holiness and honor, not in the passion of lust like [those] who do not know God" (1 Thes. 4:3-5). [124] Scripture is clear. The sexual part of us is designed for use within the parameters of marriage.

---

124 Author's note: "Sexual immorality" in Greek is *porneia*, which means "fornication."

To be lovers or, in other words, to share sexual intimacy and literally fit together in the pro-creational act of sex, is reserved for marriage between one man and one woman. To be male or female, however, is a design and vocation for *daily use* in glorifying God. *God does not tell us to abstain from being male or female.* God does not tell us to abstain from being the human beings He created us to be, but He does tell us to abstain from sexual activity except within marriage. Sexual activity is not an intrinsic part of what it means to be human. We don't do battle with the attributes of maleness or femaleness, but with "sexual immorality, impurity, sensuality, idolatry . . . . [T]hose who belong to Christ Jesus have crucified the flesh with its passions and desires" (Gal. 5:19-24). Unmarried males and females, of any age, are not to be lovers, but they are free to practice *agape* love which is this:

> To be male or female is a ... vocation for daily use in glorifying God. God does not tell us to abstain from being male or female ... We don't do battle with the attributes of maleness or femaleness, but with "sexual immorality, impurity, sensuality, idolatry ..."
>
> ❖ ❖ ❖

Love is patient and kind; love does not envy or boast; it is not arrogant or rude. It does not insist on its own way; it is not irritable or resentful; it does not rejoice at wrongdoing, but rejoices with the truth. Love bears all things, believes all things, hopes all things, endures all things (1 Co. 13:4-7).

40. If being male or female isn't exactly being "sexual," what is it?

Let's review: male or female describes the kind of human we are. It is a specific description of our physical and spiritual being. It is also a vocation. Our maleness or femaleness is a way for us to live with purpose and bring glory to God. God did not create male and female in the same way, at the same time, or for the same purpose. The man is the steward and manager of creation. It wasn't good for man to be alone in this endeavor. He looked at all the animals, but none was an appropriate companion. Man needed someone who would complement him—someone who was like him in spirit, but different in function and purpose. He needed a "helper." "I will make him a helper fit for him," God declares (Gen. 2:18). "Fit for him" (Hebrew: *keneged*) literally means "opposite him, facing him, in front of him, corresponding to him." The two types of human beings—male and female—are different in a multitude of ways. One of those differences is sexual, but there are other compatible differences.

Both man and woman can think, reason, be creative, love, and communicate. But evidence proves that we do these things differently. As co-workers and stewards of this earth—young or old, married or single—our complementary differences serve well as we live in anticipation of Christ's return. Men and women are the "two eyes of the race, and the use of both is needed [for] a clear understanding of any problem of human interest . . . If, in viewing the human problems of life, we have the man's view only, or the woman's view only, we have not the true perspective."[125] There is more to male and female than "sexuality," "sensuality," or anything related to the intimacy of the sexual act. Men and women, married or single, can relate to one another in completely non-sexual ways and, in doing so, use their thinking skills and talents for the good of society. It is folly to think of every interaction of male and female as being sexual in nature. What an abhorrent mess that would be! Being male and female is not so much sexual as it is the partnering of our comple-

> As co-workers and stewards of this earth—young or old, married or single—our complementary differences serve well as we live in anticipation of Christ's return.
>
>

---

125 Mary Wood-Allen, M.D. *What a Young Woman Ought to Know (Purity and Truth, Self and Sex Series),* (Philadelphia, PA: Vir Publishing Company, Copyright 1898 by Sylvanus Stall, 109.

mentary differences to bring glory to Jesus Christ and affect the culture for good.

When an enlightened population decided it didn't need God, its men and women were more easily swayed to view each other as sexual rather than as spiritual persons. Men and women are capable, thanks be to God, of looking at one another as spiritual beings whose life on this earth is daily preparation for eternal life with Him. Perhaps we've never thought about our lives this way, but if not, it's time to help ourselves and our children do so. Just think! If every boy, man, brother, grandfather, uncle, or co-worker looks at a girl, woman, sister, granddaughter, niece, or female co-worker as being a "sexual being," what chaos would rein! Identity matters.

41. Because male and female do have a "sexual" side that includes more than sexual organs but also desires and feelings, shouldn't we help our children become acquainted with that part of themselves?

We have sexual organs, feelings, and desires for a special purpose, but little boys and girls are not interested in or ready for that special purpose. Children cannot be lovers and marry but they can be friends. They can work and play together. Not until they are mature should they think about relating to one another as lovers. A Christian parent or teacher should not stir up ideas of sexual love because, in God's world, sexual love leads to the establishment of the home into which new life comes. No child is ready for this privilege and responsibility.

Children need the discerning wisdom of parents who trust God's Word more than voices of the world. Christian parents are well acquainted with sin. We are born in sin. We battle sin daily; therefore, in a highly sexualized culture, it is not helpful to give detailed sexual information to adolescents who are just beginning to experience new emotions and thoughts about themselves but who do not have the ability to discern the proper use of that information. Imagine if we described to a child the most delicious candy he could ever want. We walk with that child by the candy store to look in the window, but tell him he must not go in. We promise him that the day will come when he can enter the store and enjoy some of the candy he sees on display. We talk with him about the candy all the way home. During the week, we ask him if he has any questions about candy. What desire have we stirred in him? What will he think about candy? Will he be curious about candy and desire a taste right now?

Our sinful human flesh too easily desires what it should not have. Our flesh, like human instinct, cannot be trusted. Obeying human instinct is like obeying people. But people, with all kinds of opinions, tell us different things. So do our instincts. In *The Abolition of Man*, C.S. Lewis reminds us that our instincts are at war; each instinct, if we listen to it, will claim to be gratified at the expense of the rest. So it is with our flesh. Our flesh carries the sin inherited from our first parents. Our sinful human flesh is fickle, selfish and easily deceived. *Better than helping young people be at ease with their flesh is helping them to stand guard.* In Gethsemane, Jesus knew His disciples would intend to be faithful. Nevertheless, He said, "Watch and pray that you may not enter into temptation. The spirit indeed is willing, but the flesh is weak" (Matt. 26:41). For this reason, the faithful parent or instructive adult begins early to teach a child their identity and purpose in Christ, explain the order of God's creation and set boundaries for behavior. God's Word teaches self-control. Parents need to help children practice self-control even as they model it themselves. We are like athletes in training, but our prize is not perishable (1 Cor. 9:25-26; 1 Tim. 4:7-12).

> Our sinful human flesh is fickle, selfish and easily deceived. Better than helping young people be at ease with their flesh is helping them to stand guard.
>
>

CHAPTER EIGHT

Mature Manhood & Womanhood

is Not Sensually Driven

42. One of the reasons given for sex education in the Church is so that we might share perspective on "God's gift of sex" and "sexuality." What do you say to this?

First of all, we need to discern the language. Does God speak about His "gift of sex" or "sexuality" in Scripture or is this phrase coming from another source? The words we use matter. When we speak about "God's gift of sexuality," we turn eyes toward the created; but when we speak about God's *design* for sexuality, we turn eyes toward the Creator. God's design for sexuality is within the boundaries of one man/one woman marriage, but His design for mature manhood and womanhood is not bound by marriage and, therefore, does not have to be sensually or sexually driven.

One of the failures of sex education in the Church becomes evident once we acknowledge the foundation upon which it was built. Sex education was intended to make children who are "sexual from birth"

> Sex education was intended to make children who are "sexual from birth" understand how central their "sexuality" is to their humanity and to express that sexuality in ways different from their parents.
>
>

Mature Manhood & Womanhood is Not Sensually Driven

understand how central their "sexuality" is to their humanity and to express that sexuality in ways different from their parents. It was important to both humanists and feminists that boys and girls see themselves not compatibly different as male and female, but the same as uninhibited "sexual beings." Denying God's design and created order is doomed to failure and there are many casualties. When the Church brought in the language of social scientists, the faithfulness of instructing in biblical manhood and womanhood was set aside. Many girls and women I talk to are comfortable with their "sexual identity" but uncomfortable with being a woman. Boys and men in my relational circle are bombarded by a feminized and sexualized culture but don't know how to engage as mature men.

43. What is mature manhood and womanhood?

Here is perhaps one of the most important questions for Christian parents to help their adolescent children answer. If we place emphasis on an identity as a "sexual being," we miss the opportunity to discuss what masculine or feminine personhood really is. Men are not men and women are not women because of their sexual urges or desires, nor does marriage make a person more fully male or female. By labeling children or adults as "sexual beings," we can actually distort the purpose and vocation of manhood and womanhood.

> Men are not men and women are not women because of their sexual urges or desires.

❖ ❖ ❖

Genesis 1:27 tells us four things about the first man and woman. They were created by God to be human, not the same but male or female, in the image of God (not animals) and, because they were created in God's image, they were created to be holy. There is no mention of anything of a sexual nature ("one flesh") until God brings man and woman together as husband and wife (Gn. 2:24). Too many of us scurry from Genesis 1:27 and skip straight to that union. But in doing so, we miss something very important about the essence of male and female. We are more than sexual beings because God first spoke to Adam about being a man. Man was put in the Garden to "work and keep it" (Gn. 2:15). Man was to be a good steward over all of creation. In faithfulness to God, he was to defend life and avoid death (Gn. 2:16-17). "Then the Lord God said, 'It is not good that the man should be alone; I will make him a helper fit for him'" (Gn. 2:18). The creation was incomplete without woman. Man had no one like himself nor did he have a way to procreate. God made (literally "built") woman from man's rib. In marriage, the woman is her husband's "helper" (Hebrew: *ezer*), assistant and ally. The vocation of "helper" is not inferior. Jesus called the Holy Spirit a "Helper" in John 14:16 which can be translated as "comforter," "encourager," or "advocate." In her "one flesh" union with Adam, Eve became the bearer of life who would nurture, comfort and encourage husband and children.

> Too many of us scurry from Genesis 1:27 and skip straight to [the one flesh] union. But in doing so, we miss something very important about the essence of male and female.
>
>

Sin distorted God's perfect design and rhythm of life. Sin causes the relationships of men and women—married or not—to be difficult. But even in chaos, God's order of creation stands. Whether married or single, men are stewards of creation. Whether married or single, men are called to defend life and avoid death in faithfulness to God. In or out of marriage, women help men do good or evil, be encouraged or discouraged, build up or tear down. Mature manhood and womanhood are not dependent on being married; thus, neither are sensually or sexually driven. Do you see that boys can be mentored to work, build, protect and engage in life without sensual implications? Do you see that girls can be mentored to help, encourage, counsel and build relationships without sensual suggestions?

44. Some say that the "gift of sexuality" is a glorious thing which can be celebrated. What do you say to this?

Once again, we do better to focus on the Creator rather than the created; thus, on God's *design* for sexuality rather than the "gift of sexuality." God says we are "fearfully and wonderfully made," (Ps. 139:14), but who should we celebrate for such amazing craftsmanship: the Potter or the pot? Once we turn ourselves over to celebrating the pot, are we more easily tempted to define the purpose of that pot (Isa. 45:9-11)? Psalm 8 reminds us of our glory; yes, we are indeed just "a little lower than the heavenly beings . . . [with] all things under [our] feet" (v. 5-6), but to whom does the glory belong? Who is celebrated? "[W]hat is man," the Psalmist asks, "that you [the Lord God] are mindful of him" (Ps. 8:4)? When we encourage ourselves and others to celebrate the glory of our sexuality, might there be risk of spiritual danger? Using proper distinction of Law and Gospel, we remember that God is to be celebrated for all He has made. We give Him our praise, especially for the fact that He has brought us into a light and knowledge that does not spring up out of our own flawed and human reason but out of Christ.

45. How should we view the Song of Songs? Doesn't this book of Scripture celebrate sexuality in a very open and less than modest way?

Christopher W. Mitchell, the author of *The Song of Songs – Concordia Commentary*, admits to wrestling with the question of how detailed a discussion in his commentary on sexuality should be. "In the end the decision was made to follow the text by discussing its features with approximately the same degree of detail (no more and no less) than the Song itself possesses." Careful to "avoid the egregious excesses found in some other expositions" and not to "cause offense or to inflame prurient interests that are all too easily aroused in every sinful human being," the Rev. Dr. Mitchell began the discussion of sexuality first with "The

Protective City Wall" and "The Lovers Are Married."[126] He offers the following for consideration:

> 1) "The most suitable context" for considering "sensual, even arousing" passages "may be for a married couple in private so that passions kindled may be satisfied without sin in a God-pleasing manner."[127]

> 2) "Pastors and other ministers, especially those who work with youth, need to be keenly aware of the appropriateness of the material and its effect upon their particular audience (age, gender, marital status, etc.). Even solidly biblical material or Scripture itself, if presented inappropriately, may stimulate impure thoughts and actions regardless of the intent of the presenter."[128]

> 3) "The interpreter of the Song should pay close attention to what it does not say (as well as to what it does say) . . . the Song never refers to the external genitalia or to genital sexual activity. An interpreter who claims to find such references in the Song must resort to philological contortions and convoluted distortions that reveal more about the interpreter's mind than about the biblical text . . . Also, in the present author's opinion, some well-meaning Christian authors have perceived in the Song more specific sexual references than may actually be there."[129]

---

126 Christopher W. Mitchell, *The Song of Songs – Concordia Commentary* (St. Louis, MO: Concordia Publishing House, 2003), 275.

127 Mitchell, *Song of Songs*, 286.

128 Mitchell, *Song of Songs*, 287.

129 Mitchell, *Song of Songs*, 288-289.

46. Is it possible that sex education may have a negative impact on marriage?

It seems fair to note that with over five decades of sex education in the Church, we have also seen an increase in cohabitation, divorce and tolerance of same-sex "marriage" among those who call themselves Christian. Mary Calderone founded SIECUS and worked her way into churches because she feared that parents did a poor job of teaching their children about sexuality. She believed there were too many boundaries placed around anything of a sexual nature. She wanted children to experience the "wow" factor of sex. Many in the Church agreed, so they begin early talking about sex with the hopes that boys and girls will grow up to be husbands and wives who know the "wow" factor of sex. From kindergarten on, children hear sex described in these ways:

- God created sex to be beautiful within marriage.

- It is the best thing ever.

- It is worth waiting for.

- It is the time when we are the closest to God.

- It is so amazing, dear child, that we are going to talk about it a lot.

Sin permeates all relationships, including marriage, so it is possible that years of fantasizing on the ecstasy of sex might have an impact on a husband and wife. Sexual expectations might be so high that when marriage is put to the everyday tests of real life, husbands and wives are disappointed. They might be so disappointed, in fact, that they are tempted to believe that sex might be better with someone else, or maybe even with someone of the same sex who might better understand their partner's needs. After so many years of "cradle to grave" sex education—from kindergarten continuously into old age—we should ask:

Might there be even the slightest connection between sex education and cohabitation, divorce or even the acceptance of same-sex "marriage"?

Sex matters, but marriage matters more. Some pastors take care during pre-marital instruction not to overemphasize sexuality because they believe that it could threaten the hierarchy of values in marriage and assume too predominant a place in terms of producing a well-grounded and joyful marriage. The "wow" factor of sex can be wonderful, but it is the friendship, trusted companionship, communication, and *agape* love of a husband and wife that carries them through good times and bad, sickness and health. With an identity that is primarily "sexual," we are limited in the ways we can serve others. Not so with our holy identity; for indeed, "uncommon" and set apart for use not just by anyone but by God, our opportunities to serve are many.

> Sex matters,
> but marriage
> matters more.
>
>

Instead of such intense sex talk, parents do better—with the support of the Church—by preparing young men and women for the realities of married life. Because of the Fall, marriage is hard work. It requires appreciation of our differences as male and female, the commitment to work together, trust, friendship, and more *agape* than *eros* love. Marriage can be a beautiful relationship, not just because of the sexual union, but sometimes even in spite of it. Marriage of man and woman is the nest for new life. It is the foundation for home and family. It is, even in its most difficult moments, the amazing teamwork of two completely different sexes and personalities. Intimacy in marriage is not all about the sexual act. It is the most perfect trust, companionship and faithfulness this side of heaven. It is the unity of two spirits in this life—male and female, each encouraging the other to journey well to a sure and certain destination.

> Marriage can
> be a beautiful
> relationship, not
> just because of
> the sexual union,
> but sometimes
> even in spite of it.
>
>

47. How do "cradle to grave" sex education and an emphasized identity as a "sexual being" impact single men and women?

The single man or woman might ask, "If God created us to be sexual beings, am I not fully human?" The mistaken identity of "sexual" (from birth) may tempt us to think that we'll never be all we were meant to be if we don't marry and enjoy sexual intimacy. But this tempts us to forget Jesus Christ. Let's recall once again that Jesus Christ was not married and yet He was fully human. It is our personhood that defines us and not our sexual desires or urges. Oh, but some insist, our sexuality is part of our personhood; we would be incomplete without it. But Jesus Christ, fully human, never entered into a sexually intimate relationship. There is liberation in this truth for the single man or woman. Let's also remember that in heaven there will be no marriage. We will be the person— body and soul—that we were on earth only perfect in every way. This, too, refutes for the single man or woman that our identity is "sexual."

The exaggerated place of sexuality in cradle to grave sex education is destructive to all relationships between men and women, married or single. It takes our focus off the identity bestowed upon us at Baptism. For Christians, mature manhood and womanhood is about relating to one another as brothers and sisters in Christ, being thankful for the gift of self-control and enjoying the respectful interaction of male and female perspectives on life. It means men assuming the role of leader and protector but in ways that vary from how a husband would lead and protect his wife. It means that women assume the role of helper, ally and even counselor but in ways that vary from how a wife would submissively yet confidently help her husband. Personally, I find it humorous, productive and comforting to interact with my brothers in Christ. Seeing my identity as fundamentally "sexual" would potentially change every relationship I have with the men in my life. That would be a tragic loss for me.

The baptized child of God in Christ can live fully as a male or female without ever being sexually intimate. Self-control, as evidenced by the Apostle Paul (1 Co. 7:7) is a gift. We can say that with the gift of self-control comes order and strength for life. [130] Mature manhood and womanhood receive the gift of self-control and are not dependent upon sexual intimacy. Man does not become man by getting married and being "one flesh" with his wife, nor does woman become woman by getting married and being "one flesh" with her husband.

48. Does the sexualized identity threaten to diminish manhood and womanhood and even impair the daily relationships of male and female?

Yes, it can. Sex education that has taken its cue from the secular model misses something vitally important when it focuses primarily on God's "good" creation of sex and sexuality, but gives very little time to God's "good" creation of manhood and womanhood. We do not need sexual intimacy to be a man or to be a woman, but men and women do need to be relational. We do this best when we see ourselves in light of our Baptism. As sons and daughters of God in Christ, male and female can see each other as brothers and sisters. They can work together, enjoy life together, pair up different perspectives in order to problem-solve, serve in church or neighborhood together, and always trust that God knows the desires of their heart.

The Tenth Commandment has something to say to the single man or woman. We are not supposed to covet "anything that is your neighbor's." This includes our neighbor's sexuality. Marriage is the sacred

---

130 Author's note: It might be helpful here to consider the Fourth Petition of the Lord's Prayer which is "Give us this day our daily bread." What is meant by daily bread? Martin Luther answers, "Daily bread includes everything that has to do with the support and needs of the body, such as food, drink, clothing . . . house, home . . . good government . . . peace, health, *self-control* . . . and the like." *Luther's Small Catechism* (St. Louis, MO: Concordia Publishing House, 1986).

place for all things sexual, but being a husband or a wife is a vocation for some and not for others. It is important for the Body of Christ to see each member as fully human as opposed to sexual and, therefore, an instrument for God's purpose and glory whether a child or adult, single or married, in this circumstance or that. We see in Scripture that singleness is not an affliction or lessening of personhood; rather it is an opportunity to serve the Lord Jesus in a different way than in marriage.

> It is important for the Body of Christ to see each member as fully human as opposed to sexual and, therefore, an instrument for God's purpose and glory whether a child or adult, single or married, in this circumstance or that.

God does want our undivided attention. St. Paul writes, "The unmarried man is anxious about the things of the Lord, how to please the Lord. But the married man is anxious about worldly things, how to please his wife, and his interests are divided. And the unmarried or betrothed woman is anxious about the things of the Lord, how to be holy in body and spirit. But the married woman is anxious about worldly things, how to please her husband" (1 Co. 7:32-34). The commentary in *The Lutheran Study Bible* reads, "Neither Christ nor Paul praise virginity because it justifies, but because it is freer and less distracted by domestic occupations in praying, teaching, and serving."[131] Pleasing God is the priority for a Christian. Be honest—do you think sinful men and women in this world are more encouraged to please God when they see themselves as "sexual," or when they see themselves as baptized sons and daughters of God in Christ? The right identity matters.

49. How does emphasis on life as a "sexual being" help our brother or sister in Christ who practices celibacy but battles homosexual desires? What are we saying to them when we educate early and long about God's "gift of sexuality"?

---

131 Commentary in *The Lutheran Study Bible*, 1956.

In kindness, we should seriously consider this question. It is, first of all, understandable that Christians want to affirm sex as the "good," "one flesh" union of husband and wife that God created it to be. However, when even Christians repeatedly define men and women as "sexual human beings," how are we helping our brother or sister who struggles with sexual temptations? It was disappointing to read the following in *The Lutheran Witness*:

> Jesus said, "I have come that they may have life, and have it to the full" (John 10:10). This includes life in all its fullness regarding one's sexuality and the gift of sex.[132]

When Jesus says, "The thief comes only to steal and kill and destroy. I came that they may have life and have it abundantly" (English Standard Version), He is describing a battle for our eternal body and soul. Jesus promises the believer an abundantly full and holy life with the Father in eternity, but Satan wants to steal away all hope of such life and leave us in despair. Abundant life is not found in the promises of this sin-filled world but in Jesus Christ and His promise of everlasting life with God. This passage is not about sexuality and our temporal life, but salvation and our eternal life. In heaven there is no marriage; therefore, no sex. The Christian who struggles with homosexual desires on this earth but trusts their identity as a baptized child of God in Christ has the promise of abundant life in heaven, not where they will find fullness of sexuality, but complete holiness and eternal life with God.

> The Christian who struggles with homosexual desires on this earth but trusts their identity as a baptized child of God in Christ has the promise of abundant life in heaven, not where they will find fullness of sexuality, but complete holiness and eternal life with God.
>
>

---

132   Roger Sonnenberg, "The Gift of Sexuality" (*The Lutheran Witness*, October 2013), 10.

Once again, we do better to speak of God's *design* for sexuality rather than His "gift" of sexuality. We do better to focus on the Creator rather than the created. Let's remember the words of Christopher Yuan who, even in his temptation and struggle, began to understand that God was calling him to be holy. "My identity was not 'gay' or 'homosexual' or even 'heterosexual,' for that matter. But my identity as a child of the living God must be in Jesus Christ alone . . . God never said 'Be heterosexual, for I am heterosexual.' He said, 'Be holy, for I am holy'."[133]

In this sinful world, it is rather depressing to think of my identity as being "sexual." What will happen when I'm not thinking, looking or acting "sexual"? What if it isn't the driving force of my life? What happens when sexual appeal fades, the pace is slowed and I require more patience and care from others? How will my value be measured? In this sinful world, it is refreshingly hopeful to know my identity as a daughter of God. I am a treasure of great worth because of what Jesus Christ did for me. I am a vessel for honorable use until the day God calls me to His home where I, indeed, will enjoy the fullness of holy and abundant life. Instruction in purity helps encourage this truth.

---

133 Yuan, *Out of a Far Country*, 187.

CHAPTER NINE

Parents Teach Children God's
Design for Love, Sex and Marriage

50. To whom does God entrust children?

God entrusts the education, mentoring, and care of children to parents. "Children, obey your parents in the Lord, for this is right . . . Fathers, do not provoke your children to anger, but bring them up in the discipline and instruction of the Lord" (Eph. 6:1-4.) Many Christians would agree that discussions about morals, sex and sexually-related behavior with children or adolescents are best accomplished in the home. The governing idea in society as a whole is that the "sex talk" should be left to parents but, at the same time, too many Christian parents are intimidated into believing that they don't have the relevant knowledge to be qualified to talk to their kids about sex. Some educators may point out that parents are too busy to teach their children or too "uptight" to comfortably discuss this particular subject. So, believing that something had to be done about teaching God's "gift of human sexuality," the Church offered its services and provided sex education.

It would follow that since the advent of sex education in the Church, we should see evidence of healthier and safer children, more joyful marriages, and stronger families. Do we? Has K-12 sex education in Christian schools shaped young people to be distinctively different in their attitude about premarital sex, cohabitation or homosexuality?

As parents, what do we know about sex education in the Church? Some questions we might ask ourselves include:

- If my child is in a sex education or family living class, do I know what is being taught?

- Have I been asked to review the material?

- How regularly is the program evaluated?

- Is there measurement of the effectiveness?

- Has my child been taught that he or she is "sexual from birth"? In fact, do I identify myself as a "sexual being"?

We have all been influenced by humanistic sex education. But Christian parents can do what Christian parents have always done in the midst of changing cultures. We can trust God, know His Word and not be ashamed to use it. We can resist compromise of faith and practice. While having parents do the teaching about love, marriage and sex will not be enough to solve some very serious problems, it is a step in the right direction. It stands to reason that moms and dads will more effectively restrain their children from pre-marital sex activity than any "professional" sex educator. Parents are compelled by both Law and Gospel—God's command and promise of blessing—to guard the souls of sons and daughters. If parents are in the habit of teaching their children from Scripture and catechizing them in the "way they should go" (Pr. 22:6), then it is quite likely that curious

> While having parents do the teaching about love, marriage and sex will not be enough to solve some very serious problems, it is a step in the right direction.

children will have no hesitation in coming to their parents—the ones they trust— for information on sex and sexual behavior as well. God's Word on modesty, the procreative act of sex, and the patience and unselfishness of agape love provides everything needed by Christian parents to instruct their children in a lifestyle of purity.

51. Why do Christian parents willingly let others educate their children about sex?

The reasons are many. Some admit that "Christianized" sex education is a reaction to worldly sex education. "Our kids are going to hear it anyway, so we want them to hear it right." Parents who were sexually intimate before marriage may wonder, "How can I tell my child not to do what I did?" Parents may be weary, exhausted from work and the demands of life. Some parents confess, "I don't feel qualified," or "To be honest, I don't want to appear dumb or completely old-fashioned in an area my child seems to know more about than I did at that age." Some parents, deceived by the lie that children are "sexual from birth," may assume that their child will naturally experiment with sex (especially in this highly-sexualized culture) and, therefore, is in need of more information at an earlier age.

As modern people, we may be tempted to think God's Word was written for another time or doesn't address today's issues. Fearing for the health and future of our children, we may doubt that God's Word is sufficient and be tempted to put our trust in sources that actually conflict with or add to that Word. Eve did not think God's Word sufficient, so she not only spoke for God but added some words of her own (compare Gen. 2:16-17 with 3:3). The consequences were deadly. The Christian parent is called to beware of deception. "See to it that no one takes you captive by philosophy and empty deceit, according to human tradition, according to the elemental spirits of the world, and not according to Christ" (Col. 2:8).

When God's people returned from captivity to rebuild the decaying walls of Jerusalem, they were overwhelmed and wearied by the work. They were ready to accept the help of resourceful neighbors, but God said "No!" Why? Because those neighbors were influenced by opinions contrary to His Word. Parents have always been daunted by their responsibility. Moms and dads do best when they don't react to things of this world but, instead, remain faithful to the task divinely entrusted to them. Parents are parents, but we are also children of God. The heavenly Father never forsakes His children. He gives wisdom in His Law and Gospel.

52. Because children are growing up in a different world today, aren't parents more challenged? Don't they need the help of trained or professional experts?

The world is always changing, but God does not. Parents are to model and instruct in the Lord's ways. Satan may ask, "Did God really say . . . that you are capable to parent your child?" He may attempt to wrestle from parents the authority given to them by God. But God gives to parents His Word—the treasure of true wisdom. God's Word speaks clearly to parents about their role as educators (Deut. 6; Prov. 1:8).

Those who inspired modern sex education did not intend that parents do the teaching. Bear in mind the goals of the Frankfurt School and their followers, one of them being to separate children from their parents (see chapter one). Sanger, Calderone, Kinsey, and others worked hard to separate children from their parents and to promote classroom or group instruction by a so-called expert. It is true that most Christian sex education materials have been developed for parents to use in the home. However, if "parents aren't doing their job," the Christian school must. But wait! Because some parents aren't doing what they should, do all of our sons and daughters have to join together in a classroom for sex education? Are parents who instruct their child in purity at home and who don't want their child discussing the intimacies of sex in a classroom forced to pull their child out of sex education in a Christian school just like they would in public school?

Martin Luther wrote *The Small Catechism* for the head of the family— the fatherly steward—to teach God's commandments to his household. The First Commandment to father and mother, son and daughter is this: "You shall have no other gods." This means we are to "fear, love, and trust in God above all things."[134] Satan knows that with this command comes the promise of life for people who will live forever in the presence of God. For this reason, he comes into the home through every nook and cranny, hissing, "You're a pitiful parent. Doesn't your child deserve better?" Outside the home, others are ready and willing to assist fearful, weary, or doubting parents. Every parent needs encouragement, sound biblical resources, and support from their church family, pastor, and Christian teachers, but what children need most is a parent who courageously accepts their God-given role.

Parents serve their children best by putting every thought or idea under the microscope of Wisdom. Guarding the body and soul of a child, preserving modesty, and teaching self-control grows out of the purity of Truth. Sex education that defines people as fundamentally sexual, details the "one flesh" sexual union of marriage, and discusses everything from masturbation to contraceptives with mixed groups of boys and girls is not pure; rather, it is stained with earthly colors. The palette of sex education is tainted by the very things that fooled our first parents: deception, doubt, pride, flesh, fear, and words that God has never spoken. A parent may attempt to use only the best of secular material and pair it with God's Word. But when God's Word

---

134 Luther's Small Catechism (St. Louis, MO: Concordia Publishing House, 1986).

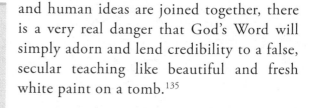

When God's Word and human ideas are joined together, there is a very real danger that God's Word will simply adorn and lend credibility to a false, secular teaching like beautiful and fresh white paint on a tomb.

❖ ❖ ❖

and human ideas are joined together, there is a very real danger that God's Word will simply adorn and lend credibility to a false, secular teaching like beautiful and fresh white paint on a tomb.[135]

Parents can help their children identify themselves in light of their Baptism, vocation, and sanctification. What does this mean? Our Baptism makes us sons and daughters of God in Christ. Our vocation of engaging life as His son or daughter is to be practiced daily whether we are married or not. Our sanctification through faith in Jesus is God's work in our life through the Holy Spirit who helps us resist the sensual world and be transformed to what is holy. Parents can help their children be like the wise virgins who had their oil lamps ready when the bridegroom came (Mt. 25:1-13).

53. What happens when Christians believe the premise of sex education that "children are sexual from birth?"

Fearing that his daughter might get pregnant, a Christian father told me he put her on the Pill. Later, he made sure she had the Gardasil injection to prevent HPV. "I know how I was at her age," he told me. "What can I say? We're sexual creatures!" Had he forgotten to see his daughter as God does? This man's daughter would often come to my house or we would go for long walks. She was completely ignorant about hormones like oxytocin (the "cuddle" hormone), the effect of bonding, that the

---

135 "Woe to you, scribes and Pharisees, hypocrites! For you are like whitewashed tombs, which outwardly appear beautiful, but within are full of dead people's bones and all uncleanness. So you outwardly appear righteous to others, but within you are full of hypocrisy and lawlessness" (Matt. 23:27-28 ESV).

Pill can actually make a girl more vulnerable to diseases, that sex is more than just intercourse, or that boys think differently than girls![136]

A Christian mom told me she raised her children to practice abstinence but, as they prepared to leave for college, she put her daughters on the Pill and encouraged her sons' use of condoms. Why? She believed the lie and, because (after all) her children were "sexual," she was afraid they could not resist the temptation. Had she forgotten to see her sons and daughters as God does?

A pastor confessed to me that he's taken more than one girl from his congregation to have an abortion. Kids are sexual, too, he explained. They're "going to do what they do." He is among those who see "sexual children" becoming sexually-active but because he does not want to see "children raising children," he believes in eliminating the "problem" with or without parental consent. Has he forgotten to see boys and girls as God sees them?

Think about your own congregation in the last 30 years:

- Do you think less or more adults assume young people will be sexually intimate before marriage?

- Do you think there is a decrease or increase in the number of parents who defend their son's use of a condom or their daughter being on the Pill?

- Does your pastor see fewer couples living together before the wedding than when he began his ministry?

- Has the problem of single parenting decreased or increased?

---

136 Author's note: You may be interested in reading "Maura's" story to learn how a sexually-saturated society leaves young women vulnerably ignorant about their own anatomy and psychological make-up. The story is found at www.ezerwoman.wordpress. com/ 2011/05/17/unhooked-set-free/ followed by part two at www.ezerwoman.word-press.com/2011/05/18/hooked-part-ii/

54. Surely Christian professionals who emphasize the "goodness of sex" and "sexuality" have some positive influence on young people, don't they?

Perhaps C.S. Lewis offers the best answer. "In the first place," writes Lewis,

> our warped natures, the devils who tempt us, and all the contemporary propaganda for lust, combine to make us feel that the desires we are resisting are so 'natural,' so 'healthy,' and so reasonable, that it is almost perverse and abnormal to resist them.[137]

In time sexuality becomes an identity, one to which we may tightly cling. But this is a lie. C.S. Lewis continues,

> Like all powerful lies, it is based on a truth—the truth . . . that sex in itself (apart from the excesses and obsessions that have grown round it) is 'normal,' and 'healthy,' and all the rest of it. The lie consists in the suggestion that any sexual act to which you are tempted at the moment is also healthy and normal.

Boys and girls have experienced the secular or religious classroom environment of sex education since the late 1960s. Continuing education takes place outside the classroom via the internet, advertising, TV and movies, magazines, and a trip to the mall. Has it worked for the good of our young people? At my own small-town pregnancy center, we see high-school freshman girls who are "hooking up" or having casual sex sometimes with boys their age but often with older boys. Many of the girls are very comfortable with their sexuality and use it to keep a boy's attention, but they seem less happy and, in fact, more depressed about life.

---

137   Lewis, *Mere Christianity*, 93.

In my community and across the country, adults fear teenage pregnancy. Sexually-transmitted diseases have increased among the teen population. (Teens actually contract gonorrhea and chlamydia more often than adults.) So, for these reasons, students as young as 11 or 12 are instructed about contraceptives that might protect one part of their body but leave heart and soul unguarded. There is an old, but falsely identifying, saying that goes like this: Boys will be boys, you know (wink, wink). To avoid discrimination, feminists insist that girls must be treated like boys. *We're all just sexual, after all. Let's just make sure no babies come from being who we are.* Consider those under age thirty in your own congregation. How many live together before getting married? How many appear to tolerate "gay rights" and even same-sex "marriage"? What has been produced by the seed of identifying ourselves as "sexual"?

55. Is there such a thing as "good" sex education as opposed to "bad" sex education?

If you are thinking of the "sex talk" that happens in a Christian home, then we could call that "good" sex education. Identity determines the kind of instruction. If the earliest education is about the child's identity as a son or daughter of God in Christ and not a "sexual being," then it will be much easier to train the child in the "way he should go" (Pr. 22:6). The parent, obedient to God, is on guard keeping the walls up and acting as the child's good judgment. The parent helps a child "have nothing to do with irreverent, silly myths" but instead "train for godliness" (1 Tm. 4:7).

> If the earliest education is about the child's identity as a son or daughter of God in Christ and not a "sexual being," then it will be much easier to train the child in the "way he should go."

Doing things together, a mom has opportunity to get to know her daughter. She senses when it is time to encourage questions or promote conversation about changing bodies, moods, the differences between boys and girls, love, and preparation for marriage. Mentoring a daughter in the way of seductiveness is foolish. A wise father is attentive to the changes of his son and ready to instruct with the treasure of God's commandments. Like the father in Proverbs 7, he warns his son away from the temptress. He strives to mentor self-restraint and respect for women by example. He engages his son in work and helps him to see the blessings of honest labor for the sake of family. Awkward or not, articulate or not, the information of life is shared at home. If there is an information overload, the attention of son or daughter drifts away, but mom or dad remain accessible for future conversations. A son can learn much from his mother about the way girls think and why they act as they do. A daughter who receives the appropriate affection of her father learns how to be patient for love and what qualities to look for in her someday husband.

Bad sex education is built on an identity, too, but it is a mistaken identity. Any sex education founded on the assumption that "children are sexual from birth" is wrong and potentially harmful. This sex education tears down the walls that Christians are reminded over and over again to build up for the sake of holiness and virtue. Focusing on an identity that is "sexual," walls crumble and doors are opened.

> Although called a "science," sex education that gives early and much information disregards the developmental/cognitive capabilities of children and adolescents.
>
>

Prior to 1960, there were critics who worried that sex was *only* being talked about in the home or by those committed to religion and morality. That would not do. In time, and using Kinsey's statistics (which relied heavily on the behaviors of criminals and sex deviates), SIECUS and a bevy of sexologists squeezed the authority out of parental hands. They turned the faces of children away from their parents.

Sex education as we've known it since the 1960s has not been good for children or society. Sexually transmitted diseases, abortion and experimentation with homosexuality have only increased in both secular and Christian communities. Boys and girls are intentionally placed together in a mutual encounter of joyful sexuality. Although called a "science," sex education that gives early and much information disregards the developmental/cognitive capabilities of children and adolescents. Parents are not in the classroom to discern their child's understanding or monitor information overload; instead, a teacher facilitates the encounter. Because sex education is a human concept, it is not clearly defined; rather, it is driven by prevailing human opinions and popular culture. The teaching environment is shaped by questions such as: What should we tell children to think about themselves and others? How do we make sure that girls aren't discriminated against by being taught differently than boys? Who will shape the decision-making of young people and to what end?

> Sex education is not science at all. It is, rather, the teaching of an ideology first promoted by people who abandoned one faith for another.
>
>

56. How can Christians respond to the assertion that "sex education is science-based, but purity is faith-based"?

Anatomy and biology are true science. They are science in perfect harmony with the biblical worldview because, after all, God is the Creator of our bodies. You don't have to deny Jesus Christ to discuss the science of human organs, hormones, and fetal development. Holiness, or purity, is a lifestyle protective of the body and its proper procreative function within marriage and family, which benefits the whole of society.

Sex education is not science at all. It is, rather, the teaching of an ideology first promoted by people who abandoned one faith for another. Many of these people are humanists and eugenicists with little if any regard for human life created in the image of God or His institutions of marriage and family. The work done at the Institute for Sex Research at Indiana University (Kinsey Institute) beginning in the late 1940s that opened the door to formalized sex education was hardly scientific. Reisman writes,

> Replication and validation are two key attributes of authentic scientific investigation, but Kinsey's data has yet to be validated, and his methodology has not been replicated. One wonders how it could be. Would the abusive treatment of infants and children that became a sordid hallmark of the Kinsey investigation be tolerated today, even in the name of "science"? Subjects of all ages were anonymous, some coerced, and data were clandestinely altered and destroyed at whim . . . [T]he "new academic discipline" of sexology is a shaman's trade; its claim of sound "methodology" is hokum. No sensitive-or sensible-person, including a scientist who understands the dynamics of marriage, real human love, and the absolute trust and commitment they require, would propose or participate in perverse studies such as those conducted by Alfred Kinsey and his team.[138]

"The discredited founder of 'sexology' has been dead for over a half century, yet he holds more influence on sex education than today's eminent neurobiologists."

"The discredited founder of 'sexology' has been dead for over a half century," writes Dr. Grossman, "yet he holds more influence on sex

---

138 Reisman, *Crimes and Consequences*, 67.

education than today's most eminent neurobiologists."[139] The so-called "science" of sexologists may claim that parents either aren't doing their job right or that they don't know enough to be truly helpful, but the ethical science of adolescent brain specialists proves why moms and dads are needed as much as ever to help their children think. Science proves that children are not ready for sex. Today's Christian parent has access to everything God tells us about guarding the bodies and souls of children and the amazing science that testifies to the need for instruction in purity. (This will be detailed in chapter thirteen: "Hard Science Destroys the Myths of Sex Education".)

---

139 Grossman, inside front book jacket of *You're Teaching My Child What?*.

CHAPTER TEN

The Church is Influenced
by Humanism, Kinsey & SIECUS

57. Who influenced the Church to provide sex education materials for home and classroom study?

The Church was influenced by the "social scientists" and followers of Kinsey. (Let's remember that prior to the 1960s, children were not understood to be "sexual" in the way Kinsey and SIECUS saw them.) Claire Chambers explains the SIECUS influence on American church bodies in *The SIECUS Circle*. In 1961, Mary Calderone, co-founder of SIECUS, "lectured on the role of the churches in sex education before the First North American Conference on Church and Family, convened by the National Council of Churches (NCC) of the U.S. and Canada, which was attended by 500 delegates from thirty-eight Protestant denominations. According to SIECUS, of the seventeen professionals from many disciplines who served as resource persons for the five-day conference, four became co-founders of SIECUS, and five others became SIECUS board members."[140] Chambers continues, "In 1968, at the start of the national sex education controversy, an *Interfaith Statement on Sex Education* was approved for release by the NCC in cooperation with the Committee on Family of the Synagogue Council of America and the United States Catholic Conference's Family Life Bureau. This pamphlet has since become a so-called religious backing and frequently used support for sex education, often being displayed at PTA meetings and committee meetings for the study of home and fam-

---

140   Chambers, *The SIECUS Circle*, 259.

ily living programs."[141] The Interfaith Statement was drafted, Chambers explains, "by a thirty-member Interfaith Commission on Marriage and Family Life" whose officers included "Rev. William Genne, one of the original SIECUS founders" and "humanist Helen Southard of SIECUS and the Rev. Jesse Lyons of the Riverside Church in New York City, both of whom were later to become top officials of the National Association for the Repeal of Abortion Laws."[142]

Chambers explains that in 1968 the NCC published *Sex Education in Major Protestant Denominations*. This booklet presented a study of sex education materials most frequently used by church schools and youth groups. Given special commendation in this booklet was the Concordia Sex Education Series of The Lutheran Church-Missouri Synod which was lauded as "the most complete direct approach to sex education" and to be considered as one of three "tentative models for comprehensive programs."[143] Also commended were *Sex and Selfhood* of the United Presbyterian Church, U.S.A., authored by SIECUS director William G. Cole,[144] and the program of the Southern Baptist Convention entitled *A Christian View of Sex* which "included lengthy excerpts from the writings of SIECUS official Evelyn Duvall and her husband Sylvanus, as well as from SIECUS-recommended authors Seward Hiltner and humanist Hugh Hefner of Playboy magazine.[145]

58. Was The Lutheran Church-Missouri Synod influenced by secular humanism, Kinsey and SIECUS?

Yes. In chapter one, we were introduced to the 1961 book from Concordia Publishing House entitled *Sex and the Church* [146] which made use of Kinsey research and statistics. The book reads,

---

141 Chambers, *The SIECUS Circle*, 259.
142 Chambers, *The SIECUS Circle*, 260.
143 Chambers, *The SIECUS Circle*, 260-261.
144 Chambers, *The SIECUS Circle*, 261.
145 Chambers, *The SIECUS Circle*, 261.
146 Feucht, et al., *Sex and the Church* .

We cannot close this section of the chapter on proper and improper use of sex without a further reference to the studies of Alfred C. Kinsey and his associates. These studies were variously evaluated as invalid and exaggerated or as revealingly real, presenting the status quo. They gave some new insights and further opened up the whole area of sexual behavior. Even conservative scholars feel that these studies cannot be ignored. Christian writers agree that they expose the extent of human weakness.[147]

The editors of *Sex and the Church* then direct the reader to a footnote which quotes Russell L. Dicks, head of the department of pastoral care at Duke University who wrote the following in *The Pulpit* (March 1955):

The best reply to the Kinsey reports is not to question their accuracy. It will not help to dismiss the sex behavior or misbehavior of his subjects as unimportant because his figures are believed to be inaccurate . . . some ministers have been so busy moralizing over Kinsey's figures that they fail to see the need for a better understanding of sex . . . We should turn our attention and energy to the ways in which we neglect, or sexually mis-educate, our children and recognize our failures to prepare young people for marriage . . . Ministers need to seek opportunities for training to help them achieve objective standards in sex education for the children and youth in their church schools and provide adequate premarital and marital counseling for their adult members.[148]

Rather than questioning the reports and methodology of Kinsey or his humanistic faith, my own church body as well as others chose to heed the

---

147 Feucht, et al., *Sex and the Church*, 203.
148 Feucht, et al., footnote in *Sex and the Church*, 203.

advice of "social scientists" and develop formalized sex education with the help of SIECUS. [149] It is fair to ask:

- What does it mean to "open up the whole area of sexual behavior"?

- Did pastors and church leaders reinterpret Scripture in light of the "new insights" of nonbelievers?

- Why was it that neither Kinsey nor his reports were questioned?

- What happens when Christians fail to discern cultural trends or test new ideology against biblical teaching practiced through the ages?

Christian marriage and family were dealt a hard blow by Kinsey's claims. His purported scientific data showed an obscenely high number of WWII generation men and women having pre-marital, adulterous and homosexual sex. Did husbands and wives begin to doubt each other's faithfulness or wonder, "What sexual pleasure am I missing?" Were children tempted to doubt the morality of their own parents or consider them hypocrites for not teaching them enough about sex or giving too many negative messages? In school and at the university, were children told that their parents were too sexually inhibited and, therefore, forced to cover up their sexual escapades?[150]

Even well-intentioned sex education in the Church leans the wrong way if it is built on the wrong foundation. Worldly "philosophy and empty deceit" (Col.

---

149 Author's note: SIECUS members reference in *Sex and the Church* include Jerome Himelhoch, Sylvia F. Fava, William G. Cole, Evelyn Duvall, and Seward Hiltner.

150 Author's note: Judith Reisman helps us understand the significance of Kinsey's attack on the so-called "greatest generation." No generation is above reproach or free of sin, but Reisman reminds us that people of the WWII era had high standards for marriage and family. Soldiers married their sweethearts just so they could spend a few short nights together before being shipped off to the beaches of Normandy. Didn't anyone cry "foul" when Kinsey spoke ill of such men and women? Reisman suggests that just as propaganda was used to demoralize the soldiers in the European and Pacific theaters of war, so Kinsey used propaganda to demoralize the family and society. I suggest you read *Sexual Sabotage*.

2:8)—indeed, the language of another faith—does not blend with Jesus' Word. Instead, it compromises the life of a Christian and leads to undesirable consequences. Christian parents or churches and schools that develop or teach sex education may have the best interests of children in mind, but a Christian cannot obey God or protect children by teaching false identity and doctrine.

> Even well-intentioned sex education in the Church leans the wrong way if it is built on the wrong foundation.
>
> ❖ ❖ ❖

59. Are there more examples of secular humanism's influence on sex education in Lutheran and other Christian churches?

Yes. Let's consider three examples from the same publisher. The book entitled *Life Can Be Sexual* was published in 1967.[151] Many years later, I purchased the book to help me prepare to mentor my own sons but, after reading it, I changed my mind. There were several reasons why, including the recommended list for further reading. In the author's bibliography were the works of SIECUS directors Evelyn Duvall and William G. Cole as well SIECUS-recommended publications by humanists Margaret Mead, Betty Friedan and Hugh Hefner. Other works listed were John A.T. Robinson's *Christian Morals Today*, which supports the use of situation ethics, and Donald Kuhn's *The Church and The Homosexual* which was published by the Glide Urban Center in San Francisco. The Glide Center was a vanguard in the movement to legitimize homosexuality in the U.S.[152] To be sure, *Life Can Be Sexual* (out of print, but available on Amazon) is filled with biblical language but there is

---

151   Elmer N. Witt, *Life Can Be Sexual* (St. Louis, MO: Concordia Publishing House, 1967).

152   Authors' note: In 1963, winds of change were blowing mightily through San Francisco. Nowhere were these forces of transformation more visible than at GLIDE Memorial United Methodist Church. That year, a young African-American minister named Cecil Williams came to GLIDE determined to bring life back into the dying congregation. Williams changed both policies and practices of the conservative church, helping to create the Council on Religion and Homosexuality in 1964. In 1967, Williams ordered the cross removed from the sanctuary, exhorting the congregation instead to celebrate life and living (Source: www.glide.org)

no description of male and female as spiritual beings; rather, the reader learns that "everyone is born with a sex urge,"[153] and

> We are sexual beings not only when at certain times we experience specific sexual desires; rather we are sexual beings in all that we are and all that we do. Sexuality means understanding sex as an expression of the human personality."[154]

Later, the book states,

> Leaders in education, government, science, and religion are only now beginning to recognize the importance of sexuality— the way sex invades and influences all of life—and what can be done about it.[155]

It is fair to ask: Who were those "leaders" and upon what did they base their new discovery of "the importance of sexuality"?

The book *Parents Guide to Christian Conversation About Sex*, published in 1967, states that "some medical authorities now regard masturbation as a step in preparation for adult sexual feelings."[156] This quotation, according to Claire Chambers, is "from SIECUS-recommended author Marion Lerrigo's *Your Child From 9 to 12*."[157] The topic of abortion is also discussed in this book for Christian parents: "There is no easy answer to every situation, but many Christians believe that an abortion not judged necessary to save the life of the expectant mother is the taking of a life. Today the church

---

153   Witt, *Life Can Be Sexual*, 14.

154   Witt, *Life Can Be Sexual*, 15.

155   Witt, *Life Can Be Sexual*, 16.

156   Erwin J. Kolb, *Parents Guide to Christian Conversation About Sex* (St. Louis, MO: Concordia Publishing House, 1967), 71.

157   Chambers, *The SIECUS Circle*, 213.

is facing the question of whether an abortion should be permitted in other situations." [158] Concerning the issue of homosexuality, the book echoes the SIECUS concept that homosexuality may at times be considered "a temporary step in the process by which emotions mature."[159]

Parents Guide to Christian Conversation About Sex offers Scripture and what appears to be a sincere effort to help parents and children; however, the foundation crumbles immediately in the first chapter which attempts to explain the "Christian understanding of sex."[160] If this were true, why do the footnotes reveal the influence of so many people with a faith that opposes Christianity? The book directs the reader's attention to the high cost of misunderstanding sex and then uses as his proof "the famous Kinsey reports."[161] The book quotes what we now know to be skewed and manipulated statistics from Kinsey's books *Sexual Behavior in the Human Male* and *Sexual Behavior in the Human Female*.[162] Footnotes and an annotated book list also include the works of humanists Wardell Pomeroy, Deryck Calderwood and Helen Southard (all SIECUS directors), Evelyn Duvall and Reuben Hill (SIECUS directors), and *What To Tell Your Children About Sex*, prepared by the humanist-founded Child Study Association of America.

> [The book] attempts to explain the "Christian understanding of sex." If this were true, why do the footnotes reveal the influence of so many people with a faith that opposes Christianity?
>
>

The book for teachers and church leaders entitled *Christian View of Sex Education* was published in 1986. It has a "Resource List for the Christian Sex Educator" and offers additional

---

158 Kolb, *Parents Guide*, 89.

159 Kolb, *Parents Guide*, 103.

160 Kolb, *Parents Guide*, 11-22.

161 Kolb, *Parents Guide*, 20.

162 Kolb, *Parent's Guide*, 22.

aids for the development of a Christian sex education program. The list includes materials authored by Evelyn Duvall and Reuben Hill (SIECUS directors), Alan F. Guttmacher (humanist associated with Planned Parenthood), Lester Kirkendall (SIECUS founder and humanist), Paul Popenoe (member of American Eugenics Society's board of directors), Isadore Rubin (SIECUS director and humanist), and Helen Southard (SIECUS director and humanist). Also included in the resource section and under the heading "Organizations Offering Assistance" *to church sex education committees* are SIECUS and SIECCAN (Sex Information and Education Council of Canada).[163]

60. The books you have referenced are all out of print. What impact do they have on us today?

Yes, the books are out of print, but they helped to set the stage for sex education in church schools and homes. They were used for many years by parents, pastors and teachers. What impact did they have on the Christian community as a whole? The books remain in many church libraries. When revisions are published, old books are not necessarily replaced. I ordered old copies of the books from Amazon booksellers that still have library cards from Baptist and Methodist congregations. In what ways did these books influence children and grandchildren?

Once again, I commend my church's publishing house for listening to informed and on-guard parents, making some good changes in the *Learning About Sex* series, and striving to do right. However, missing from the most recent books in the series are citations and sources of information. Bibliographies are not included. Every parent needs to know the source of what their child is learning. We need to know what the language is and from where it comes.

---

163 Martin Wessler, *Christian View of Sex Education* (St. Louis, MO: Concordia Publishing House, 1986), 79-87.

61. How did sex education come to be accepted in Catholic schools and how does this explain the shift of parental role as a child's primary mentor to a secondary position behind the school?

A lecture given by Charles Donovan to the Human Life International's conference on sex education in 1994 may shed some light for us. What follows are excerpts from the lecture that pertain to Catholic sex education in the U.S.

> Sex education, taught in a very delicate and moral manner, was the role of the parents, exclusively. Moreover . . . the idea of treating sexuality separately from the other commandments, from the other responsibilities to practice self-discipline and moral virtue, simply hadn't occurred [to pastors] . . . Again and again, up until the mid-1960s, the burden of proof was on those who would usurp or take some portion of the parental role; and in this case the parents must be incompetent.

> In 1944, Bishop Thomas Toolan of Mobile, AL., called sex education "a pagan doctrine." In 1949, the New York Catholic Conference, then called The Welfare Conference, went to battle over two sex education films called "Human Growth" and "Human Reproduction" in the New York public school system. The bishops . . . quoted Pius XI . . . on the dangers of classroom teaching . . . Bishop Joseph Flanelly in the presence of Cardinal Spellman in St. Patrick's Cathedral that same year called one of the films "immoral, bad, and invasion of parental rights."

> In 1962, a book titled *The Mysteries of Marriage* from Sheed and Ward . . . had this to say: "Sex is a holy and happy thing if we make it to serve God as it should; and not only fills the

Earth, it fills Heaven with more and more saints." He went on to say: "The initiative in sex education should come from the children." What he meant by that was that their natural curiosity would lead them to questions and that it was a violation of their innocence for an outside authority to presume the competence to eject this information onto their lives.

"The biggest danger [was] the demystification of sex and the placing of sexuality on the plane of the everyday and the pedestrian."

❖ ❖ ❖

Ignaice Lepp (a psychologist and Catholic convert from Communism), talking about sex education in 1966, wrote: "As experience has shown, so-called sex education is really the beginning of many painful traumas in countries where it is generally taught collectively in the classroom." [Lepp] was strongly opposed to it. He felt it was best that mother teach it, particularly to daughters. The biggest danger [he believed was] the demystification of sex and the placing of sexuality on the plane of the everyday and the pedestrian.[164]

Given this emphasis in Church teaching, Christian ethics, university texts, and marriage counseling, Donovan wondered: How did Catholic school sex education come to be accepted? In 1991, Donovan co-authored a book on Planned Parenthood together with Bob Marshall.[165] To prepare for the project, Marshall went to the archives on sex education at the National Catholic News Service where he discovered the process of change in the Catholic approach.

---

164 Donovan, "The History of Sex Education in the U.S."

165 Charles Donovan and Robert Marshall, *Blessed Are the Barren: The Social Policy of Planned Parenthood* (San Francisco, CA: Ignatius Press, 1991). (Author's note: At the time Robert Marshall researched sex education in the Catholic schools, he was serving as Director of Congressional Affairs for the American Life Lobby, Inc., in Stafford, VA.)

Here is my summary of what Marshall learned. A Catholic position endorsing early classroom sex education was first endorsed in 1966 by Sister Mary Jacob of St. Vincent's Hospital in Philadelphia as a "prevention" of unwed teenage pregnancies. That same year, a Jesuit priest named Fr. Francis Phillus called for sex education in the Catholic classroom in seventh grade for the purpose of social hygiene. In 1966, the first major conference for sex education in the Catholic Church was held at the Catholic University of America based on the premise that parents had fallen down on the job and the schools must step in. Fr. James McHugh, director of the U.S. Catholic Conference of Bishops' Family Life Bureau, organized the conference with the goal of creating a complete program of education in sexuality. One of the session presenters was Fr. John Thomas, a member of SIECUS. By the end of 1970, one third of U.S. Catholic dioceses had sex education.[166]

From this time on, the Catholic church began radically departing from the teachings of the Old and New Testaments, the early Church, and Christianity in general. Donovan said that, in 1910, perhaps a dozen books on some form of sex education could be found in the Library of Congress. "One was written by R.C. Bowl. It was not a sex education book as we know them today, but had a 30 or 40 page discourse on the dangers of bad companions."[167] Calderone and others were ready to affect societal change. For them, Kinsey's reports were timely. They made the study, teaching and learning about sex and sexuality a "science." And, if parents wouldn't teach the "science" of sexuality, then someone else would.

---

166 Donovan, "The History of Sex Education in the U.S."
167 Donovan, "The History of Sex Education in the U.S."

CHAPTER ELEVEN

Sex Education in the Church is Not

Distinctively Different

62. Knowing the temptations that young people face, wouldn't a good youth leader want to teach abstinence by way of attention-getting object lessons?

Probably, but in what manner and environment? Some time ago, I was invited to speak about biblical manhood, womanhood and chastity at a Christian youth event. Mindful of the mixed group, I spoke about the different ways that men and women think, feel, love, and communicate; from where we get our identity and value as persons; and how we can treat one another as we want our someday-spouse to be treated. During the break between speakers, a youth leader asked for volunteers from the assembly of high school students. Not knowing what they would be asked to do, the hands of a dozen youth waved in the air. Invited to come forward, they were placed in a line: boy, girl, boy, girl. The youth leader handed a glass of water to the first in line, explaining that it represented bodily fluid from sexual intercourse. Each boy, then girl, was to spit into the glass before passing it on to the next person. Now you know, the youth leader explained, how easy it is to transmit STDs among multiple partners. I wanted to cry "foul" as I watched the young ladies blush and the young gentlemen focus on the floor. Did the youth leader intend to desensitize the boys and girls? I'm sure he did not. But what was happening to each girl as she passed the "STD" on to the boy beside her? What was happening to each boy as he passed the "STD" on to the girl beside him?

SIECUS, Planned Parenthood and websites such as Teenwire and Go Ask Alice aggressively seek to remove shyness and embarrassment from young people. From their perspective, shyness and embarrassment are nurtured by parental or religious hang-ups and are unnecessarily counterproductive to good, natural and wholesome sexuality. "Don't be fearful or shamed by talking about sex," chants the sex educator; rather, "Be fearful or shamed by not talking about it." Is this what God wants the Church to say?

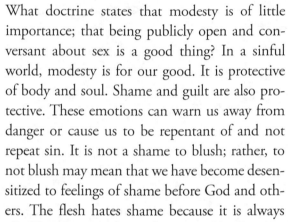

What doctrine states that modesty is of little importance; that being publicly open and conversant about sex is a good thing?

❖ ❖ ❖

What doctrine states that modesty is of little importance; that being publicly open and conversant about sex is a good thing? In a sinful world, modesty is for our good. It is protective of body and soul. Shame and guilt are also protective. These emotions can warn us away from danger or cause us to be repentant of and not repeat sin. It is not a shame to blush; rather, to not blush may mean that we have become desensitized to feelings of shame before God and others. The flesh hates shame because it is always working to resist the sin that "self" so loves. Bearing that in mind, Christian adults should take care not to desensitize boys and girls. Instead, they should help young people appreciate an active conscience and protective modesty that may, at just the right time, cause them to blush and flee danger.

63. When Christians think about sex education, isn't abstinence education what they have in mind?

Probably, but even abstinence education can bring the language and methods of humanistic sex education into the classroom. "I had years of abstinence education in school," a college graduate told me. "It was just lots of talking about sex on top of all the rest of the sex talk I was hearing from TV, movies and magazines." Well-intentioned Christian adults may want to help children correctly learn about the created differences between boys and girls, hormones, sexual organs, the procreative act of sex, and why and how to patiently wait for the "one flesh" union God designed for one man and one woman in the faithfulness of marriage. Abstinence may, indeed, be the goal. But think about it. If we really want to help young people resist sensuality and abstain from sexual immorality, will we:

- Talk to them about it in great detail?

- Dangle like a carrot a provocative thought or image at every turn?

- Keep something beautiful and "good" in view but out of touch?

Abstinence education can bestow the wrong identity if it assumes "children are sexual from birth." If it starts young, like sex education, and teaches boys and girls together in the same classroom, then it, too, runs the risk of desensitizing youth. Can we say for sure that even abstinence education does right by our children in a "one-size-fits-all" classroom? Some teachers and parents liken certain text, graphics and group conversation to soft porn that stimulates a part of the brain. In a group setting, do we really know how each individual girl or boy will receive the information? What are the boundaries of abstinence education? Does it take into full account how easily human nature can be tempted? The secular world saturates children with sexual images and topics. Is there anywhere a kid can get a break from all the sex talk?

> If we really want to help young people resist sensuality and abstain from sexual immorality, will we keep something beautiful and "good" in view but out of touch?

We see that knowledge of and comfort with sexuality has increased. But has other knowledge kept pace? It is long past time to turn the attention of children away from their sexuality to help them busy their minds with thinking, work and communication skills; character development;

goal-setting; practice of good manners; training in godliness and preparation for spiritual warfare. We should strive to transform a child "by the renewal of [their] mind, that by testing [they] may discern what is the will of God, what is good and acceptable and perfect" (Ro. 12:1-2).

64. Is abstinence education the same as instruction in purity?

No, not exactly. Abstinence focuses on what a person is not supposed to do, but instruction in purity focuses on things that we can do. Instruction in purity (holiness) encompasses more than sex or sexuality; in truth, it nurtures a lifestyle. Holiness is both a command (6th commandment) and an invitation from God to say "Yes!" to a life that more safely leads to eternity with Him. It is saying "yes" to living one's vocation of male or female to the glory of Jesus Christ—young or old, married or unmarried.

> Abstinence says, "I must wait for sex until marriage." Purity says, "I don't have to wait to be the woman (or man) God created me to be."
>
> ❖ ❖ ❖

Abstinence says, "I must wait for sex until marriage." Purity says, "I don't have to wait to be the woman (or man) God created me to be." Abstinence says, "Because we are sexual beings, I must be cautious with the opposite sex." Purity says, "Because we are persons more than sexual beings, I can respect, talk to, learn from, work beside, and be patient with the opposite sex." Purity is not captive to a fickle heart, but is always training for godliness. The practice of purity blesses us with eternal implications. Purity always journeys toward hope with the encouragement of the Holy Spirit. In fact, because of Jesus Christ, we can be restored to a life of purity even after we've failed to abstain.

There are several abstinence programs across this country used by church youth groups and Christian schools; but sadly, teaching purity as a lifestyle is far too rare. The best book series I have found on sexual purity was written in 1898 by a woman physician, Dr. Mary Wood-Allen, and described by Vir Publishing Company as "Pure Books on Avoided Subjects." The series is titled *Purity and Truth: Self and Sex Series*. Four books for girls/women and four books for boys/men made up the original series. I found one of the books, *What A Young Woman Ought to Know*," in my grandmother's collection. Modern people may scoff at such an ancient book, believing that we are more enlightened on sex and sexuality. But with sophistication, Dr. Wood-Allen talks to the young woman about the care of her "house" (body and soul), wrong ideas of beauty, how conduct and behavior affects the way she views God, and the practice of self-control. She writes,

> The conduct of a pure woman should be the safeguard and not the destruction of a man . . . You cannot think that the buckling on of the knight's armor by his lady's hand was a mere caprice of romantic fashion. It is . . . an eternal truth – that the soul's armor is never well set to the heart unless a woman's hand has braced it; and it is only when she braces it loosely that the honor of manhood fails.[168]

Wood-Allen discusses emotions and longings, love and preparation for marriage and family without sexualizing the young woman or compromising holiness. She writes,

> It is because of sex that we are fathers, mothers, and children; that we have the dear family life, with its anniversaries of weddings and birthdays. It is through sex that we are set in families, and love and generosity have sway instead of selfishness. For this reason, we ought to regard sex with reverent thought, to hold it sacred to the highest purposes,

---

168   Wood-Allen, M.D., *What A Young Woman Ought to Know*, 163.

to speak of it ever with purest delicacy and never with jesting or prurient smiles.[169]

65. Sex education in the Church is certainly different from "modern" or "comprehensive" sex education, isn't it?

"Comprehensive" means "including many, most, or all things; covering completely or broadly; inclusive."[170] Sex education in secular and Christian classrooms commonly address the following topics: personality, values, decision-making, peer and social pressures, affection, love, intimacy, body image, sex (as in male/female), sex (as in sexual intercourse), human sexuality (as in urges, desires, and feelings), abstinence, masturbation, pornography, birth control, abortion, sexually transmitted diseases (STDs), dating relationships, parental relationships, marriage, homosexuality, and guilt. The manner in which the subjects are addressed depends on the teacher. Christian educators may tell us that they are helping young people value sex and sexuality as gifts from God and certainly not teaching comprehensive sex education, but what should we call any discussion about the topics listed above? Very real emotions of fear and guilt may be discussed in any sex education class, but in what way and to what end? Fear and guilt will always exist for the Christian, but might someone encourage us (intentionally or not) to shift what we are fearful or guilty about?

Comprehensive can also mean "integrated." *Parents Guide to a Christian Conversation About Sex* defines the "integrated approach" as being

> sex education . . . built into the everyday teaching of children as they go through the grades. Much sex education also occurs in the informal relationships between teacher

---

169 Wood-Allen, M.D., *What A Young Woman Ought to Know*, 116.

170 Comprehensive: accessed September 11, 2013 www.merriam-webster.com/dictionary/comprehensive.

and pupil outside the classroom. A boy, for example, will often get more help from his coach than from any other adult with whom he has contact [therefore] . . . the qualifications of the teacher are very important.[171]

The book continues,

Schools ought to go beyond the 'integrated approach' and informal teaching, however . . . A school may set up a program in which the elementary grades include units of sex instruction in health education or science classes. Junior high courses may include units on personality growth and boy-girl relations. The high school may offer classes on courtship, marriage, and parenthood.[172]

This book, although out of print, helped to set the integrated, age four through high school approach that the current *Learning About Sex* series from the same publishing house now has in place.

Pastors or Christian teachers may continue to insist that "Christian sex education" is nothing like "comprehensive sex education." But let's remember that the Concordia Sex Education Series of the LCMS was lauded as "the most complete direct approach to sex education" in 1968 by the NCC and recommended as one of three "tentative models for comprehensive programs."[173] In the early 1960s, the only "experts" training both public and parochial school teachers on how to convey attitudes about sex to children were Kinsey associates using Kinsey data. These "experts" included Deryck Calderwood, Wardell Pomeroy, William Masters, Virginia Johnson, and

---

171 Kolb, *Parents Guide*, 32.

172 Kolb, *Parents Guide*, 32.

173 Chambers, *The SIECUS Circle*, 260-261. (Author's note: The Concordia Sex Education Series was lauded in the 1968 booklet *Sex Education in Major Protestant Denominations* published by the National Council of Churches.)

Mary Calderone. The only training for sex and human sexuality educators was provided by the Society for the Scientific Study of Sex (SSSS), the American Society for Sex Educators, the Advanced Study of Human Sexuality (IASHS), and SIECUS. SIECUS persevered to become one of the most powerful forces in American education (public or parochial) in the area of comprehensive sexual health and sexuality education.[174]

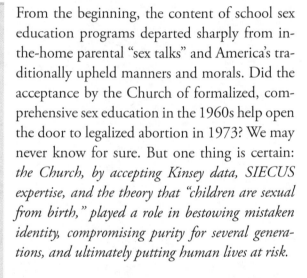

The Church, by accepting Kinsey data, SIECUS expertise, and the theory that "children are sexual from birth," played a role in bestowing a mistaken identity, compromising purity for several generations, and ultimately putting human lives at risk.

❖ ❖ ❖

From the beginning, the content of school sex education programs departed sharply from in-the-home parental "sex talks" and America's traditionally upheld manners and morals. Did the acceptance by the Church of formalized, comprehensive sex education in the 1960s help open the door to legalized abortion in 1973? We may never know for sure. But one thing is certain: *the Church, by accepting Kinsey data, SIECUS expertise, and the theory that "children are sexual from birth," played a role in bestowing mistaken identity, compromising purity for several generations, and ultimately putting human lives at risk.*

66. Knowing what we know, wouldn't it be true that revised sex education materials for the Christian classroom would be less comprehensive?

We would hope so. A recent review for parents of the *Learning About Sex* series notes, "Concordia publishes what is probably one of the most comprehensive series on sex education with resources for all ages . . . [the books] for older children might treat controversial topics in ways with which you disagree or may require additional input and guidance from you. Parents also need to ensure that the content is appropriate for each of their children

---

174 Reisman, *Sexual Sabotage*, 176-178.

at that point in their lives; be careful not to present too much information too early."[175] Topics in the most current book in the series for thirteen to fifteen year-olds, *Sex and the New You*, include birth control, abortion, pornography, masturbation, sexual experimentation, oral sex, STDs, homosexuality, and guilt. Questions for parents remain. Where and from whom should your child (ages four through high school) learn most about themselves and behavioral decisions that affect their health and well-being? Should it be in a classroom of peers facilitated by a well-meaning teacher or in your home by you?

67. The desired outcome of sex education in the Church contrasts that of the secular; therefore, to imply that the two have anything in common is unfair, isn't it?

No, it would not be unfair. The mission of sex experts, writes Dr. Miriam Grossman,

> is to mold each student into what is considered "a sexually healthy" adult—as if there was universal agreement on what that is. From a review of many of today's sex ed curricula and websites, it would appear that a "sexually healthy individual" is one who has been "desensitized," who is without any sense of embarrassment or shame (what some might consider "modesty"), whose sexuality is always "positive" and "open," who respects and accepts "diverse" lifestyles, and who practices "safer sex" with every "partner."[176]

To be sure, most sex education in the Church does not encourage "diverse lifestyles" and "safer sex." However, one wonders how we can teach the "yeses" of sexuality and desensitize young people away from

---

175   On-line review for home-schooling parents, accessed September 2, 2013, www.cathyduffyreviews.com/science/learning-about-sex-series.htm.
176   Grossman, *You're Teaching My Child What?*, 8.

embarrassment and shame without opening the door to "comfortable" expression of "my personal sexuality." Dr. Grossman notes that common

> If sex education in a Christian classroom teaches the "yeses" of sexuality at the same time it desensitizes the child, then we might be naïve to think that the child will be armed for battle in a sexualized culture.
>
>

sex education programs assert that they're giving children the same information and advice as parents and that their curricula are science-based and age-appropriate. But parents, explains Grossman, are being conned by the sex education industry. "Children are inundated from a tender age with a 'sex positive' message; they're taught that sexuality is a life-long adventure, 'who they are' from cradle to grave, and that the freedom to explore and express their sexuality is a sacred 'right.'"[177] If sex education in a Christian classroom teaches the "yeses" of sexuality at the same time it desensitizes the child, then we might be naïve to think that the child will be armed for battle in a sexualized culture.

68. We know of congregations that have offered a type of sex education class for parents and their pre-teen children. Is such a class a good idea and, if so, who should teach it?

There are many who believe that sex education, secular or Christian, should only be taught by specially-trained teachers. These people believe that such teachers should ideally have completed academic courses or programs such as human sexuality or family living in schools of higher education. In the 1980s, my congregation encouraged parents and their sixth grade sons and daughters to attend a class that prepared boys and girls for adolescence.[178] The woman who facilitated the class was a public school teacher who had

---

177 Grossman, *You're Teaching My Child What?*, 11.

178 Author's Note: The study book used was *Preparing for Adolescence* by Dr. James Dobson (Colorado Springs, CO: Focus on the Family).

attended classes in family life, values clarification and encounter groups for her own continuing education. She was generous with Scripture passages but also detailed information on sexual urges and intimacies. She explained to the mixed group of students (with parents present) what their moms and dads were doing under the sheets in the privacy of their bedrooms. A father of two daughters finally spoke up in defense of their modesty. "Thank you very much," he said, "but my daughters' mother and I prefer to decide when and how we will discuss our married intimacy with our children at home."

The next year, I was asked to teach the class. Never knowing of a bride and groom who were clueless about what to do on their wedding night, I didn't think it necessary to detail the intimacies of marriage to sixth-graders. Instead, I explained to the boys what it means to be a man, to the girls what it means to be a woman, and how both are called by God to respect each other and their complementary differences. When delicate questions arose, I connected the act of sex to procreative, married love without offending the little ones entrusted to my care. I never identified the students as sexual beings, but as sons and daughters of God in Christ. Parents who attended with their child were encouraged to trust God for wisdom and courage to mentor chivalry, virtue, modesty, patience, and holiness in all areas of life.

In time, I found myself out speaking to parents and teens in Christian schools and at congregationally-sponsored youth events. At first, I spoke to mixed groups of boys and girls about the ways that biblical manhood and womanhood guard life. But I soon committed myself to speaking to girls and their moms separate from boys and their dads. The subject matter did not tantalize sexually, but encouraged moms to talk with their daughters about *agape* love, the influence of maturing hormones, decision-making, why boys think and act differently, why God clothed Adam and Eve, how not to be a temptress, how to choose friends, what qualities to look for in a someday husband and the culturally-influential vocation of motherhood. As a mother of sons, I spoke with great respect to the dads and their sons. I did not cover intimate topics, but explained the importance of chivalry, the noble vocation of fatherhood, how to avoid the temptress, how to treat girls like they want their sisters or someday wife treated, and why Jesus is the model (and forgiveness) for all men.

69. Where does a Christian go to become a "sex educator"?

Sexologists and so-called sex experts originally came out of the Kinsey Institute or organizations started by Kinsey's followers. Sexologists became well-entrenched in American universities. By 1957, Kinsey associates were organizing to credential one another as "sexologists." Wardell Pomeroy, an associate of Kinsey, founded the Society for the Scientific Study of Sex (SSSS). John Money was an early president. Today, the SSSS lists undergraduate studies at such universities as Yale, Johns Hopkins and Washington University in St. Louis. Doctoral programs at universities across the U.S. and Canada are offered in family relations, family social science, human development, sociology, psychology, health sciences, and human sexuality.[179]

> Credited students created sex-education curricula for all ages and then marketed these materials to public, private and religious schools.
>
>

In 1971, the Institute for the Advanced Study of Human Sexuality (IASHS), with Pomeroy as academic dean, began giving college credits and degrees to sexuality students for participating in a program called Sexual Attitude Restructuring (SAR). Credited students created sex-education curricula for all ages and then marketed these materials to public, private and religious schools.[180] I did not have to try very hard to find evidence detailing what SAR is all about. A power point curriculum, for example, is available on-

179 www.sexscience.org/resources

180 Reisman, *Sexual Sabotage*, 177-179. (Author's Note: SIECUS started in 1968 under the direction of Pomeroy and with funds from Hugh Hefner. Figure 12 on page 184 of *Sexual Sabotage* diagrams the funding, institutions granting degrees and collaborators of sexuality programs and accreditation.)

line which is no more than a multi-media onslaught of pornography and every type of sexual behavior.

A 2012 YouTube with Martha Tara Lee explains the technique of SAR: 1) to have students watch videos of sexual behaviors and then discuss their feelings about what they saw, 2) to break down inhibitions, and 3) to motivate students to question who they are. [181] One can learn from the websites of the SSSS, IASHS and Institute for Sexual Health (ISH) that SAR is commonly used today. The ISH offers SAR to students wanting to be certified not as a therapist, per se, but as people "moved into a zone of greater knowing, acceptance, and tolerance of human sexuality in all of its possible dimensions."[182] The ISH describes SAR as a "highly provocative, experiential, cognitive and affective experience, which is designed to push comfort levels, elicit feelings and confront attitudes, beliefs and values about sexuality."[183] Among those trained and counseled, for example, by SSSS using SAR are theologians; medical, child development, and family life consultants; organizations such as SIECUS, Planned Parenthood, and the American Psychology Association (APA); medical schools and human services.[184] Among those trained by IASHS are teachers, ministers, physicians, social workers, marriage and family therapists, business people, and others.[185]

---

181   Explanation of SAR technique by Martha Tara Lee. Accessed September 21, 2013, www.youtube.com/watch?v=bFg!75CnJy4.

182   Center for Positive Sexuality, accessed September 21, 2013, www.positivesexuality. org/?p=468.

183   Center for Positive Sexuality, www.positivesexuality.org/?p=468.

184   Accessed June 16, 2013, www.sexscience.org/continuing-education.

185   Accessed September 23, 2013, www.iashs.edu/faqs.html (Author's Note: Every student in the Master's program of the IASHS must have 18 units of Wardell B. Pomeroy lecture Series, students in the Ph.D. and Ed.D. programs must have 24 units and students in the D.H.S. program must have 16 units. Credits are awarded when the student turns in a written report on what the course meant to him/her in a personal sense. Courses cover desensitization and a multitude of sexual subjects, see: www.iashs.edu/ courses.html)

By the 1970s, courses in human sexuality or family living were offered on Christian campuses. If one carefully studies the changes in education, one begins to recognize what Dr. Grossman calls a "social movement one child at a time." This agrees with Dr. Coulson's explanation that sex education was introduced almost in tandem with values clarification, relativism, diversity, sensitivity education and a growing interest in marriage therapy.[186] If we are deceived by humanistic ideas that "children are sexual from birth," that they are pleasured by sex, and that society needs to affirm the "gift of sexuality," then how much easier it becomes to tolerate pornography, pedophilia, teen sexting, and sexual experimentation among children. "Claiming to be wise, [we] become fools" (Ro. 1:22). Foolishness leaves us ill-equipped to guard the purity of the most helpless in the human family: the little ones Jesus calls His own. "Let the little children come to me," He says, "and do not hinder them" (Mt. 19:14).

70. Might sex education raise the curiosity of a young Christian?

Yes. With every good intention of protecting children, we might, nevertheless, raise a child's curiosity and unintentionally put them more at risk. Let's consider an experience shared with me by my friend Sandy. In third grade, her son went through the DARE anti-drug program. The DARE program is intended to instruct kids away from drug use by providing them with knowledge. One day, Sandy's son brought home information on drugs complete with colorful illustrations. She explained to me that "the illustrations were eye-catching with all those pretty pink and blue pills." Together, mother and son carefully studied the information. "I have to admit," Sandy told me, "that both of us were made more curious about the different kinds of drugs, how they looked, what they did, and where they could be found."

---

186   Personal notes taken during Dr. Coulson's workshop hosted by LFL of Iowa at St. Paul Lutheran Church in Ames, IA., in April, 1991 while I was serving as LFL of Iowa president. More from Coulson can be found on pages 7-11 in chapter one.

People can look at pictures of drugs or learn about them but not desire them. It is different with sex. It has been said that God created man to be visually appreciative of a woman's body. However, sin has a way of distorting that appreciation into lust. When a boy is no longer "grossed out" by girls and, instead, is intrigued by the feminine form, his imagination stirs. So does evil. Easily accessed internet sites are bold temptation. More subtle but perhaps just as intoxicating is frequent discussion of the pleasures of marital love in sex education class. How many not-ready-for-marriage-boys are frustrated by the conflicting thoughts of "just imagine," but "don't touch"?

71. Are there more examples that prove sex education in the Church is not substantially different from any other sex education?

Let's begin by reviewing a few common phrases repeated by both secular and Christian educators. They include:

- "Children are sexual, too."

- "Children shouldn't be embarrassed by sex."

- "We should celebrate our sexuality."

- "More knowledge is always better."

- "Parents are not doing their job" or "parents are teaching too many 'noes.'"

- "Cradle to grave sexuality."

- "Boys and girls should be taught together in the same classroom."

Now, let's consider the subject matter, teaching manner and environment.

- A pastor told me that he once asked a Christian educator who promotes sex education if he could explain how such teaching in the Church differs from the secular in the area of modesty. The educator replied that modesty means teaching sexually explicit material in a biblical way. The pastor responded that the Word of God never treats sex as something to be spoken of openly and shamelessly.[187] Ah, you may say, did he overlook that "sexual" book of Scripture entitled The Song of Songs? No, he did not. Nor have other pastors and those faithful to Scripture. In his 1300-page *The Song of Songs Concordia Commentary*, Christopher W. Mitchell writes, "Many scholars consider the Song to be erotic in a humanistic sense. This commentary believes that such a perception derives from the sinful condition of readers, not from the Song itself. Only when the wall is broken down and the garden is plundered does the holy become profane and the exquisite yearning of the Song become narcissistic eroticism."[188]

> "Many scholars consider the Song to be erotic in a humanistic sense. This commentary believes that such a perception derives from the sinful condition of readers, not from the Song itself. Only when the wall is broken down and the garden is plundered does the holy become profane and the exquisite yearning of the Song become narcissistic eroticism."

- Dr. Philip Ney, a respected pro-life psychiatrist, writes, "Many kinds of sex education, including 'chastity' education, leave a young person with the impression that any kind of sex except vaginal intercourse is okay when

---

187 Author's Note: The Word of God shows no visual images nor does it tantalize or eroticize, but it does occasionally use explicit language to shock and put people to shame.

188 Christopher W. Mitchell, *The Song of Songs Concordia Commentary*, 277. (Author's note: More of the Rev. Dr. Mitchell's commentary can be found on pages 102-103 of this book.)

it's not."[189] I know a young woman who attended a Christian school K-12. There, she had classes in health and "lifetime fitness." During her first year in college, she asked her dad, "If my boyfriend and I engage in oral sex, I'm still chaste, aren't I?"

- We should not ignore the influence of feminism on all sex education. We may hear comments such as, "Whatever boys are learning I want my daughter to learn, too," or "If girls are taught separately from boys, then we're saying they're not equal." Such statements disregard the science that proves boys and girls are, indeed, equal but not the same. They mature, think, visualize, respond, and communicate in different ways. It is shamefully unfair for feminists to ignore the influence of oxytocin on a girl's brain. A feminist-influenced classroom also means that clothing is not likely to be discussed because it is either a woman's choice or a thing indifferent.[190] Do girls who go through "Christian sex education" dress less sexy or provocatively than those who go through secular sex education?

- Do we know how often any sex education is evaluated? Are such evaluations documented? Are parents asked to evaluate the program? Is sex education taught openly as "sex education" or as family living, health, or integrated into other subjects? A good place to go for an honest evaluation of any kind of sex education would be your community's CPC (caring pregnancy center). Do they see fewer or just as many young women from the Christian school or congregations that teach sex education, family living, or human sexuality as they do from public schools?

Post-1960s "Christian sex education" may see itself as a more sophisticated version of the parent-child "sex talk." It may be generous with Scripture

---

189   Philip G. Ney, M.D., "Sex Education," posted April 18, 2008, accessed September 10, 2012, www.messengers2.com.
190   See Chapter 14.

and attempt to lead on the high road of chastity or purity. But, perhaps, might it be the most dangerous of all? If it teaches all things and claims that knowledge of sexuality is what God intends for His children, but fails to regard the tenderness of youth, puts boys and girls together, breaches the barrier of natural embarrassment, and innocently leads young people to identify themselves as "sexual beings," then does it also compromise purity? God's Word does not provide a model for sex education, but it consistently tells us to train in holiness. Being holy means resisting our own sinful passions and replacing false sentiments with godly ones.

CHAPTER TWELVE

The Learning Environment
Influences Boys and Girls

72. God made our bodies, so why shouldn't children from an early age—boys and girls together—learn about the ways their bodies function and be encouraged to maturely discuss them?

It is one thing for boys and girls in anatomy class to discuss the heart, glands, and reproductive system; to know how the body functions; or to learn that God intricately weaves us together in our mothers' wombs, with every day written in His book of life (Ps. 139:13-16). It is entirely different, however, to put boys and girls together in sex education or human sexuality class in order to discuss "sexual identity," talk about pleasure, detail the emotions and feelings that go with physical touch, assure that sexual thoughts and fantasies are normal, detail the intimacies of marriage, discuss sodomy, or explain masturbation.

Feminist thinking might conclude that boys and girls should encounter sexuality together, but God's model for mentoring in Titus 2 does not agree. Sex educators might conclude that since God made us to be sexual, it is a beautiful thing and children should learn of its glories. But this world is fallen. We might want to believe that children can mature with an untainted perspective on sex and sexuality but children are not untouched by sin. "In sin did my mother conceive me" (Ps. 51:5). The fallen nature of humanity must be considered when teaching children. Do we want them at ease with—or prepared to resist—Satan, the world, and their own fallen human nature?

73. Aren't we being prudish when we insist on modesty and separation of boys and girls in a classroom?

No, we are not being prudish; we are being prudent. Prudence is what the ancients called wisdom. John Stonestreet writes, "The one who is prudent possesses the understanding to practice all the virtues in the right time and right circumstance. Prudence is a virtue of the intellect rather than of the will, and it's needed to regulate all the other virtues. Without it, our bent toward practicing vice is given free rein."[191] To be modest is to be prudent. If some people call modesty "prudish," they are just name-calling without engaging the issue.

> To be modest is to be prudent.
>
> ❖ ❖ ❖

In 2002, U.S. Attorney General John Ashcroft modestly curtained semi-nude statues in the Great Hall at the Department of Justice. Soon after the pragmatic modesty, sniggering began. He's "uptight," "too religious," "sexless," "a prude." But *modesty is a gift from God in a sinful world*. Modesty is a kind of "conscience" for the body. "There is an innate modesty in children," said Jeffrey Murrah, licensed marriage and family therapist in Pasadena, TX. "Once we become self-aware, we become modest. But among the sophisticated, modesty isn't hip."[192]

74. We have watched a sex education film for the Christian classroom where boys and girls together are instructed to repeat the names of sexual organs and then told to laugh and get it out of their system. Is this helpful?

The purpose of such a film may be to help children be comfortable with what God has created, but natural and protective boundaries might be

---

191   John Stonestreet, "The Power of Prudence: No Hindsight Needed," accessed May 24, 2012, www.breakpoint.org.
192   Jeffrey Murrah quoted by Ellen Makkai, "Modesty Isn't Just For Prudes", www.wnd.com/2002/02/12721.

trespassed in the process. Parents, with the support of other adults, are to guard the natural and protective inhibitions of children as well as the created differences between boys and girls. 1 Corinthians 12:22-23 speaks about the body with many members. It reads, "[T]he parts of the body that seem to be weaker are indispensable, and on those parts of the body that we think less honorable we bestow the greater honor, and our unpresentable parts are treated with greater modesty." What are the "unpresentable parts?" The commentary in *The Lutheran Study Bible* tells us that "modesty accentuates the importance of the sexual organs, which God located out of view and behind hair to reserve them for special, honorable use."[193] An arm is an arm, a breast is a breast, but King Solomon, when describing his wife, skips from the navel to the thighs (Song of Sol. 7:1-5). "Private parts" are, in God's Word, set apart for the marital and procreational union between husband and wife.

St. Paul mentions sexual immorality, but then goes on to say, "Let there be no filthiness nor foolish talk nor crude joking, which are out of place, but instead let there be thanksgiving" (Eph. 5:4). Why would we want to make common a discussion of body parts that God wants covered? Why would we want to train boys and girls together to commonly reference the cervix or vulva or penis as if they were an arm or leg or neck? The purpose of each body part gives us a clue about its honorable and proper use. Let's be honest about our human condition. Where do the curiosities of our minds too often lead our behaviors? When the conversations of adult men and women take a sexual turn, what can easily happen? We may think it modern to speak openly of intimacies, but can we honestly say it's a good thing for us or our children? Where is the wisdom in desensitizing boys and

> Where is the wisdom in desensitizing boys and girls or making common what God intends to be uncommon for His honorable use?
>
>

---

193 Commentary: *The Lutheran Study Bible*, 1967. (Author's Note: Rev. Dr. Mitchell concurs in *Concordia Commentary Songs of Songs*, 290.)

girls or making common what God intends to be uncommon for His honorable use? Adults and young people can be sexually immodest in the way they talk without doing or touching anything. This is "out of place," writes St. Paul, for those people made holy through faith in Christ Jesus.

75. Today's children are learning about sex from a sexually-saturated culture; therefore, isn't it true that we need to teach boys and girls together about something God declared "good"?

That appears to be what some Christians believe. One pastor writes:

> We live in a world where sex education is taking place daily with the same sexes being together at movie theaters and in classrooms . . . [W]hen we divide boys from girls, we are subconsciously saying that sex is a dirty subject and should never be talked about openly in mixed company! Needless to say, there should never be a time when anything sexual should be talked about in a way that offends or lightens the gravity of the subject. "Do not let any unwholesome talk come out of your mouths, but only what is helpful for building others up according to their needs, that it may benefit those who listen" (Eph. 4:29)." Professor John Money of Hopkins University coined a phrase, "Lovemap." He referred to it as a type of "Rorschach love blot." It is a template formed in a person between the ages of five and eight, deciding whether a specific situation is arousing or not. His research discovered that this "Lovemap" can be distorted in different ways. One significant distortion takes place when a family or parent(s) do not talk about sex or cast a negative judgment about anything sexual."[194]

194 Rev. Roger Sonnenberg, "Sexuality: What Congregations, Parents, Pastors and Teachers Need to Teach," *Issues in Christian Education*, Vol. 46, No. 2 (Spring 2013): 22, accessed April 2, 2013, http://www.cune.edu/about/publications/issues-in-christian-education/issues-Spring-2013/

Let's think about this. Boys and girls may be forced to learn together about sex in common and public venues, but Christian parents and educators are called to instruct in an uncommon and dissimilar way. The message we want to share with children about male, female and anything having to do with sexual activity runs counter to the sin-warped world. The manner in which we instruct should, too. All things sexual should be treated with reverence and held to the highest purpose.[195] Male and female are not common to be used by anyone, but uncommon and to be used by God for His holy purpose. Neither is the marital, "one flesh" union common but sacred and for holy and procreative purpose.

> The message we want to share with children about male, female and anything having to do with sexual activity runs counter to the sin-warped world. The manner in which we instruct should, too.

Second, some blame concern for modesty on being afraid to discuss the goodness of sex. Daniel Heimbach writes,

> This is completely false. The reason Christians value modesty is not because sex embarrasses us, but because we think sex is so honorable that we are embarrassed by anything that corrupts it. We are modest, not because we think sex is bad, but because we think sex is only good when it is pure, and anything compromising the purity of good sex is therefore horribly bad.[196]

---

195 Author's note: If we were to do a Bible word search on uncleanness or impurity or filthiness, we would find that it is nearly always in connection with sex. The Bible is where people got the idea that engaging in sex outside of marriage is dirty, that sensuality is a "work of the flesh" (Gal. 5:19), and that "God has not called us for impurity, but in holiness" (1 Th. 4:7).

196 Daniel R. Heimbach, *True Sexual Morality*, 215-216.

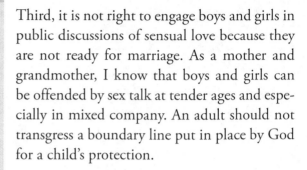

"We are modest, not because we think sex is bad, but because we think sex is only good when it is pure, and anything compromising the purity of good sex is therefore horribly bad."

❖ ❖ ❖

Third, it is not right to engage boys and girls in public discussions of sensual love because they are not ready for marriage. As a mother and grandmother, I know that boys and girls can be offended by sex talk at tender ages and especially in mixed company. An adult should not transgress a boundary line put in place by God for a child's protection.

Fourth, sexual modesty includes what we say, how we dress, what we see and how we express ourselves. We should not mentor children to speak casually about things of a sexual nature nor should we lighten the gravity of the subject with humor. Male, female, and God's design for sexuality are not to be treated as common, but uncommon.

Fifth, we should build up and do what is beneficial for young people. This is nearly impossible, however, in a classroom where two different sexes from different families and at different levels of maturity and understanding sit side-by-side for discussions of sex and sexuality. There is no shame in acknowledging boys and girls as the complementary but different persons God created them to be and teaching them accordingly.

Finally, we must know the source of information. John Money accepted as normal the idea that children between the ages of five and eight can be aroused and, thus, enjoy sex. He found nothing wrong with adult-child sex and would "never report a pedophile".[197] He believed "child sex-play" to be healthy and used it along with nudity and pornography in his work.[198]

---

197   See page 56.
198   John Colapinto, *As Nature Made Him: The Boy Who Was Raised As A Girl* (New York, NY: HarperCollins Publishers, 2000), 86-96.

Could this be why he believed that parents who choose to delay discussions about sex and sexuality with their five or six-year-old are "distorting" the thoughts of their little one? Scripture tells us, "Do not stir up or awaken love until it pleases," (Sg. 2:7; 3:5). The time for arousal is not a time set by the individual or anyone else, but the time of marriage which is the order ordained by God.

CHAPTER THIRTEEN

Hard Science Destroys the

Myths of Sex Education

76. Sex education depends on the theories of men like Kinsey and Money, but does the hard science of neurobiology prove such thinking to be dangerous folly?

Yes it does. The feminist movement, SIECUS and Planned Parenthood depend upon so-called experts like Kinsey and Money, but Christians should be skeptical of any research "findings" from elite universities that claim evidence for profoundly unbiblical ideas and behaviors. This includes putting boys and girls together in sex education class. Demanding that boys and girls learn together about sex in the same classroom ignores the amazing discoveries of neurobiology, a science that actually supports one-sex classrooms.[199] Dr. Grossman offers some history.

Christians should be skeptical of any research "findings" from elite universities that claim evidence for profoundly unbiblical ideas and behaviors.

---

199 Author's note: In 2008, Concordia Publishing House re-wrote its sex education series, one set of books for boys and one set for girls. I am appreciative. However, there

In 1955, John Money introduced the concept that humans develop an internal sense of maleness or femaleness, separate from chromosomes and anatomy. Infants are born gender-neutral, he claimed, without a predisposition to think, feel, or behave in a masculine or feminine manner. '[M]en impregnate,' Money wrote, 'women menstruate, ovulate, gestate, and lactate.' All other distinctions are due to socialization. . . . [W]hile Baby Jill has two X chromosomes, she has the potential to feel like a man. Little Jack has a penis, but if he's dressed in pink, given Barbies, surgery, and estrogen, he'll do fine as Jacquelyn. Jack and Jill's gender identity will depend on messages they receive in the first years of life from family, friends, school, religion, and media. [200]

Money believed he could settle the "nature or nurture" debate. His theory that genders could be reassigned or nurtured was put to the test when Bruce Reimer, at eight months of age, suffered a tragic loss during a botched circumcision. The parents turned to Money, wanting to believe that all it would take to make everything better was some surgery, estrogen, and a pink blanket. Money advised that Bruce be raised as "Brenda" but the boy fought his "therapy" at every turn until, at 14, he returned to living as the boy he was. Money continued to call the macabre experiment a success, but it was a nightmare for Bruce, his twin brother and their parents. Journalist John Colapinto captured Bruce's story in *As Nature Made Him*. "To Money," writes Colapinto, "the issue of childhood sexual rehearsal play had assumed the dimensions of a crusade."[201] Money believed that explicit sexual pictures (or pornography) should be used in sex education in order to help reinforce a child's sense of being a boy or girl. At age six, Money had Bruce ("Brenda")

---

continues to be a strong voice in favor of mixed classrooms in spite of the evidence that weighs against it.

200 Grossman, *You're Teaching My Child What?*, 158-159.

201 Colapinto, *As Nature Made Him*, 90.

mimic coitus with Brian, his twin brother. Money showed them pictures of adults engaged in sex, saying, "I want to show you pictures of things that moms and dads do."[202]

As Nature Made Him has been on my library shelf for years. From a biological and psychological perspective, it serves as a reminder to me of why feminists do great harm when they insist that girls be instructed in the same environment and for the same purpose as boys. "The blurring of differences between male and female," writes Grossman, "is a radical agenda unsupported by hard science."[203]

> "The blurring of differences between male and female is a radical agenda unsupported by hard science."
>
>

77. Is it possible to frustrate boys and girls by putting them together in sex education?

Yes. Secular models of sex education too easily corral male and female as one and the same. But girls and boys know they are *not* the same! "Eight weeks after conception—seven months before the pink or blue blanket," writes Dr. Grossman, "a fetus has a boy-brain or girl-brain . . . when it is the size of a kidney bean."[204] Putting boys and girls together in the same sex education classroom may appease feminists but it risks the unhealthy frustration of both male and female students.

78. Do we deny teen girls the opportunity for straight talk about their bodies in a sex education classroom with teen boys?

The answer from Marianne J. Legato is "yes." Legato is the founder and director of the Partnership for Gender Specific Medicine at Columbia University.

---

202 Colapinto, *As Nature Made Him*, 86.
203 Grossman, *Unprotected*, 149.
204 Grossman, *You're Teaching My Child What?*, 165.

> We want to guard the physical and spiritual health of a young woman just as we want to guard her right to a childhood, right to girlhood, and right to maidenhood.
>
>

She sees women's health as more than a political or feminist issue because women differ from men in every system of the body. Those differences affect the diagnosis and treatment of disease.[205] If parents or teachers really want to help prevent pregnancy outside of marriage, abortion, STDs that may never go away or result in infertility, cancer from the human papilloma virus (HPV), broken hearts and depression, then they will teach girls separately from boys about their very unique, but far more vulnerable anatomy. We want to guard the physical and spiritual health of a young woman just as we want to guard her right to a childhood, right to girlhood, and right to maidenhood.

It is feminist folly to insist that girls and boys are both sexual beings and, therefore, should be taught in the same classroom and be treated just the same. It is not to a girl's benefit to speak of bodily hygiene, menstruation and gynecological matters in the presence of boys. If a girl is inclined (or enticed) toward the reading of sensually romantic love stories at a tender age but no one addresses the power of written and visual images (can this be done with boys in the room?), she could be tempted into behavior that later in life makes her ashamed to remember. We fail young women by not helping them understand how maturing sexual organs and hormones direct them to think and feel in ways different from men. At the same time, they need careful instruction in how to resist "irreverent, silly myths . . . train yourself for godliness" and not be despised "for your youth, but set an example in speech, in conduct, in love, in faith, in purity" (1 Tm. 4:7-8, 12).

---

205 Marianne J. Legato, accessed September 27, 2013, www.nlm.nih.gov/changingthefaceofmedicine/physicians/biography-197.html (Author's note: Dr. Legato edited the medical textbook *Principles of Gender Specific Medicine* and authored *Eve's Rib: The New Science of Gender Specific Medicine and How It Can Save Your Life.*

Girls need to learn how they differ from boys in an environment where they are not distracted by boys. Teen girls need to learn, for example, that they have a more sensitive "eco-system" than boys. For example, the immature cervix of a girl under the age of twenty is far more vulnerable than that of a woman over the age of twenty. Dr. Grossman explains, "The more mature cervix is protected by twenty to thirty layers of cells. In contrast, the cervix of a teen has a central area called the transformation zone. Here the cells are only one layer thick. The transformation zone is largest at puberty, and it slowly shrinks as the cervix matures . . . the T-zone can be seen during a routine pelvic exam. It makes the cervix look like a bull's eye, which is fitting, because it's exactly where the bugs want to be."[206] Girls under age twenty are being hit the hardest by cervical infections that can cause ectopic pregnancies, miscarriages and infertility later in their lives. Dr. Grossman writes, "Being on the pill may enlarge the transformation zone, increasing the risk of infection."[207] Will the girls really hear all of this while boys are in the room? What will boys, who typically mature later than girls, do with a discussion of "T-zones" and "bull's eye" targets?

Sex education typically explains that people kiss, hug, and touch to show love or feel good. This sounds normal and acceptable. But, girls need to know that intimacy of any kind promotes attachment and trust. Dr. Grossman explains:

> Intimate behavior floods [a girl's] brain with a chemical that fuels attachment. Cuddling, kissing [and touching] releases oxytocin, a hormone that announces: I'm with someone special now. *Time to switch love on, and caution off.* . . . When it comes to sex, oxytocin, like alcohol, turns red lights green. It plays a major role in what's called 'the biochemistry of attachment.' Because of it, [a girl] could

---

206 Grossman, *You're Teaching My Child What?*, 77.
207 Grossman, *Unprotected*, 27.

develop feelings for a guy whose last intention is to bond with [her]. [She] might think of him all day, but he can't remember [her] name.[208]

With oxytocin at work, a girl can be hooked into repeating the behaviors that felt so good. If she bonds at a young age but does not marry, she may bond again and again with many different boys or men. But each time a relationship is broken off, it may feel like a divorce. The search for love may continue in a desperate and depressing sort of way.

> The woman is the bearer of life. She deserves to know why her chemicals, hormones and procreative organs are worthy of respect. Purity and motherhood should never be compromised by callous disregard for modesty.

❖ ❖ ❖

The woman is the bearer of life. She deserves to know why her chemicals, hormones, and procreative organs are worthy of respect. Purity and motherhood should never be compromised by callous disregard for modesty. It may be the trendy thing to do, but it is not wise nor is it safe. Far better than the boy/girl classroom is moms and grandmothers who set aside special times for "girl talk" with daughters and grand-daughters. Dads and grandfathers honor God the Father by doing the same with sons and grandsons.

79. Is a boy-girl sex education classroom in the best interest of a young man?

No, but there is wisdom in giving boys their own time away from the girls for discussions of manhood and godly behavior. Boys learn and mature in their own male way, so why would we deny them opportunity to do so? Boys are

---

208   Miriam Grossman, M.D., *Sense & Sexuality* (Herndon, VA: Clare Booth Luce Policy Institute, 2009).

structurally and chemically different from girls, so why would we want to blur or diminish their created differences? Girls tend to "input or absorb more sensorial and emotive information than males do".[209] More verbal than boys, they typically want to talk about their feelings. Boys may not want or be ready to process, analyze and discuss information or feelings especially in front of girls. How can a boy concentrate on learning about his changing body and how to treat girls as a brother wants his sister to be treated when girls are watching or bantering about? Even better than teaching a group of boys together about sex and expecting them to ask lots of questions in front of their peers is teaching them one-on-one: father with son. In the past, when there was no father involved in the life of a boy, grandfathers, uncles, cousins and older brothers saw mentoring of a young man's body, mind and soul as a sacred duty.

Because the culture is so saturated with sex, it is simply backwards to teach boys about sex before they've put on their armor and been trained in self-control. Boys need to know the rules of engagement. Yes, engagement is a military term and boys need to know who they're up against: the devil, the world and their own sinful nature. If they're going to "run the race" toward the prize and wrestle powers and principalities, they need training in godliness. Too much sex talk desensitizes a boy and encourages him to let down his guard.

> Because the culture is so saturated with sex, it is simply backwards to teach boys about sex before they've put on their armor and been trained in self-control. Boys need to know the rules of engagement.
>
>

There cannot, however, be too much talk about or mentoring in the "good feeling" of work, manners, and service of others. Boys need training not to become better "sexual beings," but better citizens and men

---

209 Gregory L. Jantz, PhD and Michael Gurian, *Raising Boys by Design* (Colorado Springs, CO: Waterbrook Press, 2013), 26.

of justice, kindness, and courage. When the questions from a maturing boy show that he is curious about things of a sexual nature and capable of understanding, we should resist stirring up his feelings and desires. Instead, we can help him do what boys most often do so well—figure out what makes things work! Older men can help younger men figure out the science of things.

There is a science to male and female thinking and behavior. Girls have the neurochemical oxytocin, but boys have vasopressin. Vasopressin plays an important role in sexual bonding and bonding between fathers and children. But vasopressin is values-neutral. If boys begin early to think about girls, are encouraged to spend time with girls, then touch and be intimate with girls, they will bond with every girl they are intimate with. In God's perfect creation, vasopressin (like oxytocin) works to bond husband and wife and also attach father and mother to their children. In a sinful world where lust is aroused and boundaries transgressed, boys may bond to one girl, then another, then another. After a rush of good-feeling chemicals flood his brain with each sexual image or personal encounter, he seeks more. Powerful neurochemicals at work may lead a young man to return to a "temptress" even though he knows she isn't good for him. If the biblical skills of self-control, steadfastness and good work have not been mentored first, a young man may find it very difficult to commit to one woman and find joy in the faithfulness of marriage and family.

> For the adolescent boy, in or out of the classroom, arousing discussions or visual images might stimulate dopamine neurons to make him feel good or excited. There may be a desire to seek more of that kind of talk or imagery even if risk is involved.
>
>

Boys need to know about dopamine, a messenger chemical of the brain that sends a kind of reward signal when we do something exciting.

Dopamine floods the brain with good feeling when a boy rides his bike without training wheels for the first time but also when he isn't caught in the act of accidentally breaking a window. Dopamine is values-neutral. For the adolescent boy, in or out of the classroom, arousing discussions or visual images might stimulate dopamine neurons to make him feel good or excited. There may be a desire to seek more of that kind of talk or imagery even if risk is involved. Fathers, grandfathers and godly big brothers need to help boys navigate from childhood into manhood by explaining the science of their bodies. "Bodily training is of some value, godliness is of value in every way, as it holds promise for the present life and also for the life to come" (1 Tm. 4: 8). "Older men are to be sober-minded, dignified, self-controlled, sound in faith, in love, in steadfastness" (Ti. 2:2) so that, in a sexually saturated world, they can "urge the younger men to be self-controlled" (2:6).

80. We can help young people make better choices when we give them more information and the earlier the better, right?

No, not according to the wisdom of experience and the science of neurobiology. Parents have always known that their children have some foolish and thoughtless behaviors. They are not self-aware, self-disciplined, or even rational people. Children and teens are not miniature adults in mind and body; therefore, parents should reject the madness of giving too much sexual information, too soon. Many sexologists believe that kindergarteners need to develop a healthy sexuality and parents should provide information even if the child doesn't ask for it. They believe that five-year-olds should know about intercourse. They say that failure to discuss a little girl's vulva with her could cause trauma in later years. But a young child does not think logically. She is self-centered. Why did her daddy get mad at her mommy? Because little Susie did something bad. Why did it start snowing? So Susie can wear her new mittens and hat. She does not process large amounts of information and may, in fact, misunderstand. Dr. Grossman gives this example of a boy "who concluded, 'If I grew from an egg, I must be a chicken,' and refused to eat his breakfast. 'Egg' meant just one thing to him. What if, instead of being born, he'd been made into an omelette?"[210]

> "We can no longer assume that teens make poor choices—drug use, high-speed driving, unprotected sex—because they are uninformed or unclear about the risks … It's not lack of information—it's lack of judgment."

"We can no longer assume," Grossman writes, "that teens make poor choices—drug use, high-speed driving, unprotected sex—because they are uninformed or unclear about the risks … It's not lack of information—it's lack of judgment."[211] This is affirmed and explained by scientists, writes Dr. Grossman, who studied the brain scans of children and adolescents. The area of the brain called the prefrontal cortex (PFC) is the last to mature. It may not completely develop until the mid-twenties. The PFC is located behind the forehead and is responsible for the executive functions of the brain: judging, reasoning, decision-making, self-evaluation, planning, suppression of impulses, and weighing the consequences of one's decision. The PFC, like a chief executive officer, needs time to mature. Not yet "on the job," how will the PFC of an adolescent serve him or her, particularly in risky situations? Dr. Grossman writes, "The rates of death, disability, and health problems of teens is 200 percent to 300 percent higher than children, due primarily to their poor control of behavior and emotion. A portion of this burden is a consequence of sexual activity: pregnancy, sexually transmitted infections and emotional turmoil. In devising an effective public health response to this crisis, the process of adolescent decision-making must be examined."[212] We might note that statutory rape laws are in effect because an adult is taking advantage of someone under age 18, most of whom are not yet capable of reasoning, setting boundaries,

---

210 Grossman, *You're Teaching My Child What?*, 33.
211 Grossman, *You're Teaching My Child What?*, 74-75.
212 Grossman, *You're Teaching My Child What?*, 72-73.

or weighing consequences. Due to the corruption of sin, giving information about sex will not lead to good decisions. Young people do need to learn about sex, but the time when they need to be informed will vary from child to child. In all cases, the message needs to be communicated in all modesty so as not to tempt toward sinful thoughts, words and deeds.

Educators hold up knowledge as a good thing. But can we all agree that some things are too difficult for children and teens with undeveloped PFCs to understand? A teenage boy, for example, is capable of respecting a girl when he identifies her as a creation of God and His daughter in Christ. But he may not be ready to comprehend exceedingly detailed knowledge or process it in his or that girl's best interest.

81. A good sex educator will take adolescent brain development into consideration, won't they?

We hope so. But in what way do they factor in what we might call the "cool" and "hot" conditions of the classroom vs. real life? The classroom is an environment where the intensity or level of emotion is "cool;" in other words calm, unpressured, and disciplined. The teen might demonstrate excellent executive functions when given a hypothetical dilemma in class. There, together with the teacher and other students, he engages in deliberate, logical, and non-pressured thinking. He may conclude the following: 1) Being sexually involved is a big deal, so I'm going to go slow and weigh the consequences; 2) Knowing the risks of STDs and pregnancy, I will keep myself informed of contraceptives and birth control; and 3) Should my relationship with the one I love grow to the next level, I will act responsibly. A Christian teen may even confidently proclaim, "I'm going to wait for marriage." But the "cool" conditions of the classroom differ from real life situations.

Now imagine the same boy in an unexpected situation, for example, at a friend's house with no parental supervision. The girl he is with appears ready and willing. Other couples are disappearing into bedrooms. Functional brain scans (MRIs) tell us that in the midst of "hot" conditions—intense, exciting and stimulating—this boy is more likely to make use of his amygdala (ah-MIG-di-lah), or the feeling part of his brain, rather than the PFC, or reasoning and weigh-the-consequences part of his brain. His ability to think and use good judgment can be hijacked by his strong emotions. Adults are most often capable of reasoning things through or applying brakes to their emotional feelings and responses because they, literally, engage their frontal lobe. Adolescent brains are just beginning to develop that ability.[213] Parents and teachers do best to help children and young people avoid situations where self-control will be put to the test.

82. If all the risks of sexual intimacy and benefits of waiting are laid out, won't boys and girls get the picture? Won't they set goals and consider the consequences of any decision?

> Christians should know that due to sin's corruption, having sexual information is not sufficient to make good sexual decisions; in fact, if that sexual information was acquired at the loss of modesty, it has actually weakened the child's resistance to sexual temptation.

We should support the teaching of sexual ethics. Parents, with the support of pastors and teachers, should set forth the risks of sexual intimacy and the benefits of patiently waiting for such intimacy until marriage in accord with God's plan. The problem is, however, that sex education based on humanism does not take original sin into account. Christians should know that due to sin's corruption, having sexual information is not sufficient to make good sexual decisions; in fact, if that sexual information was acquired at the loss of modesty, it has actually weakened the child's resistance to sexual temptation.

For at least two generations, parents have been tempted to believe that sex education is a science. If we just pour all information—risks

---

213 Grossman, *You're Teaching My Child What?*, 73-74.

and benefits—into the minds of children and teens, then they will process it. Using role-play, discussion groups, and visual resources, so-called experts in the field of sexuality may drill boys and girls every school day, but all the best intentions in the world won't produce a sexually responsible teen. "The wiring isn't finished," writes Dr. Grossman. "The circuits aren't complete. The driver is unskilled."[214] And, we must add, extremely vulnerable.

"With the onset of puberty," continues Dr. Grossman, "the brain is flooded with sex hormones … strong drives, excitement, and emotional intensity." New experiences are sought in order to produce a greater high or good feeling. Into the mix, add the youthful myth of immortality and the naïve notion that it can't happen to me. "There is substantial evidence," notes Dr. Laurence Steinberg, "that adolescents engage in dangerous activities despite knowing and understanding risks involved."[215] It is for this reason that parents need to act as the pre-frontal lobe or PFC of their sons and daughters. This means leading away from temptation rather than encouraging early dating. It means giving girls time to be girls and boys time to be boys. Young people might resist, but parents must be consistent in setting and maintaining boundaries, monitoring friendships and activities, and never giving up on biblical instruction in purity.

83. Some people believe that sex education in a Christian classroom, more than discussing the act of sex, is really an opportunity to discuss the common understanding of masculinity and femininity. There is no harm in a mixed group of boys and girls discussing this, is there?

Yes, there could be because we're forgetting something about our identity. We may speak of common things in public and in mixed company; but male and female, created by God for His purpose, are certainly not common. By virtue of Baptism, all Christians are "holy ones," saints set apart

---

214 Grossman, *You're Teaching My Child What?*, 76.
215 Grossman, *You're Teaching My Child What?*, 75.

for God through the death and resurrection of Jesus Christ. God creates male and female to compatibly live and work together in more than just intimate ways; therefore, it is important for us to teach young men and women how to interact with one another when marriage is not in view. Christians can highlight the different ways that God uses male and female for holy purpose in vocations of brother or sister, neighbor, co-worker and friend. Admittedly, this will require boldness because drawing attention to the distinctive differences between male and female has been out of vogue for a very long time. So has comfort with the building of non-sensual relationships. Those who oppose God tend to diminish all that is uncommon, holy and complementarily different about male and female.

Ever since the Fall, men and women have been perplexed by and even at odds with each other. The Christian community has the unique opportunity to do something beyond teaching about sex and sexuality; we can mentor manhood and womanhood. We do this best using the Titus 2 model: older men teaching younger men and older women teaching younger women. This is not the way of popular culture. It is not what sex educators are trained to do nor is it what feminists want to do. But Christians don't live by worldly opinions and values.

Sin causes boys to be puzzled and frustrated by girls—and vice versa; therefore, Christian parents, pastors and teachers do both boys and girls a great service by teaching them separately about themselves and one another. I discovered long ago that girls have many questions about themselves, feelings, boys, relationships, marriage, motherhood and so on, but they will not ask a great many of these questions in the presence of boys. What a joy for an older woman not to pit the girls against the boys, but to describe the created differences; not to withhold information for fear of betraying the feminist agenda, but to share medical science without fear of betraying faith. Girls can learn a lot about boys from their fathers and older brothers; but not just any older man will do in such an instructive position. The same is true with boys. They can benefit from a mother or grandmother's instruction, but not just any older woman will do in such a mentoring role.

Parents and teachers are called to honor God's created order and guard the virtue of youth. We are to create environments for instructing in purity that do not compromise the child's identity as God's son or daughter. It does not please God for an adult to remove the protective fence of healthy embarrassment or natural modesty. Embarrassment was a new emotion after sin entered the world, given by God to men and women—even married men and women like Adam and Eve—for their own protection against the temptations of their own sinful nature.

> Embarrassment was a new emotion after sin entered the world, given by God to men and women—even married men and women like Adam and Eve—for their own protection against the temptations of their own sinful nature.
>
>

CHAPTER FOURTEEN

God is the Designer
of Modest Clothing

84. Sex education taught in the Church probably differs from the secular by providing discussion of modest clothing... or does it?

It should. However, only when the books in the *Learning About Sex* series from Concordia Publishing House were recently rewritten for girls separate from boys was a significant discussion about clothing included.[216] With eyes open, however, it appears that clothing even for Christians is a thing indifferent. Younger (and older) women too often approach the Lord's Table clothed in eye-catching attire not dissimilar from the women one might see working the corner of Hollywood and Vine. From time to time, I ask teen girls and their moms if they would be comfortable wearing their lingerie or bra and panties out in the front yard or going shopping. "Of course not," they proclaim, "no way!" But how is their bikini any different? As a wife and mom, I strive to see the world through the eyes of my husband, sons and grandsons. They are sorely put to the test. For example, there was the time when a beautiful and well-endowed woman waited on the table of my family. The cross the server was wearing hung low and visible between her breasts, but where were the eyes of my husband and sons invited to focus: upon the cross or somewhere else?

---

216 *Love, Sex & God* (2008), 54-55.

Sex education most certainly turns the eyes of boys toward the bodies of girls. It turns the eyes of girls to the bodies of boys. Sex education teaches that there is no shame in the human body. After all, as this thinking goes, God made our wondrous bodies. But, we must not ignore the fact that sin has corrupted our desires. Sex education may unintentionally encourage girls to become temptresses. Sometimes a young woman is completely unaware that she is being a temptress. She is, perhaps, uneducated in godly womanhood, dressing "like everyone else" or unaware that immodest clothing draws a man's attention. There are other women who know full well that sensual clothing invites attention and this is how they exercise power over men. We may hear people claim that clothing is a matter of "Christian liberty;" it is simply a personal choice. "Sexy," they say, is just part of being female. It is, as I have been told, "showing my best assets." But showing them to whom and for what reason? To believe it is a "liberty" to wear clothes designed to highlight certain parts of the body is to be fooled. Foolishness puts us at risk.

For the sake of young women and men, let's be honest. There is a reason why the marketing industry uses scantily-clad women to sell products. There is a reason why the procurers of prostitutes want their "working girls" to dress the way they do. That reason is sin. It is sin when one person uses another person to gain power or financial profit. Young women need to know that they are more—far more—than objects of pleasure for display. Failing to speak about clothing as God's protective covering for their bodies puts them at risk of being identified, not as He created them but as the world sees them. It removes respect. It places them in conflict with themselves and compromises their true identity. It sets young men up for temptation, frustration, and trouble. A young Christian woman in college told me that she never gave much thought to the way she dressed until the day her boyfriend blurted out, "Do you know what you're doing to me?"

A classroom educator might try to explain to a young woman that a man's eyes rest easily on a woman's body. It is, however, far more appropriate and protective when a father explains the virtue of modesty to his daughter. He can explain to her that before sin Adam could gaze upon Eve's body in appreciation for what God had made, but that after sin his eyes would distort that appreciation. It is also the father who best explains to his son how to avoid the temptress. The father's warning away from the temptress in Proverbs 7 is wisdom to his son.

85. Some Christians believe that Scripture speaks of a woman's modest apparel only for those times when she is in the presence of God and men in corporate worship. What do you say to this?

The outward adornment of a woman who professes faith in Christ should reflect her inner beauty and identity as a baptized daughter of God. This is true especially in worship but, because women are always in the presence of God and men, it is true for all times. 1 Timothy 2:9-10 encourages women to "adorn themselves in respectable apparel, with modesty and self-control, not with braided hair and gold or pearls or costly attire, but with what is proper for women who profess godliness—with good works." The Christian woman is called by God to profess godliness every day of the week in her vocation of "helper" (Gn. 2:18) whether she is in class, at work, or having fun. She should refrain from being proud and sensual but can be generous with "good works" that help men think about what is honorable and pure.

Identity matters. How we dress says something about who we think we are. Focused on an identity of being "sexual," it is easier for girls and women to disregard self-restraint and responsibility in favor of personal rights. Dressing "sexy" can have a powerful influence on our feelings and, therefore, the decisions made based on those feelings. But if girls learn to see themselves as daughters of God in Christ, then they will be encouraged to dress in a way that calls attention not to themselves, but to their Father. Women who see themselves as God sees them

> Identity matters. How we dress says something about who we think we are.
>
>

help their brothers in Christ better navigate the journey of life to their eternal destination.[217]

> Women who see themselves as God sees them help their brothers in Christ better navigate the journey of life to their eternal destination.
>
>

86. Adam and Eve were naked and without shame; therefore husbands and wives can celebrate God's design for sexuality and be unashamed in nakedness, isn't that true?

Husbands and wives in Christ can be pleased by God's design for sexuality and be unashamed in nakedness, but our corrupted nature reminds us that we no longer live in the Garden. At the time when Adam and Eve were completely naked and without embarrassment (Gn. 2:25), the world was perfect. Man and wife had no lustful thoughts. There was no such word as "sexy;" instead, the word was "holy." God covered animals with fur, feathers, scales, and so on. But God covered man and woman with His glory. And why wouldn't He? He made male and female in His image. God Himself is covered in glory (Ps. 104:1-2; Isa. 61:3-10). Sin changed everything for Adam and Eve—and all of us. Their eyes were opened and they knew that they were naked (Gn. 3:7). Nakedness was no longer "good." Their sin left them exposed and vulnerable. New emotions of embarrassment and shame caused them to cover themselves with fig leaves. They sewed for themselves a loincloth and bikini of fig leaves but, still very embarrassed, ran to hide. God could have left Adam and Eve in their naked and hopelessly sinful state but He had loving compassion. Before He sent Adam and Eve out of the Garden, God did something for

---

217 Author's note: For a number of years, I presented a purity lifestyle show using vintage and modern clothing to illustrate the language of clothing and its effect on the culture. In 2006, I was asked to adapt the program into a Bible study for young women, their moms and mentors. The ten-lesson study is entitled *Dressing for Life: Secrets of the Great Cover-up*. It is available as a downloadable PDF file from www.lutheransforlife.org or www.cph.org. (Order #LFLDFLWEB.)

them that only a merciful God can do. He knew that a bikini or loincloth of fig leaves would not be enough covering in the sinful world so He covered them with garments of skins.

Martin Luther writes,

> Here Adam and Eve are dressed in garments by the Lord God Himself. Whenever they looked at their garments, these were to serve as a reminder to them to give thought to their wretched fall from supreme happiness into the utmost misfortune and trouble. Thus they were to be constantly afraid of sinning, to repent continually, and to sigh for the forgiveness of sins through the promise Seed. This is also why He clothed them, not in foliage or in cotton but in the skins of slain animals, for a sign that they are mortal and that they are living in certain death.[218]

No man or woman on this earth, not even husbands and wives, would ever look at one another in the way that Adam and Eve did before sin. Original sin put corruption into our human nature and radically impaired our desires. Now what God created to be "good" nearly always brings forth evil desires. Not even the loving and procreative act of sex made for the faithfulness of marriage between one man and one woman would, on this earth, be quite the same.

87. From Scripture, we learn that a Christian is both sinner and saint. How does clothing remind us of these conflicting identities?

Every person conceived and born after the Fall is a sinner. Every person who believes in Jesus Christ as their Lord and Savior is a saint. Clothing, which is significant in Scripture, speaks to both of these identities. After the Fall, a loving God provided Adam and Eve with two kinds of clothing. Coats of

---

218 Commentary on Genesis 3:21, *The Lutheran Study Bible*, 20.

animal skins covered their physical body, but the covering of Jesus Christ was promised for their spiritual body. As forgiven sinners, we are clothed in the garment of salvation which is the robe of righteousness given freely to us by Jesus Christ (Isa. 61:10). Wearing the robe of His Son, God sees us as holy. However, it is a consequence of the fallen world that men and women see each other through sin-tainted eyes. For this reason, God tells women to dress modestly—in a way that professes faith—so that they do not tempt an admiring man by way of false glory to sinful thoughts or deeds.

> There was absolute necessity for the full covering and righteousness of the Savior, Jesus Christ. Today, whenever we consider clothing, we can remember that its purpose is to cover our bodies and protect us from our own corrupted thoughts.

Adam and Eve covered only certain parts of themselves with fig leaves, but God designed clothes to cover their bodies. From this we know that Adam and Eve could not sufficiently cover themselves physically (nakedness) or spiritually (works righteousness). The work of their hands was neither acceptable nor enough. There was absolute necessity for the full covering and righteousness of the Savior, Jesus Christ. Today, whenever we consider clothing, we can remember that its purpose is to cover our bodies and protect us from our own corrupted thoughts. Here is where instruction in purity does what sex education does not. Clothing is not usually considered very significant in sex or sexuality education. But to help male and female of any age understand that we are called to a lifestyle of purity means that we must talk about clothing.

88. What more can we say about the significance and permanent place that clothing has for God's people?

Let's look at some specific passages beginning with Matthew 22:11-12. "But when the king came in to look at the guests, he saw there a man who had no wedding garment. And he said to him, 'Friend, how did you get in here without a wedding garment?' And he was speechless." The *Lutheran Study Bible* explains: "Israelites expected invited guests to wear festive wedding garments, which the host could provide. Thus, this fellow's failure to dress in appropriate clothing, which was freely given to him, offends the host. This garment signifies the righteousness of God, which covers our sin" (cf Is. 61:10; Gal. 3:27).[219]

We can also look at Revelation 16:15: "Behold, I am coming like a thief! Blessed is the one who stays awake, keeping his garments on, that he may not go about naked and be seen exposed." White garments serve as a symbol for Christian righteousness which is bestowed through Christ at Baptism. Here, again, we are reminded of our earthly and eternal identity: we are holy as opposed to sexual; uncommon and useable by God as opposed to common and useable by anyone. Revelation 19:8 speaks about the marriage of the Lamb (Jesus) to His Bride (the Church), saying: "It was granted her to clothe herself with fine linen, bright and pure for the fine linen is the righteous deeds of the saints." The bride's preparations for the marriage are the result of God's grace and Spirit, not simply her own efforts . . . the saints' righteous deeds, which are here identified with spiritual adornment, are a gift granted by God, not a human achievement.[220]

89. So if nakedness, modesty, and clothing take on new meaning for children of God, then might we actually do a disservice to children and ourselves if we infer that embarrassment is unnecessary or unnatural?

There is no shame in blushing. It's natural, too! When the wind whips up a woman's skirt, she quickly responds by pulling it down. To be embarrassed about nakedness is God's natural protection for our body and spirit. We

---

219 Commentary on Matthew 22:11-12, *The Lutheran Study Bible*, 1630.
220 Commentary on Revelation 19:8, *The Lutheran Study Bible*, 2228.

cannot separate the physical and spiritual, or the lower and upper stories of our house (body). The two affect each other. In this world, men and women see each other through sin-damaged eyes. We are too easily tempted to wrong thought or action by a warped vision and perspective. We owe our sons and daughters the truth about nakedness and the reason for clothing. The world cares little, if at all, about our vulnerability. It is God, because of His great love for us, who wants us covered. When we are not, God uses natural emotions of shame and embarrassment for our benefit.

Physical clothing actually affords brothers and sisters in Christ—married or single—more freedom to interact with one another in their vocations of male and female. They are less distracted and able to do the work laid before them, whether that is studying in class or clerking in a store. As baptized sons and daughters of God in Christ, we are dressed in preparation for heaven. We are not left naked—physically or spiritually. God covers our body and spirit with appropriate clothing so that we are less vulnerable and tempted to stray away from Jesus who waits for our meeting with Him in heaven.

It cannot please God when an adult tries to remove a child's embarrassment. Embarrassment and shame, like guilt, can move all of us to the Cross where repentant sinners can robe up in Jesus' righteousness. More than anything, we should want to help our children appreciate Jesus' robe of righteousness which makes them holy in God's eyes. Wearing that robe, children of God are called not to sensual living, but holy living.

CHAPTER FIFTEEN

Sex Education is

A Form of Child Abuse

90. Might sex education be considered a form of cruelty or abuse?

Some have thought so, and their reasons are worthy of consideration. The first time I heard sex education referred to as "child abuse" was in a personal e-mail written to me from Douglas Gresham, the step-son of C.S. Lewis. I had contacted him about coming to the U.S. to do some speaking. In our correspondence, I expressed concern about sex education in our public and parochial schools. Mr. Gresham responded that I was right to be concerned. He wrote, "Sex education is child abuse because it is ill-planned and poorly thought out, thus adding to the very problem it is trying to address and eroding the structure of a healthy family." Mr. Gresham is the founder of Rathvinden Ministries in Dublin, Ireland. He and his wife minister to those who have suffered child abuse and to women who grieve children lost to abortion.[221]

Over a period of thirty years, Dr. Judith Reisman researched and exposed the work of Alfred Kinsey and other sexologists. I have already explained who she is and quoted frequently from two of her books. Dr. Reisman

---

221 Author's note: Douglas Gresham is the co-producer of *The Chronicles of Narnia: The Lion, The Witch and the Wardrobe*. He and his wife, Merrie, came to have a personal understanding of child abuse through their ministry at Rathvinden House and by affiliating with the International Institute of Pregnancy Loss and Child Abuse Research and Recovery.

documents Kinsey's abuse of children in gathering research for his reports and the damage that was to follow because of his betrayal of true scientific study. She writes,

> In 1976, Stanford University historian Paul Robinson, observed in *The Modernization of Sex* that Kinsey's statistics were designed "to undermine the traditional sexual order" and that paying heed to Kinsey would gut all sex laws, including age of consent.

The sexologists always fought back, since the notion of infant sexuality is powerfully entrenched in sexology. We see this in statements by Mary Calderone, MD, past president and co-founder (with Lester Kirkendall) of SIECUS, and past medical director of Planned Parenthood. Speaking before the 1980 annual meeting of the Association of Planned Parenthood Physicians, Calderone said the primary goal of SIECUS was teaching society "the vital importance of infant and childhood sexuality."

Infant sexuality?

This theory, that sexualized children are prey for pedophiles, is staggering. Children's "sexuality," she said, should "be developed in the same way as the child's inborn human capacity to talk or to walk, and that [the parents'] role should relate only to teaching the child the appropriateness of privacy, place, and person—in a word, socialization."

To sexualize an infant before his or her ability to walk or talk, never mind before their developmental maturity and reproductive readiness, is criminal—a cruel torment that interferes grotesquely with children's natural developmental sequence and produces unnatural behavioral, psychobio-logical, and psychological deviance. [222]

Lynette Burrows is the mother of six. In her October 2011 comments on the BBC and her presentation to the Society for the Protection of Unborn Children (SPUC), she explains why sex education is a form of child abuse:

> I do believe that all "sex education" as practiced today is wicked because it has, in terms of human misery, an unacceptable number of casualties. All of which can be re-used as further propaganda for the necessity of their product. With little children . . . we are on holy ground and Christ Himself warned that those who lead children astray would deserve hideous punishment. "Better for him that a millstone were hanged about his neck and he were drowned in the depth of the sea." We often refer to protecting their innocence—but what do we mean by it? Is innocence simply the absence of useful information; is it simply not knowing something or other? I don't think so. I think it is something much more vital and akin to a mental immune system that operates in young children for as long as they need it for their growth and development and for the protection of their mental well-being. I don't believe they can grow up healthily without certain areas that they have not got the emotional maturity to understand or deal with, being veiled from them. . . . To force sex ed on to them, before they are ready, is therefore to enact mental violence on them for some theoretical reason that is far closer to paedophilia than anything else.[223]

---

222 Reisman, *Sexual Sabotage*, 302.
223 Burrows, "The Worst Sexualisation of Children is Happening in Schools."

91. Isn't it going too far to accuse well-meaning Christians of cruelty or child abuse?

This book is not written to accuse any parent, pastor or teacher of child abuse. *It is written to sound an alarm within the Church. We have not been on guard, carefully discerning between human opinion and God's Word. We have flirted with humanism and embraced skewed social science. We reinterpreted Scripture in light of "new" information presented by unbelieving neighbors in the land.* When the Israelites blended with the Canaanites, children paid the highest price with their lives. The Canaanites did not fear and love God, but worshiped at a sexual altar. Archaeological excavations at Gezer in the Canaanite region revealed the ruins of temples where Baal and Ashtoreth were worshiped. Found in the ruins were excessive sexual images and plaques designed to raise curiosity and foster sensual feelings. Under the debris of the High Place were also found a great number of jars containing the remains of children who had been sacrificed to Baal. A child was sacrificed and its body built into the wall so that the family might have a brighter future.[224] What is the lesson for us?

> We have flirted with humanism and embraced skewed social science. We reinterpreted Scripture in light of "new" information presented by unbelieving neighbors in the land.
>
> ❖ ❖ ❖

The Church, true to God's Word, has always upheld instruction in purity. Parents were to instruct in the lifestyle of a Christ-follower, answer the questions of their children, catechize them, help them develop skills for

---

224 Author's note: An excavation at Megiddo near Samaria (in the stratum of Ahab's time) found the ruins of a temple of Ashtoreth, goddess wife of Baal. Just a few steps from the temple was a cemetery where many jars were found containing remains of infants who had been sacrificed in this temple of sexuality.

life, mentor self-control, help them discern right from wrong, judge what young minds are not yet capable of judging, set boundaries, and prepare their sons and daughters for the faithfulness of marriage and family. The Church was to support the Christian parent in their responsibility and, if the parent was not honoring God or shirking their duty, the Church was to remind them and work with them. But those of the humanist faith did not like the cautionary tone that most parents took with their children when it came to sex. People like Kinsey, Pomeroy and Money wanted to believe that most people thought about sex the way they did. Giving themselves up to dishonorable passions, they committed shameless acts. Since they did not acknowledge God, it appears that God gave them up to do what should never be done. These men and others were zealous in their "mission" to set children and adults free from repressive religion, but they were neither ethical nor honest. Worse than their betrayal of science was the door they opened to pornography, pedophilia, incest, and human trafficking. Because they did not see children as God does, they helped shape a world more dangerous for children.

In 1961, when the National Council of Churches held the first conference on sex education, how many who attended could have known the secrets of Kinsey, his immoral methodology or his fraudulent statistics? How many within the Church could have known about his abusive experiments on little children or his utter violation of science? What some leaders within the Church might have feared was that the world was changing and they needed to keep pace. But God's Word does not change. It is wisdom for every generation. A sane and sensible dialogue on sex education was needed, but any "new information" should always be interpreted in light of God's Word. The "authority" at that conference was not God's Word but Mary Calderone of SIECUS who subscribed to Kinsey's human sexuality model.

92. But didn't Christians attempt to take sex education in a different direction?

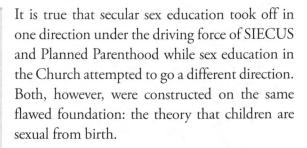

The goals of secular sex education and abstinence have always been different, but their resources, methods and teaching environment have been too much the same.

❖ ❖ ❖

It is true that secular sex education took off in one direction under the driving force of SIECUS and Planned Parenthood while sex education in the Church attempted to go a different direction. Both, however, were constructed on the same flawed foundation: the theory that children are sexual from birth.

It has been said that there is nothing wrong with taking the best and throwing out the rest; in other words, even people who reject Jesus Christ may still have some good ideas useable by Christians. I believe that most Christian educators, pastors, or parents who favor comprehensive, formalized sex education do so because they care about young people. I believe they faithfully tried, in writing Christian books on sex and human sexuality, to sort the good from the bad. The goals of secular sex education and abstinence have always been different, but their resources, methods and teaching environment have been too much the same. Sex education, in or out of the Church, has:

- Recognized Kinsey as "authority" in the area of sex and sexuality and referenced the work and statistics of Kinsey, Pomeroy and C.E. Martin's *Sexual Behavior in the Human Male* and *Sexual Behavior in the Human Female.*[225]

- Believed that parents fail to teach the "goodness" of sex.

225 Author's Note: This book does not pretend to offer the depth of research on Kinsey and his associates that Judith Reisman, the Family Research Council and others do. Reisman's books simply must be read by any concerned Christian in order to fully grasp what was set in place by humanists and those who oppose God. Once children were seen as "sexual," then the pornography industry and pedophile predators gained a power that

- Encouraged sex education beginning at an early age.

- Violated the biblical modesty of children by putting boys and girls together for discussion of sex and sexuality.

- Accepted "children are sexual from birth" as fact and, in so doing, made them more vulnerable in a sexualized world.

- Promoted a primary identity of "sexual" which too easily compromises purity.

In too many ways, sex education brought into the Church is an unholy alliance with opposing doctrines and faith. The identity of "sexual" has been declared the cultural holy of holies, but it is poison to the Church. It targets the absolutes of God's Word. Whenever the people of God no longer find His Word sufficient but fall into idolatry, the Church is hard-pressed to affect the culture. Idolizing our sexuality, the culture dangerously becomes more acceptant of promiscuity, adultery and divorce, homosexuality, counterfeit marriage, and abortion.

> In too many ways, sex education brought into the Church is an unholy alliance with opposing doctrines and faith. The identity of "sexual" has been declared the cultural holy of holies, but it is poison to the Church …Whenever the people of God no longer find His Word sufficient but fall into idolatry, the Church is hard-pressed to affect the culture. Idolizing our sexuality, the culture dangerously becomes more acceptant of promiscuity, adultery and divorce, homosexuality, counterfeit marriage, and abortion.

influenced laws, psychology, and medicine. In the Acknowledgments of *Kinsey: Crimes & Consequences*, Reisman notes the difficulty of "grappling with Kinsey's statistics," thus she was most grateful to W. Allen Wallis, past president of the American Statistical Association and past editor of the journal of the American Statistical Association for his "critical approval of my work on Kinsey's statistical maze." Wallis confirmed that Kinsey's report was not an objective, factual study of sexual behavior in the human male or female. (*Crimes & Consequences*, xiv)

93. Is it fair to say that sex education brought into the Church is an unholy alliance with an opposing worldview?

Yes, it is fair to say this because the purpose of sex education as its earliest proponents envisioned it was philosophical. It was about change; changing the way we view sex, marriage, and the family. We must not forget that Kinsey, Sanger (Planned Parenthood) and Calderone (SIECUS) were all evolutionists, humanists, eugenicists and not particularly fond of the biblical family. They believed that education creates a modern point of view. But what does this mean? It means progressing out of antiquated ways to a better, utopian world. A modern point of view, to a secular humanist, rejects the biblical worldview. I have no difficulty imagining that the Christians who attended the conference on sex education hosted by the NCC in 1961 were hoping to learn how to help young people and their parents. They were, perhaps naively, seeking the counsel of the "best minds" on the subject of human sexuality.

Jacqueline R. Kasun writes,

> In the words of Calderone, "Change is the new reality . . . the unchanging . . . is unreal, constraining, a false goal." Children must "become familiar with change, feel comfortable with it, understand it, master it, and control it." [Calderone] summed up the task of sex education: "If man as he is, is obsolescent, then what kind do we want to produce in his place and how do we design the production line?— that is the real question facing . . . sex education." Calderone answered her own question. The new human beings will be "consciously engineered" by society's "best minds," who also will provide the necessary "conditioning." These "best minds" will, of course, be "mindful of the facts now known to science," and Calderone emphasizes that her sexual teachings are indeed one of the marvels of modern science. The task is great, she acknowledges,

but she and her colleagues will press onward and upward. Confident that "where religious laws or rules about sex were made on the basis of ignorance of facts now known, laws and rules need to be reexamined and recast to be consonant with these facts."[226]

I don't know if Calderone was this frank and open when she addressed the representatives of 38 Protestant denominations at the NCC conference on sex education in 1961. But if she was, were those Christians so enamored with the "best minds" that they were ready to return to their church bodies and publishing houses to interpret Scripture in light of such "modern science"? In the desire to return to the Garden of Eden (utopia) and make sex "good" again, did they fail to take into account the effects of original sin? Children suffer and the lives of young people are put at risk whenever adults are taken "captive by philosophy and empty deceit, according to human tradition, according to the elemental spirits of the world, and not according to Christ" (Col. 2:8)?

94. Wouldn't any Christian become indignant if accused of child abuse, especially if they were trying to teach a child about something "good from God"?

Yes, understandably so. But a Lutheran pastor's wife helped me to see sex education in the Church from a new perspective. She wrote to express gratitude for the Titus 2 Retreat she had attended. Of greatest value, she said, was the opportunity to contrast a sexualized identity with our true identity in Christ. She had believed most abortions were the consequence of promiscuity resulting from immodest dress, media influence, and a "me first" attitude. She understood the deceit of the feminist movement and the absence of biblical fathers. But there was a piece of the abortion puzzle,

---

226 Jacqueline R. Kasun, "Sex Education: The Hidden Agenda," *The World and I*, 499. (Author's note: Kasun is quoting from Calderone's "Sex Education and the Roles of the School and Church," *The Annals of the American Academy of Political and Social Science* 376 [March. 1968], 57, and *The Family Book About Sexuality* authored with Eric W. Johnson [New York: Harper & Row, 1981], 171.)

she believed, that was missing. That piece, she believed, would significantly impact the number of abortions, health risks, and hurting women in our country if it were addressed.

This woman, following a confidential discussion with other Lutheran women, was motivated to research the prevalence of childhood sexual abuse and its connections to promiscuity and abortion. She encouraged me to address this missing piece of the abortion puzzle. When we think of childhood sexual abuse, we tend to think about sexual sins committed against children by relatives or neighbors. If such behavior is known, it is typically covered up by those who feel powerless to do anything about it. Is it possible, do you think, that childhood sexual abuse might also occur in the classroom where boys and girls together are desensitized by sexual talk and visual images? The theory is that children should feel at ease with their sexuality, but what if they are not ready for such dialogue? What if there is too much, too soon? What if the encounter group of the classroom actually strips them of their innocence? Will they feel powerless to do anything about it?

> What if the encounter group of the classroom actually strips them of their innocence? Will they feel powerless to do anything about it?
>
> ❖ ❖ ❖

It is not my intent or desire to heap guilt upon any Christian brother or sister. God knows my own doubts, failures and acceptance of teachings that are not His. I did not want to write this book, but after hearing "Well, I'm a sexual being" or "Children are sexual, too" so many times over the course of 30 years in pro-life work, I was compelled to learn the source of such thinking. In short, I came to understand that this mistaken identity makes abortion and same-sex "marriage" thinkable. It makes child with child or child with adult sex thinkable. I have quoted Reisman many times in this book. I believe it is important for you to understand why. She writes,

In 1966 . . . my ten-year-old daughter, Jennie, was molested by a 13-year-old adored and trusted family friend. She told him to stop, but he persisted. He knew she would like it, he said, he knew from his father's glossy magazines, the only "acceptable" pornography of the time. The boy left the country a few weeks later, after it came to light that my daughter was but one of several neighborhood children he had raped, including his own little brother. . . . [M]y daughter slipped into a deep depression. Only after I promised not to call the police would she talk about what happened. After assuring her this was not her fault, I called my dependable, staid aunt who listened sympathetically and declared, "Well, Judy, she may have been looking for this herself. Children are sexual from birth." Stunned, I replied that my child was not seeking sex, and I dialed my Berkeley school chum, Carole, still seeking confirmation of my righteous indignation at my daughter's violation, which I badly needed to hear. Instead, Carole counseled, "Well, Judy, she may have been looking for this herself. You know children are sexual from birth." . . . I had entered the world according to Kinsey. [227]

It bears repeating: It is *never* a child's fault when he or she is abused. A child has not sinned when they are forced to do something against their will or learn something they're not equipped to understand. So what does the person who experienced childhood sexual abuse do? He or she finds hope and healing in God's promises: "Those who look to him are radiant, and their faces shall never be ashamed. . . . The angel of the Lord encamps around those who fear him, and delivers them. . . . The Lord is near to the brokenhearted and saves the crushed in spirit (Ps. 34:5, 7, 18).

---

227 Reisman, preface to *Kinsey: Crimes & Consequences*, xviii.

95. Would it be fair to say that sex education—too much, too soon, too frequent— is cruel?

> Sex education, although only a part of the problem, has certainly not been as effective as those dreaming of "utopia" thought it would be.

Yes, it would. Sex education, although only a part of the problem, has certainly not been as effective as those dreaming of "utopia" thought it would be. It is not very helpful to give early and much information, strip away modesty and then expect young people to "wait."

Wanda Franz, a professor of child development and family studies at West Virginia University, writes,

> We should be very sensitive to the amount of sexual arousal in our children's lives. They should be protected from excessive arousal and arousal to the wrong circumstances. Attempting to "desensitize" children to sexual arousal by forced contact with sexual topics is cruel and detrimental. . . . [W]e must take into account the developmental/cognitive capabilities of our young people. Until we do this, our attempts at [reforming sexuality education] will be doomed to failure. [228]

Let's fast forward to the teenage years. By now, a girl has been desensitized sexually but aroused emotionally. She has been desensitized sexually by shopping at Victoria's Secret or Abercrombie & Fitch, watching Miley Cyrus on YouTube perform "We Can't Stop," learning the secrets of "turning a boy on" from her most recent teen magazine, and sitting

---

228 Wanda Franz, "Sex and the American Teenager," *The World and I*, Vol. 4, No. 9 (Washington, D.C: *The Washington Times* Corporation, September 1989), 484-485. (Author's note: Dr. Wanda Franz served as president of National Right to Life for several years.)

through years of sex education. She has been aroused emotionally by countless romance stories, love songs and movies. There is really very little left to the imagination of boys. They have seen Miley Cyrus, too, and wonder if the girls in youth group who seem comfortable showing their bodies might also be comfortable with some intimate touching. Even in the Christian classroom, sitting next to that girl he saw wearing the "fig leaf" bikini at the pool and with the teacher speaking of the glories of sex, lustful ideas are hard to suppress. Information is faithfully followed by the word "wait," but for how long?

Do you remember the 20-something-year old woman who told me that she had had years of abstinence education which was, in her words, "just lots of talk about sex"? Could we admit that:

- Those who feared not enough talk about sex are now providing information overload?

- Lots of talk about sex starting very young and continuing for years might desensitize our sons and daughters?

> Could we admit that those who feared not enough talk about sex are now providing information overload?
>
>

- "You are sexual from birth" and the "wow" factor of sexual intimacy in marriage might tempt boy and girl to experience the natural feelings of their sexuality even though they are not ready for the commitment of marriage?

Think about it. What does Satan do with the message "you are a sexual being" in this "whatever is right for me world"? Adults help young people in the daily spiritual battle, not by focusing on children as common "sexual beings," but as uncommon holy ones: sons and daughters of God set apart for noble purpose in Jesus Christ and strengthened by the Holy Spirit.

96. Do we frustrate young people today with an identity as "sexual" and "cradle to grave" sex education, but recommendation of delayed marriage?

Yes, we do. Perhaps the "ancients" knew something that we "moderns" have chosen to ignore. Many Christian parents understood their role as mentors, not to help their child get in touch with their sexual side, but with their thinking and faith. A parent wanted their child to read, write, do math, know history, practice self-control and pursue happiness through work and service of others. Parents, for the most part, knew the friends of their children. Did "things" happen? Sometimes, yes, but many parents knew the wisdom of not pairing boys and girls, thinking it was "cute," and then letting them find their own way. Instead, when bodies were urged to respond to the desires of their hearts, a young man and woman were encouraged to marry, start their family and, in so doing, positively affect church and community. Now think of what we've been doing for the past 50 or so years. We have taught boys and girls that they are "sexual from birth" and described the "wow" factor of marital intimacy but told them to wait to experience that joy until after getting a degree, securing a good job and being able to finance a luxurious wedding reception. Are we really surprised when they don't wait for marriage or move in together "because it's a financial no-brainer"?

97. Do well-meaning parents and sex educators, perhaps, disrupt the rhythm of life?

That's a good way of putting it. Some educators in the Church believe that the sexualization of children by social media must be countered with sex education citing biblical principles. But there's the problem. The Bible instructs in purity, not education in sex or sexuality. Purity is a lifestyle, a way of turning in a direction that reflects God's purpose rather than our own. As the One who calls us to purity, God knows that, in proper time, heart and body desire love. That desire is natural and, by His design, motivates a young man or woman to prepare for marriage and family. It is the rhythm of life! But has this rhythm of life been disrupted by:

- Early and long sex education that almost expects premarital sex (of some form) but nostalgically urges the young to "wait for true love"?

- The very education that we pride ourselves on—that university education which, today, has expanded to the necessity of a master's degree or doctorate?

- Well-meaning parents who encourage sons and daughters to great heights of career with little emphasis on vocations of fatherhood and motherhood?

- Waiting so long for marriage and the start of a family that the wife's biological clock stops ticking?

98. Is it possible that sex education or abstinence education, as some prefer to call it, might actually damage marriage by delaying it? Is there a case for early marriage?

We can answer "yes" to both questions, but not be popular for it. Our preoccupation with sex has turned our attention away from the damage being done to biblical marriage by well-intentioned Christians who delay it. Even abstinence training is preoccupied with sex, but provides very little mentoring toward marriage. Many Christians perceive a sexual crisis today, but not a marital one. There are plenty of books written about battling sexual desires, but are we being encouraged to do this for a longer period of time than our Creator intended? Most Christians want to be married someday but modern opinion seems to demand that, in addition to obtaining that college degree and securing a job worthy of one's education, there is

> "True love waits," they say. To that, other Christians may respond, "No, true love marries."
>
>

that "bucket list" of things to be accomplished before the wedding day. "True love waits," they say. To that, other Christians may respond, "No, true love marries."

This book does not allow long discussion about the advantages of early marriage, i.e. in the early to mid-20s, but here are a few things to ponder. Financial security is rather nebulous, so waiting until the day when that happens may actually kill a relationship that God is already knitting together. Good marriages grow in the midst of struggle. Some parents threaten to withdraw financial support if a son or daughter in college seeks to marry, but those parents will be far more helpful when they understand the blessing of marriage for a child who displays maturity and appreciation of marriage as the covenant it is. Married couples who refuse to be deceived by an identity that is "sexual" will go a long way in nurturing a healthy realism about marriage in their children. Yes, sex is good and connectional because God made it that way for a husband and wife, but there are other parts of the marital relationship that extend well beyond the sexual. Young people need to see that when sin messes with marriage—and it does—it is those other joys of marriage that sustain it. Those joys include shared faith in Jesus Christ, friendship, trust, laughter in the midst of difficulty, attitude adjustment, patience, kindness and selflessness.

99. Can you give more reasons why sex education—in or out of the Church—might be cruel or abusive?

Perhaps the following will bring order to some of the concerns we've previously expressed about sex education, its compromise of purity and, therefore, possible harm to children:

1. Early, explicit boy/girl sex education classes can steal the innocence of children and create mind-absorbing images, conflicts, and

preoccupations. Boy/girl classes in sex education or human sexuality can be a form of desensitization that eventually strips away defenses and induces acceptance of alternative values.

2. Early, explicit sex education offers a great deal of information to teens whose prefrontal cortex is not fully developed and who are, therefore, not equipped to use good judgment in real world, fast-moving and intense situations.

3. Sex education removes the natural and protective covering of modesty. Putting boys and girls together in a classroom for an intimate discussion of human sexuality based on the premise that "children are sexual from birth" makes children vulnerable by awakening desires before their time.

4. Sex education desensitizes girls to a point of danger. Taught to be comfortable with her body and unembarrassed about drawing attention to herself, she may receive inappropriate attention from boys, older men and perhaps even predators. Even at church events or youth activities, comfortable-with-my-sexuality girls may bring discomfort to boys, male counselors or pastors. A daughter of the heavenly Father does not honor Him when she says: "Men need to practice self-control, but I am free to do as I please."

5. Sex education is a utopian lie. Christian educators may want children to appreciate the beauty of God's creation and to rediscover the Garden experience, but we're not in the Garden anymore. Sin changed our hearts and the way we look at one another. Jesus says, "[O]ut of the heart come evil thoughts, murder,

> Christian educators may want children to appreciate the beauty of God's creation and to rediscover the Garden experience, but we're not in the Garden anymore.
>
>

adultery, sexual immorality, theft, false witness, slander" (Mt. 15:19). Do we better equip children to fight the battle with sexual immorality by telling them they are sexual beings—or spiritual beings who will live beyond this earthly life either with or apart from God? Do we help them by incessant reminders of their powerful sexual desires and urges or by mentoring them in biblical manhood and womanhood which can be practiced at all times and with "holiness and honor" (1 Th. 4:4)?

6. Sex education tantalizes the child; in other words, it presents something desirable to the view, but continually keeps it out of reach. It details sex, but always adds: "Don't use this information until you're married."

7. Sex education, even with the most noble intentions, may tempt young people to put their own desires and wants above God's Word and His will, if they think, for example, "This is who I am," "This is my identity," or "This is my right."

8. Sex education in the Church together with the sexualized culture gives little respite from daily focus on sexuality; in fact, it may only reinforce wrong identity. Jesus says we must do nothing that might cause one of His little ones to sin (Mk. 9:42).

9. Sex education might change a child's attitude toward God. Nothing we do changes the fact that God is our Creator. As a believer in Christ, God is always our Father. However, what we do can change the way we see God and dangerously expel the Holy Spirit so that our Father/child relationship suffers or does not exist until we repent and turn away from that sin.[229] If a child is given all manner of sexual information before he or she can practice self-control and

---

229 Author's note: Some sins, especially sins against conscience, do drive out faith and the Holy Spirit. See Heb. 10:38; *Book of Concord* SA III 42-43; 1 Sam. 19:23-24; Rom. 11:19-22; 2 Pt. 2:20-22.

discernment, then might the child ask, "What kind of loving God would create me with all these sexual desires and then tell me not to fulfill them?" Do we set the child up for frustration and anger toward God? Might the child ask, "What does it matter what I do if I am assured of Jesus' love and forgiveness?" Might a child redefine God according to his or her perspective of right and wrong depending upon the circumstance?

100. But what if a parent uses the sex education model at home? You would certainly not call this cruel or abusive, would you?

Parents need not refrain from teaching sons and daughters about their bodies and answering questions appropriate for their age with innocence in mind. But using a model based on the myth that "children are sexual from birth" would be wrong. It is a sad commentary on the culture that children are inundated with sex and sexuality everywhere they turn. Rather than "talking the same talk" at home, the Christian parent is called to use a different language.

- God's Word does not reveal all the details about sex or sexuality and, when talking to their children, parents don't have to, either.

- God's Word does not turn our minds to the sensual but is generous in teaching biblical manhood and womanhood, purity and virtue, patience, kindness and selflessness. Parents help counter a sexualized culture by doing this, too.

- God knows that His children, left to themselves, lack good judgment so, for this reason, He provides the bright light of wisdom needed in a dark and frightening world. Christian parents know that immature children, left to themselves, lack good judgment so, for this reason, position themselves with Scripture in hand to lead away from danger and toward a future of hope.

> In order to deal with a sex-saturated culture, parents do not have to use models based on humanism. Instead, they can make opportunities to discuss courtship, engagement, marriage and family using all that Scripture has to offer.
>
>

- In changing cultures spanning Old through New Testament, God's Word provided parents with unchanging Truth. That Truth can be trusted by modern parents today.

Christian parents are called not to see their children as "sexual from birth," but as sons and daughters of God in Christ. In order to deal with a sex-saturated culture, parents do not have to use models based on humanism. Instead, they can make opportunities to discuss courtship, engagement, marriage and family using all that Scripture has to offer. The concepts of husband and wife "knowing" each other, conception, birth and fidelity are covered by the Holy Spirit.

Charles Spurgeon wrote,

> There is nothing so cutting as the Word of God. Keep to that. I believe also that one of the best ways of convincing men of error is not so much to denounce the error as to proclaim the truth more clearly. If a stick is very crooked, and you wish to prove that it is so, get a straight one, and quietly lay it down by its side, and when men look they will surely see the difference. The Word of God has a very keen edge about it.[230]

---

230 Quoted by Charles Spurgeon. Public domain.

CHAPTER SIXTEEN

Is there No Particular

Need for Sex Education?

101. After all of this, are we to conclude that there is no particular need for sex education?

We are in great and desperate need for instruction in purity. But, sex education—Christian or not—has failed our young people. Dr. Philip Ney is a retired professor of psychiatry who taught in five universities in Canada, Hong Kong, and New Zealand. He ran child and adolescent psychiatric units and served on school boards. Dr. Ney writes, "It is from a review of the literature and from my experience that I write this brief opinion:

1. **There is no particular need for sex education.** For many centuries there was no sex education, yet children were conceived and their parents enjoyed the process. Discovery of each other and what is pleasant in bed, on the wedding night and thereafter, is an important part of the exciting and unique pleasure that bonds the couple.

2. **Sex education inhibits pair bonding**. To educate young people about something that comes naturally robs them of the spontaneity

and joy of sex that is vitally important for pair bonding and thus family stability.[231]

3. **There is substantial evidence that the more sex education, especially on technique, the more the couple is sexually inhibited**. The greater the emphasis on sexual performance, the less communication and interpersonal intimacy there is.

4. **The more sex education, the more sexual activity and all the problems that go with that**. The introduction of sex education is well correlated with the increase in abortion, STDs, and boy-girl interpersonal problems. Good education gives people the desire to try it out or learn more experientially. Paradoxically, in that respect, current forms of sex education are good education but have the wrong results.

5. **The earlier the sex education, the earlier the sexual behavior**. Thus, sexual education is sexual titillation.

6. **In preventing disease and pregnancy, sex education has been a failure**. It has had the opposite effect in preventing young people from engaging in "risky sexual behavior."

7. **There is nothing in sex education that cannot be part of a more effective general health education**. Everything of value in sex education can be integrated with the necessary knowledge of how the body and mind work. We found that by using the young person's curiosity and letting them discover how their heart, lungs, etc., work, gives them a natural desire to protect something very precious—their body and soul.

---

231 Author's note: Pair bonding is typically understood to be a monogamous affection between male and female which (in the biblical perspective) if given time and God's blessing, will lead to marriage and procreation. Pair bonding, in a sinful world, too often happens time and time again, thus making faithfulness and commitment in marriage very difficult.

8. The sex industry profits from sex education.

9. Sex education creates mind-absorbing conflicts and preoccupations. Exposing children to sexual titillation (sex education) creates conflicts and preoccupations that interfere with their mental health, education, and personal development.

10. Sex education tends to result in mental images that interfere with the appreciation of nature and art.

11. No sex education teaches the beauty and hazards of pair bonding . . . Humans are made one flesh through sex. Thus many kinds of sexual behavior create life-long pair bonds. These interfere with the intimacy and durability of a later committed marriage . . . the more "premarital" sex the more extramarital sex.[232]

12. Many kinds of sex education, including "chastity" education, leave a young person with the impression that any kind of sex except vaginal intercourse is okay when it is not.[233]

---

232 Author's note: Christians who want to teach the beauty and hazards of pair bonding will find the science of neurobiology helpful in explaining to boys separately from girls how hormones and chemicals affect emotions and decision-making.

233 Philip G. Ney, "Sex Education," accessed 9-15-2013, www.messengers2.com. (Author's note: Enter "sex education" in the "search this site" box.)

CHAPTER SEVENTEEN

There is Hope! There is Always Hope!

102. Is it possible that we have all been deceived? In our deception, is it too easy to take a defensive posture?

Yes, it is possible, and yes, we often take a defensive posture. By virtue of being a Christian, we may feel confident that we can't be deceived. That's what Chuck Colson thought before he was neck-deep in the political scandal of Watergate. "I vividly remember," Colson writes, "that sultry summer night in 1973, in the midst of the Watergate scandal, when I, a former marine captain—often called the 'toughest of the Nixon tough guys,' the 'White House hatchet man'—broke down in tears and called out to God."[234] Colson *was* deceived. He thought that because he was a Christian, he would not be deceived by wrong thinking and poor judgment. But the master of deceit is always at work. Satan weaves deception into classes at the university, into study groups, through the internet, at the coffee-house, and into discussions with intelligent but unbelieving friends. Well-intentioned Christians have been duped into wrapping Jesus around worldly ideology, secular humanism and false science.

Sex education based on "children are sexual from birth" has been actively promoted and accepted since the 1960s. That's a long time for the lie that infants and children have sexual urges and desires to infiltrate churches, schools and homes. Childhood innocence has been assaulted and parents

---

234 Charles Colson and Nancy Pearcey, introduction to *The Problem of Evil* (Wheaton, IL: Tyndale House Publishers, Inc., 1999), x.

betrayed by people who wanted to effect social change. They wanted to determine what children learn and when they learn it, define what is normal and acceptable behavior and make sure that both church and state complied. Sex education is an insidious concept that has wormed its way into curricula, workshops, conferences, sermons, counseling, books and media. It promised to make our kids happier. They are not. It promised to make our kids healthier and safer. They are not. We have all been deceived by ideas from people who opposed God. We doubted God . . . then put ourselves in the place of God by speaking what He has not. We dared to interpret Scripture in light of "new" information that "scientists" were presenting.

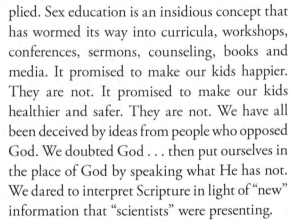

Sex education promised to make our kids happier. They are not. It promised to make our kids healthier and safer. They are not.

❖ ❖ ❖

Recognizing that we've been deceived is painful. Humiliation may turn to anger. Pride may cause us to assume a defensive posture out of loyalty to the person who deceived us or because our reputation is at stake. If a Christian brother or sister questions one of our teachings, we may initially be offended and view them as unrealistic or naïve. We may resist review or evaluation even from our peers. But prayerful and honest questions need to be asked: What is my source? Who did I believe and why? Recognizing that we have deceived others is also painful. There is guilt and regret.

103. Are there words of hope for us?

Most assuredly. For every one of us sinners there is hope. There is always hope, even in the midst of error and repetitive sin. "If we confess our sins, he is faithful and just to forgive us our sins and to cleanse us from all unrighteousness" (1 Jn. 1:9). In humility, we are strengthened by the Spirit of God who lives in us. We can express shame and regret. We can apologize for wrong teaching. We can ask for and receive forgiveness. We can squelch pride and return to the Word. We do not have to allow the deception to continue but, instead, can allow the alarm to sound.

104. But so much damage has already been done. Isn't it too late?

No, it is never too late on this earth to resist error and sin. Damage has been done but, for the sake of children—born and unborn, we can stop doing more. We don't have to be held captive by ideologies of the world or corrupted science. God's Word provides all that we need to instruct in purity and raise children to see themselves in light of their Baptism, vocation, and sanctification. King David sinned against God and hurt many people. But with broken and contrite heart, David acknowledged his sins to the Lord (Ps. 32:3-5). He received God's free grace and forgiveness. Leaving sinful ways behind, we are restored as a "vessel for honorable use" (2 Tm. 2:21).

When we begin to see ourselves as God sees us, it changes the way women see men and men see women. It changes the way we see children. It changes our behavior. It allows us to forgive those who unintentionally led us astray. It even allows us to forgive ourselves—all in Jesus' name and for His sake. At the end of Titus 2 Retreats, the women are invited to fill out an evaluation. Single, married, older and younger women typically describe the session on identity as being the most enlightening and encouraging. Why? Because, perhaps for the first time, they see themselves not in light of their sexuality, but in light of their Baptism. Because of what Jesus did for us, we are sons and daughters of God. That identity never changes, no matter our sexuality, appearance, age, health or circumstances of life. We are body and spirit: uncommon vessels for noble purpose in the hands of God. Married

> Because of what Jesus did for us, we are sons and daughters of God. That identity never changes, no matter our sexuality, appearance, age, health or circumstances of life.
>
>

or single, we are called by God to glorify Him in our vocations as male or female. In God's family, we are all brothers and sisters in Christ. What a difference identity makes!

105. What can fathers, mothers, sons, and daughters all remember?

The wisest man who ever lived wrote: "We have a little sister, and she has no breasts. What shall we do for our sister on the day when she is spoken for? If she is a wall, we will build on her a battlement of silver, but if she is a door, we will enclose her with boards of cedar" (Sg. 8:8-9).

The Lutheran Study Bible offers this explanation:

> The little sister is still very young. Her breasts have not formed. Her elder brothers have a responsibility to safeguard the chastity of their little sister until the day she will be married. The 'wall' is figurative for virginity. The girl's brothers are to continue to protect, extol, and even adorn her with all that her virtue deserves. The 'door' is figurative for promiscuity. A promiscuous girl's brothers are to do what they can to rescue her, calling her to repentance and putting a stop to her wicked ways. Families ought to curb their children's rebellion and commend them in godly living. We are to consider ourselves the keeper of our sister or brother in the faith, that the coming day of Christ's return may be a day of gladness for His people.[235]

106. What does the New Testament offer to a discussion of Christianity and sex education?

There are many verses in the New Testament that encourage purity and modesty while also warning against sensuality. But there is also a model for teaching about purity.

---

235 Commentary: *The Lutheran Study Bible*, 1076.

Titus was a young pastor who lived in the real world, too. His congregation of Cretans was enamored with unbridled excess and tolerant of new and different doctrines. Deceptive and false teachers were "upsetting whole families by teaching for shameful gain what they ought not to teach" (Ti. 1:11). Titus was in need of a model of teaching that would help the people of God reject false teaching and, at the same time, grow faithful families. St. Paul understood that this could be accomplished not by "Christianizing" the concepts, works, and opinions of false teachers, but by using a distinctively different model based solely on the Word of God. This model found in the second chapter of Titus is faithful to God's created order and is just as effective today as in the past. It respects the complementary but unique differences and vocations of male and female.

> But as for you, teach what accords with sound doctrine. Older men are to be sober-minded, dignified, self-controlled, sound in faith, in love, and in steadfastness. Older women likewise are to be reverent in behavior, not slanderers or slaves to much wine. They are to teach what is good, and so train the young women to love their husbands and children, to be self-controlled, pure, working at home, kind, and submissive to their own husbands, that the word of God may not be reviled. Likewise, urge the younger men to be self-controlled. Show yourself in all respects to be a model of good works, and in your teaching show integrity, dignity, and sound speech that cannot be condemned, so that an opponent may be put to shame, having nothing evil to say about us (Ti. 2:1-8).

Chapter two of Titus offers a model for teaching dignity, self-control, purity, and reverence in behavior. It does not lump boys and girls together as if they were one and the same. Older men are to teach younger men. Older women are to teach younger women. It is also a model with promise. God blesses the use of this model to society's benefit. It is the best way to live in anticipation of Christ's return.

> For the grace of God has appeared, bringing salvation for all people, training us to renounce ungodliness and worldly passions, and to live self-controlled, upright, and godly lives in the present age, waiting for our blessed hope, the appearing of the glory of our great God and Savior Jesus Christ, who gave himself for us to redeem us from all lawlessness and to purify for himself a people for his own possession who are zealous for good works (Ti. 2:11-14).

The biblical model of Titus 2 can be used in many ways. When I lead a Titus 2 for Life retreat, older and younger women are encouraged to see their identity not in the light of their sexuality but in the light of their Baptism and sanctified life as a woman. They learn that modern women, like Eve, have been deceived by Satan, the world, and our own sinful flesh. Deceived, we are more exposed and vulnerable. That is not the time to flaunt sexuality but humbly covet Jesus' robe of righteousness. His Word, from Old through New Testament, warns away from deception but also covers the vulnerable and repentant sinner. We don't have to remain captive to deception and the pain it causes.

107. If not sex education, then what?

Parents and grandparents can instruct children in purity by mentoring biblical manhood and womanhood. The age-appropriate chart provides a few suggestions. But first, prepare yourself!

1. Develop your parental "mission statement." What do you want your son or daughter to know about their identity in God's eyes? What do you want your child to know about sex or things of a sexual nature? Why will you strive to teach and mentor your child while also guarding the innocence of childhood?

2. Spend time with your child so that you can discern his or her questions. When your five-year-old son asks, "Where did I come

from?" don't be too quick to assume, "Oh! It's time for the full-fledged sex talk!" He might just want to know what city he came from because his friend Billy came from Denver. As the parent, you can ask questions of your child that will go a long way in determining what he or she really wants to know and is ready to hear and process, i.e. "Why are you asking me this?" or "What do you think?"

3. Follow the order of purity. When the Christian mother Laeta wondered how she could prepare her daughter for a life of purity in Christ, the Church father Jerome offered this order of instruction using God's Word: First, teach the rules of life from Proverbs, the patience and virtue of Job, the Epistles, and the prophets. Only then, and at a more mature age, is there wisdom in directing a young woman to read about marriage and the spiritual bride in Song of Songs. (With appreciation to Christopher W. Mitchell in *Concordia Commentary The Song of Songs*, 278.)

4. You may never have thought about it, but fatherhood, motherhood and grandparenthood are vocations. They are vocations that show love for God by serving others. Parents serve their children by teaching them to fear and love God, mentoring biblical manhood and womanhood, and preparing them to be good neighbors and citizens. To consider parenthood from a biblical perspective, read *God at Work* by Gene Edward Veith Jr.

5. Many resources that instruct in purity come from Christians who do not believe in original sin. With the psalmist, I believe: "In sin did my mother conceive me" (Ps. 51:5). Every Christian parent must bear in mind that even if we try to keep the walls up and the gates closed, evil still dwells within children. The purpose of instruction in purity should be to guard against temptations and attacks from the outside while we do our best with the help of the Holy Spirit to fight and clean things up on the inside, too.

Our goal is not to keep children pure, but to purify them with the grace of the Holy Spirit and guard them from daily attack. We are to help them: "Put on the whole armor of God, that [they] may be able to stand against the schemes of the devil . . . and spiritual forces of evil" (Eph. 6:10-18).

6. In every culture of madness, the unchanging Word of God gives fathers and mothers what they need to resist evil and build a future of hope. Don't let anyone tell you that you're "not progressive." Tell them you're progressing out of the insanity and chaos of this world into the sanity and order of God's Word.

7. Prepare yourselves to be uncommon parents in a highly sexualized world. Look to the example of Joshua who proclaimed, "Choose this day whom you will serve, whether the gods your fathers served in the region beyond the river, or the gods of the Amorites in whose land you dwell. But as for me and my house, we will serve the Lord" (Jsh. 24:15). Do not be faint of heart by what you see and hear. Sexualized cultures have always pressed on the Christian home. Create opportunities to talk with your child and contrast myths and half-truths with what is holy and pure.

8. Do not be afraid to question professionals and experts. If you remember, the Bereans "received the word with all eagerness, examining the Scriptures daily to see if these things were so" (Ac. 17:11). The Berean Christians questioned the Apostle Paul, the one called by God to instruct them! Contrast God's Word of purity with those who have a wall of diplomas but advocate sex education. A diploma doesn't necessarily reflect wisdom. If your discerning conscience says, "No, not for my child," listen!

9. Personalize God's call to live a life of holiness and purity. Familiarize yourself with His Word and how it contrasts "purity"

with "sensuality" or our flesh side. Then ask: Do I dress in a way that tempts the opposite sex? What books, magazines, and movies do I bring into my home? What do I look at on the internet? Do I go against the "flow" of a sexualized culture? Your child needs an example to follow.

10. As a parent, take comfort and instruction from your own Baptism and that of your child. In the flood, Noah and his family were preserved. In Baptism, Christ the Savior brings parent and child into the holy ark of the Christian Church where He marks us as His own, cleanses us from sin and, for our sake, appeals to God for good conscience (1 Pt. 3:18-22). Remind yourself of the promise of Baptismal identity and life by reading the Order of Baptism and the words of hymns. (Suggestion: *Lutheran Service Book* [Concordia Publishing House, St. Louis, MO.], page 268 and pages 594-605.)

11. As a family, pray that the Lord be in your home and drive from it all the snares of the enemy. Together, approach the Table of the Lord where, in His Body and Blood, all believers receive forgiveness, mercy, and strength to live as His sons and daughters. Develop friendships with other parents whose greater desire is to help children trust their identity as heirs of God in Christ rather than identity shaped by a restless and shallow culture.

12. Don't be ashamed by what you believe and teach; rather, be convinced that the Holy Spirit sustains you and your child. Together with your child, live as people who know that Jesus is coming again. (1 John 2:28-3:3)

MENTORING BIBLICAL MANHOOD & WOMANHOOD

GRADE LEVEL	MENTORING BOYS
Birth	Prepare yourself for raising a son in a society highly influenced by the feminist myth that "equal means being the same." One helpful resource is *Raising Boys By Design* by Gregory L. Jantz, PhD, and Michael Gurian. The authors strive to help parents learn what the Bible and brain science reveal about all that boys need in order to thrive. A second helpful resource is *Raising Real Men* by Hal and Melanie Young.
Elementary	A boy needs more time with his parents and less time with things. He needs to know God exists and that his life is not an accident. "Every son is his father's apprentice, studying not his dad's profession but his way of living, thinking, and behaving" (Meg Meeker, M.D., in *Boys Should Be Boys: 7 Secrets to Raising Healthy Sons*). A dad helps his son engage in work and fight evil. Discuss the message of great hymns such as "Onward Christian Soldiers." Use the devotional *His Mighty Warrior* by Sheri Rose Shepherd.
Elementary	John Bunyan's classic story, *Pilgrim's Progress*, anchors Gospel truth in a boy's heart. Great Commission Publications reaches boys ages 6-12 with a re-written, brilliantly illustrated edition that will inspire conversations between fathers and sons (or mothers and daughters). www.childrenspilgrimsprogress.org
Elementary	Help your son understand that his body is changing in preparation for fatherhood. What does it mean to be a father? What responsibilities come with fatherhood? Why does God want a man and a woman to marry before they become parents? Help your son learn to treat all girls in the way they want their someday wife to be treated.
Junior high	Fathers, grandfathers, and pastors offer strength and wisdom to young men in manly environments. Host a camp-out, fishing trip or weekend retreat using such resources as *Boyhood and Beyond: Practical Wisdom for Becoming a Man* by Bob Shultz. Help sons see manhood and fatherhood as vocations. Discuss the purpose of man's life: God created men to work, build, care, lay foundations, protect life, defend women and children, establish good, and resist evil. When necessary, men defend home and country. View the movies *Band of Brothers, Patriot* or *The League of Grateful Sons* (www.leagueofgratefulsons.com).

GRADE LEVEL	MENTORING BOYS
Junior high	Help sons become gentlemen. Find a copy of an early Boy Scout manual. Discuss and practice respect for women and the act of chivalry. Read the true stories of heroic men on board the Titanic (the real story is not the same as the steamy Hollywood version). Titanic men practiced the "rule of the sea" ("women and children first"). Help sons understand the sacrificial love of Ephesians 5:25.
Junior high	Fathers, take your sons apart from their sisters to offer the proverbs of life, examples of patience, and exercise in self-control. Help sons find joy in work, the very thing that man was created to do (Gen. 2:15). A healthy work ethic, along with other biblical character qualities, is discussed in *The Book of Man* by William J. Bennett and *Created for Work* by Bob Schultz.
Junior high	Follow the example of the father in Proverbs 7 and talk to sons about how to avoid girls or women who are "temptresses." What are the warning signs of a foolish woman? What are the behaviors of a wise woman who respects herself and men?
Junior high	Help sons identify the qualities of a godly father and mother. When a boy expresses interest in girls, discuss the qualities desired in their someday wife and mother of their children. How should a boy treat all girls who, most likely, will become someone's wife?
Early High School	*Fathers and Sons* is a two-book series by Douglas Bond. Volume I is *Stand Fast In the Way of Truth* and Volume II is *Hold Fast in a Broken World*. The books discuss thinking, idols, relationships, behavior, heroes, leadership, self-control, culture, and courage. Because of the shift in worship and music, many young men are less interested in attending church because they feel they have to act like women. For this reason, Douglas Bond includes lyrics (at the end of both books) in "A Young Man's Hymnal" for masculine worship and focus on spiritual warfare.
High school	When appropriate, discuss how a girl's body is different because of her creation as the "bearer of life." Her very anatomy makes her more vulnerable to bacteria and infection. In what way does a man protect the "bearer of life" before marriage? After marriage? Help sons set boundaries for behavior and hold him accountable. Let him see his father's accountability.

GRADE LEVEL	MENTORING BOYS
High school	Unmarried men abstain from sex, but not from being male. Help boys see how God calls them to reflect His glory every day as a man at school or work and in the home. Create opportunities for sons and dads to spend time together and in God's Word for men at campouts or before/after sports activities.
High school	A sexually aggressive culture too often pits girls against boys. Help sons see how they can refrain from passivity and engage themselves for good when resisting a girl's aggressiveness. Even if she is "willing," discuss how a boy can turn away from sin and, instead, guard the girl's virtue.

GRADE LEVEL	MENTORING GIRLS
Birth	Moms, prepare for the adventure of raising a daughter. Perhaps you did not have the benefit of a mentoring mother or grandmother. Perhaps you've been under the influence of feminism or resisted God's created order. Helpful resources include *Feminism: Mystique or Mistake* by Diane Passno, *Lies Women Believe and the Truth That Sets Them Free* by Nancy Leigh DeMoss, and *What Our Mothers Didn't Tell Us* by Danielle Crittenden. You may also visit www.titus2-4life.org and www.cbmw.org.
Pre-School	Be a defender of modesty and virtue. If you have a little girl, dress her like one. Even if clothing selections are limited, don't be tempted to dress your daughter like a fashion model or pop star. For your daughter's sake, refrain from dressing your little girl in "big girl" clothing, even if all the other moms are doing so. Help your daughter learn that it is not the clothes we wear that make us likeable; it is, rather, the thinking and behavior of a girl who knows God as her Father.
Elementary	Plan an etiquette night. Good manners and language are an important way of treating others like the special people God created them to be. Etiquette, every bit as important as good sportsmanship, is a skill for life useful in the home, community, school and workplace. A suggested resource is *A Little Book of Manners* by Emilie Barnes.
Elementary	Books to read with your daughter include *The Princess and the Three Knights* by Karen Kingsbury, *God's Wisdom for Little Girls* by Elizabeth George, and *The Person I Marry* by Gary and Jan Bower.

GRADE LEVEL	MENTORING GIRLS
Pre-Junior high	Help daughters see womanhood and motherhood as vocations. God said that it wasn't good for man to be alone; he needed a "helper." How does a girl/woman help a boy/man to higher standards of behavior? How does she help her husband? Male co-worker? Some material can be found at www.titus2-4life.org .
Pre-Junior high	Help daughters become women of virtue. Search the internet for Titus 2 ministries that mentor using God's Word for women. Together, mothers and daughters can practice discernment: Is what I'm reading or hearing or seeing from God or someone else? Do my friends encourage me to act like a daughter of God in Christ or to do whatever "feels right to me"?
Pre-Junior high	Do an on-line search of books for young Christian women offered by home-schooling groups. Some suggestions include *Let Me Be a Woman* by Elizabeth Elliot, *Beautiful Girlhood* by Karen Andreola and *Raising Maidens of Virtue* by Stacy MacDonald.
Junior high	Help girls understand that real life is very different from relationships portrayed by fictional TV and movie characters. Sexy look and behavior has consequences seldom explained in the media. Invite a group of moms and daughters on a "modesty" clothing expedition and invite the dads to join you for dinner that evening.
Junior high	Help girls learn skills for homemaking and how to make their someday home a warm, welcoming and safe haven for husband and children. Check out home-schooling resources on-line.
Junior high	Discuss how a girl's body is changing in preparation for becoming a mother. What does it mean to be a mother? Explain that a woman determines who the father of her child will be. She plays an integral role in determining the future of her child. What does this mean? Do not consider Planned Parenthood, SIECUS or "Go Ask Alice" as resources for your daughter's health and well-being but, instead, visit www.miriamgrossmanmd.com and www.megmeekermd.com.
Junior high	A father's love and appropriate affection of his daughter helps her to be patient and not "look for love in all the wrong places." Fathers help daughters understand what a tremendous help to boys and men a woman can be when she dresses modestly. Suggested reading includes *Strong Fathers, Strong Daughters* by Meg Meeker, M.D.

GRADE LEVEL	MENTORING GIRLS
Junior high	Prepare daughters, not to be focused on feelings and self, but on helping others and engaging the world in a positive way. Take her with you when you visit people in the hospital or nursing home. Together with her, do acts of service for those facing challenges or difficulties.
Junior high	Host a mother/daughter Bible study using *Dressing for Life: Secrets of the Great Cover-up*. Ten lessons motivate discussion on why God made clothes, the differences between men and women, emotions of embarrassment and shame, the look and behavior of love, how girls help boys make better choices, and why we wait for the white wedding dress. Look for the Bible study at www.cph.org (#LFLDFLWEB) or www.lutheransforlife.org (reproducible PDF).
Junior high	Help daughters identify the qualities of a godly father and mother. Discuss the qualities desired in their someday husband and father of their children. How can a girl act in such a way to help boys respect and honor them?
Junior high	If a popular but erotic teen magazine comes into your home, sit down with your daughter to contrast the messages of the articles, ads and photos with God's design for womanhood, purity, agape love, marriage and family.
Junior high	Replace common romance novels with books such as *Christy* (Catherine Marshall), *The Diary of Anne Frank* , and others included on the Classical Christian Education 1000 Good Books List at www.classical-homeschooling.org/celoop/1000-junior. html. Some in the early Church counseled mothers to first teach daughters the rules of life from Proverbs, the patience and virtue of Job, the Epistles, and the prophets. Only then, and at a more mature age, was there wisdom in directing a young woman to read about marriage and the spiritual bride in Song of Songs. [236]
Early high school	Be intentional with "girl talk" between mothers and daughters, grandmothers and granddaughters, aunts and nieces. One possible resource is *Girl Talk: Mother-Daughter Conversations on Biblical Womanhood* (Carolyn Mahaney and Nicole Mahaney Whitacre).

236 Author's note: This order of instruction using God's Word was offered by the Church father Jerome to a Christian mother named Laeta who wanted to raise her daughter to a life of purity in Christ. This example is shared by Christopher W. Mitchell in *Concordia Commentary The Song of Songs*, 278.

GRADE LEVEL	MENTORING GIRLS
High school	Continue discussing how a girl's body is different from a boy's because women are the "bearers of life." Explain how her anatomy makes her more vulnerable to bacteria and infection. The book *Unprotected* by Miriam Grossman, M.D., is helpful reading for moms and dads. Help a girl set boundaries for behavior. Explain ways she can help a boy by refraining from being a "temptress."
High school	Unmarried women abstain from sex, but not from being female. Help girls see how God calls them to reflect His glory every day as a woman at school or work and in the home. Create opportunities for daughters and moms to spend time together and in God's Word for women during a "girl's night only," "tea," or modesty clothing expedition.
High school	A sexualized culture, "comfort with my sexuality," and motivation by feminism to be more aggressive in sports, the workplace, or bedroom puts tremendous pressure on girls. Help daughters understand that a woman doesn't have to compete against or "rule" men but can, instead, be all God created her to be as a woman—beautifully different from a man. Two resources include *Girls Gone Wise* by Mary Kassian and *Confessions of a Boy Crazy Girl* by Paul Hendricks (book, companion guide, DVD). College-bound and mature girls who want to wait for marriage will be encouraged by *It's Not That Complicated* by Anna Sofia and Elizabeth Botkin or *What's A Girl to Do?* by Janet Folger.
High school	It may be acceptable in a "politically correct" society to place women in combat, but in what ways does this social experiment ignore the complementary differences of male and female and put purity at risk? In particular, how does it compromise the bearer of life? What does God's Word tell us? A four-session Bible study by Linda Bartlett on women in combat is available as a downloadable PDF at www.titus2-4life.org

GRADE LEVEL	MENTORING BOYS AND GIRLS
Birth	What does biblical manhood and womanhood really mean? Where do dads and moms begin in their quest to model masculinity and femininity in a world confused by gender and sexuality? A helpful website is the Council on Biblical Manhood and Womanhood (www.cbmw.org)

GRADE LEVEL	MENTORING BOYS AND GIRLS
Preschool	Worldviews are in conflict. Prepare to help your child navigate today's turbulent times by reading books such as *World Proofing Your Kids* by Lael F. Arrington. Having age-appropriate talks with your children about sex is of value, but of greater value is helping your son or daughter remember Whose they are and why their behavior and choices matter. Together with your child, practice critical thinking and become defenders of the faith you profess. This book will be a practical resource through junior high.
Preschool	Time for the "good touch, bad touch" discussion? Order the coloring book entitled *The Present* from snispel@nispelartistry.com .
Preschool	Help your child practice self-discipline when interacting with siblings and friends, in sports, in study habits, and with good manners. The highest goal in life is not satisfaction of urges and desires.
Preschool	Explain God's Genesis design for family: one man joined with one woman in marriage who have a family. Explain the child's connection to siblings, grandparents, uncles, aunts, and cousins. Families are generational. The choices made by each individual in a family affect others.
Preschool	Do things together as a family. Establish a trust between yourself and your child so that as they mature, they will know they can come to you first (rather than their peers or strangers) for wisdom.
Elementary	Engage your child in discussions about friendship. What are the most important qualities to look for in a friend? Why is faith in Jesus Christ more important than being "cool" or popular? A good friend encourages us to be the best we can be and does not tempt us to go against God or parents. If you have more than one child, stress the importance of sibling friendships. A boy, for example, who knows how to treat his sister will know how to treat female friends and, later, the girl he considers for marriage. Make yourself available for discussions about life with your child. Let them know they can bring any question, concern or fear to you at any time.
Elementary	Study biology and anatomy with your child. Help yourself and your child better know how these marvelous bodies that God has made really function. We are more inclined to take better care of ourselves when we know how miraculous our heart, lungs, skin, eyes, and ears really are and that they are entrusted to us for use to God's glory. You'll find a great many resources to help explain the human body at www.answersingenesis.org.

GRADE LEVEL	MENTORING BOYS AND GIRLS
Elementary	Teach your child his or her origin. If we don't know whose we are or from where we come, we won't know how to live as male or female on the journey to our eternal destination. A favorite source of age-appropriate creation science for parents and their children is www.answersingenesis.org .
Elementary	Remind your child that there is no sin too big for you or God to forgive. Tell them your door is always open. Sin hurts. It changes us. It can even lead us away from God. But admitting failure, confessing sin, and taking it to the Cross allows children and parents to start new each day. Remind confirmed sons and daughters of the benefits of regular Holy Communion.
Elementary	Explain your child's true identity: a creation of God and treasure of Jesus Christ, God's own possession, set apart for His holy purpose. Because of what Jesus did for us, we are adopted sons and daughters of God. Discuss the ways this affects our behavior and choices.
Elementary	Explain what happened when the first man and woman (Adam and Eve) disobeyed God and wanted to do things their way. Explain the spiritual battle between God and Satan for our body, mind, and soul. Help children understand that we can't trust our own desires, but we can trust the Holy Spirit who began a good work in us at our Baptism (1 Pet. 3:21-22).
Elementary	Explain that God created two sexes: male and female. They are equal in His sight, but not the same. They were created in different ways, at different times, and for different but complementary roles. Provide a careful study of Genesis 1-2 using the commentaries found in the Lutheran Study Bible (CPH). Other resources are www.titus2-4life.org and www.cbmw.org .
Elementary	Assure your child that he or she is "wonderfully and fearfully made." Use child-friendly resources explaining fetal development and the activity of babies in the womb. Videos of fetal development are available on-line. Preview the selection to determine what your child is ready to see. Many resources are available from www.lutheransforlife.org .
Elementary	Host a "dress up" dinner for parents and their sons and daughters. Let the dads and moms "act out" good etiquette and manners by way of a skit or drama. Include appropriate Scripture that helps explain that the way we treat one another is a way to show our love for God.

GRADE LEVEL	MENTORING BOYS AND GIRLS
Junior high	Be the scaffolding that provides sturdy and trustworthy support for your child who is God's work in progress. Your child may be academically "smart," but this isn't the same as having good judgment. Monitor activities. Be involved and ready to talk when they are.
Junior high	Explain that the biblical worldview (Creation, the Fall, & Redemption) stands in contrast to any other worldview. Familiarize your child with God's Word so he or she is equipped to recognize any message or behavior contrary to Jesus Christ. Let your children see you—the parent—in God's Word. Stand to Reason (www.str.org) and the Colson Center for Christian Worldview (www.colsoncenter.org) are two trustworthy websites to help parents be equipped for discussions with children, relatives, and neighbors about opposing worldviews.
Junior high	Talk about the fruit of the Spirit and how they contrast selfish and sensual desires of our sinful flesh and the world (Galatians 5:19-24). Help children see that Satan, who hates human life, battles God for their soul.
Junior high	Inspire your child to a life of worship. That is, indeed, what godly manhood and womanhood is all about. Worship is not just on Sunday morning in church. That's where the Christian is filled with God's Word and Sacrament and equipped for daily living. During the rest of the week, we are called to worship Him by reflecting His truth to the culture and behaving as sons and daughters of the King.
Junior high	Host cook-outs (with everyone involved in preparing food), Bible studies, and "movie" nights with other Christian families. Be intentional in contrasting the sensual relationships of TV and movies with godly and helpful friendships between men, women, boys and girls.
Junior high	Help your child learn to think rather than just "feel." Discuss and practice self-control; focus on responsibilities rather than "rights."
Junior high	Talk with sons and daughters—separately—about the qualities that a Christian looks for in a friend. Those qualities include trust, good communication, patience, kindness, selflessness, and shared worldview. Make the connection between a trusted friendship and marriage. Remember that boys and girls become curious and learn in unique ways in their own time. Try not to be intimidated by rumors that it's "not cool" for parents and children to have such honest talks. No one has a deeper interest and investment in the health and well-being of your child's body and soul than you.

GRADE LEVEL	MENTORING BOYS AND GIRLS
Junior high	Use the self-study, on-line course entitled *Teaching For Life* to help your son or daughter speak God's Word to all areas of life. Key life concepts, including chastity and purity, are offered with Bible study, short videos and opportunity for discussion. Available from www.lutheransforlife.org
High school	Talk with sons and daughters—separately—about the union between one man and one woman in the faithfulness of marriage. God brings new life and grows a family through the marital love of husband and wife. *Details of the "one flesh" union are not nearly as important as the discussion of agape love.* Marriage is more than what happens in the bedroom; it is respect, communication, selflessness, companionship, and shared faith.
High school	Trust "old fashioned" behaviors and the teachings of great-grandparents who believed in guarding the sexual innocence of children. Search for love letters written between husbands and wives married for 50 years, or married couples who endured war, poverty, and hardship. Even in marriage, "sexuality" (our flesh side) or the marital act itself does not reign supreme over a relationship of trust, friendship, enduring partnership on the hard journey of life, respect, loving communication and support, and faithfulness in joy and sorrow. Search home-school websites and classical education sites for resources on character-building, relationships, courtship, marriage, home, family, good citizenship and the culture.
High school	Parents too often develop the attitude that their older children no longer need the monitoring or personal interactions they received during childhood and adolescence. This erroneous belief has fueled sexual experimentation. Young people best protected from dangerous choices and behaviors are those who continue to spend time with and receive guidance from Christian parents. Parents are a reminder of God's created order for life. Before young people can prepare their own "nest" (marriage and family), they need to know they can count on continued mentoring in the nest of their parents.

The Conclusion of the Matter

WHO DOES GOD SAY THAT WE ARE?

The Lord identifies us in His Prayer: *"Our Father who art in heaven."* Martin Luther asks: *What does this mean? With these words God tenderly invites us to believe that He is our true Father and that we are His true children, so that with all boldness and confidence we may ask Him as dear children ask their dear father.*

Now, consider the life to which our Lord calls us in the First Petition: "Hallowed be Thy name." Luther asks: *What does this mean? God's name is certainly holy in itself, but we pray in this petition that it may be kept holy among us also. How is God's name kept holy? God's name is kept holy when the Word of God is taught in its truth and purity, and we, as the children of God, also lead holy lives according to it. Help us to do this, dear Father in heaven! But anyone who teaches or lives contrary to God's Word profanes the name of God among us. Protect us from this, heavenly Father!*

We are saints. "May you be strengthened with all power according to his glorious might, for all endurance and patience with joy, giving thanks to the Father, who has qualified you to share in the inheritance of the saints in light" (Colossians 1:11-12).

We are sinners. "The heart is deceitful above all things, and desperately sick; who can understand it?" (Jeremiah 17:9). "All have sinned and fall short of the glory of God" (Romans 3:23).

We are redeemed. "God shows His love for us in that while we were still sinners, Christ died for us" (Romans 5:8). "For by grace you have been saved through faith. And this is not your own doing; it is the gift of God, not a result of works, so that no one may boast. For we are his workmanship, created in Christ Jesus for good works, which God prepared beforehand, that we should walk in them" (Ephesians 2:8-10).

We are called by name. "But now thus says the Lord, he who created you, O Jacob, he who formed you, O Israel: Fear not, for I have redeemed you; I have called you by name, you are mine" (Isaiah 43:1).

We are the work of His hand. "But now, O Lord, you are our Father; we are the clay, and you are our potter; we are all the work of your hand" (Isaiah 64:8).

We are not our own to do as we please. "Flee from sexual immorality. Every other sin a person commits is outside the body, but the sexually immoral person sins against his own body. Or do you not know that your body is a temple of the Holy Spirit within you, whom you have from God? You are not your own, for you were bought with a price. So glorify God in your body" (1 Corinthians 6:18-20).

We are fully covered. "For he has clothed me with the garments of salvation; he has covered me with the robe of righteousness" (Isaiah 61:10). "[F]or in Christ Jesus you are all sons of God, through faith. For as many of you as were baptized into Christ have put on Christ" (Galatians 3:27).

We are not to be slaves to self, but heirs of God. "So then, brothers, we are debtors, not to the flesh, to live according to the flesh. For if you live according to the flesh you will die, but if by the Spirit you put to death the deeds of the body, you will live. For all who are led by the Spirit of God are sons of God. For you did not receive the spirit of slavery to fall back into fear, but you have received the Spirit of adoption as sons, by whom we cry, 'Abba! Father!' The Spirit himself bears witness with our spirit that we are children of God, and if children, then heirs – heirs of God and fellow heirs with Christ, provided we suffer with him in order that we may also be glorified with him" (Romans 8:12-16).

We are set apart as different. "What agreement has the temple of God with idols? For we are the temple of the living God; as God said, 'I will make my dwelling among them and walk among them, and I will be their God, and they shall be my people. Therefore go out from their midst, and be separate from them, says the Lord, and touch no unclean thing; then I will welcome you, and I will be a father to you, and you shall be sons and daughters to me, says the Lord Almighty'" (2 Corinthians 6:16-18).

We are vessels for honorable use. "Therefore, if anyone cleanses himself from what is dishonorable, he will be a vessel for honorable use, set apart as holy, useful to the master of the house, ready for every good work" (2 Timothy 2:21).

We are people with purpose. "But you are a chosen race, a royal priesthood, a holy nation, a people for his own possession, that you may proclaim the excellencies of him who called you out of darkness into his marvelous light (1 Peter 2:9).

HOW DOES GOD WANT US TO LIVE?

We are created for righteousness. "Let not sin therefore reign in your mortal body, to make you obey its passions. Do not present your members to sin as instruments for unrighteousness, but present yourself to God as those who have been brought from death to life, and your members to God as instruments for righteousness. For sin will have no dominion over you, since you are not under law but under grace. What then? Are we to sin because we are not under law but under grace? By no means! Do you not know that if you present yourselves to anyone as obedient slaves you are slaves of the one whom you obey, either of sin, which leads to death, or of obedience, which leads to righteousness? But thanks be to God, that you who were once slaves of sin have become obedient from the heart to the standard of teaching to which you were committed, and, having been set free from sin, have become slaves of righteousness. I am speaking in human terms, because of your natural limitations. For just as you once presented your members as slaves to impurity and lawlessness leading to more lawlessness, so now present your members as slaves to righteousness leading to sanctification" (Romans 6:12-19).

We are not to be conformed to the world. "I appeal to you therefore . . . to present your bodies as a living sacrifice, holy and acceptable to God, which is your spiritual worship. Do not be conformed to the world, but be transformed by the renewal of your mind, that by testing you may discern what is the will of God, what is good and acceptable and perfect" (Romans 12:1).

We put on Christ to resist self. "Let us walk properly as in the daytime, not in orgies and drunkenness, not in sexual immorality and sensuality, not in quarreling and jealousy. But put on the Lord Jesus Christ, and make no provision for the flesh, to gratify its desires" (Romans 13:13-14).

We are created to glorify God. "Whatever you do, do all to the glory of God" (1 Corinthians 10:31).

We are to be modest. "[O]n those parts of the body that we think less honorable we bestow the greater honor, and our unpresentable parts are treated with greater modesty, which our more presentable parts do not require" (1 Corinthians 12:23).

We can practice self-control. "Now the works of the flesh are evident: sexual immorality, impurity, sensuality . . . I warn you, as I warned you before, that those who do such things will not inherit the kingdom of God. But the fruit of the Spirit is . . . patience . . . self-control . . . And those who belong to Christ Jesus have crucified the flesh with its passions and desires" (Galatians 5:19).

We are called to be reverent. "But sexual immorality and all impurity or covetousness must not even be named among you, as is proper among saints. Let there be no filthiness nor foolish talk nor crude joking, which are out of place, but instead, let there be thanksgiving. For you may be sure of this, that everyone who is sexually immoral or impure, or who is covetous (that is, an idolater), has no inheritance in the kingdom of Christ and God" (Ephesians 5:3-4).

We should not be deceived. "See to it that no one takes you captive by philosophy and empty deceit, according to human tradition, according to the elemental spirits of the world, and not according to Christ" (Colossians 2:8).

We can restrain passions and desires. "For this is the will of God, your sanctification: that you abstain from sexual immorality; that each one of you know how to control his own body in holiness and honor, not in the passion of lust like the Gentiles who do not know God . . . For God has not called us for impurity, but in holiness. Therefore whoever disregards this, disregards not man but God, who gives His Holy Spirit to you" (1 Thessalonians 4:3-5).

We should help others see Christ and not ourselves. "[W]omen should adorn themselves in respectable apparel, with modesty and self-control . . . with what is proper for women who profess godliness" (1 Timothy 2:8-10).

We are in training. "Have nothing to do with irreverent silly myths. Rather train yourself for godliness; for while bodily training is of some value, godliness is of value in every way, as it holds promise for the present life and also for the life to come. The saying is trustworthy and deserving of full acceptance. For to this end we toil and strive, because we have our hope set on the living God, who is the Savior of all people, especially of those who believe" (1 Timothy 4:7-10).

We should live in anticipation of His coming. "But as for you, teach what accords with sound doctrine. Older men are to be sober-minded, dignified, self-controlled, sound in faith, in love, and in steadfastness. Older women likewise are to be reverent in behavior, not slanderers or slaves to much wine. They are to teach what is good, and so train the young women to love their husbands and children, to be self-controlled, pure, working at home, kind, and submissive to their own husbands, that the word of God may not be reviled. Likewise, urge the younger men to be self-controlled . . . For the grace of God has appeared, bringing salvation for all people, training us to renounce ungodliness and worldly passions, and to live self-controlled, upright, and godly lives in the present age, waiting for our blessed hope, the appearing of the glory of our great God and Savior Jesus Christ, who gave Himself for us to redeem us from all lawlessness and to purify for Himself a people for His own possession who are zealous for good works" (Titus 2:1-2; 11-14).

We are called to be holy. "As obedient children, do not be conformed to the passions of your former ignorance, but as He who called you is holy, you also be holy in all your conduct, since it is written, 'You shall be holy, for I am holy'" (1 Peter 1:14-16).

We must be alert to false teachers. "But false prophets also arose among the people, just as there will be false teachers among you, who will secretly bring in destructive heresies, even denying the Master who brought them, bringing upon themselves swift destruction. And many will follow their sensuality, and because of them the way of truth will be blasphemed . . . For, speaking loud boasts of folly, they entice by sensual passions of the flesh those who are barely escaping from those who live in error. They promise them freedom, but they themselves are slaves of corruption. For whatever overcomes a person, to that he is enslaved. For if, after they have escaped the defilements of the world through the knowledge of our Lord and Savior Jesus Christ, they are again entangled in them and overcome, the last state has become worse for them than the first. For it would have been better for them never to have known the way of righteousness than after knowing it to turn back from the holy commandment delivered to them" (2 Peter 2:1-2; 18-21).

We can be confident in Christ. "And now, little children, abide in him, so that when he appears we may have confidence and not shrink from him in shame at his coming. If you know that he is righteous, you may be sure that everyone who practices righteousness has been born of him" (1 John 2:28-29).

We have hope in His purity. "Beloved, we are God's children now, and what we will be has not yet appeared; but we know that when he appears we shall be like him, because we shall see him as he is. And everyone who thus hopes in him purifies himself as he is pure" (1 John 3:2).

BIBLIOGRAPHY

B4U-ACT. Accessed October 17, 2013, http://www.b4uact.org.

Bancroft, John. *Sexual Development in Childhood*. Bloomington: Indiana University Press, 2003.

Bartlett, Linda. *The Failure of Sex Education*. Lutherans For Life, 2005 (www.cph.org LFL601B).

"Be Holy, for I Am Holy." Commentary. *The Lutheran Study Bible English Standard Version*. St. Louis, MO: Concordia Publishing Company, 2009.

Bennett, William J. *The Book of Man: Readings on the Path to Manhood*. Nashville, TN: Thomas Nelson, 2011.

Burrows, Lynette. "Worst Sexualisation of Children is Happening in Schools." Presentation to the Society for the Protection of Unborn Children (SPUC) Safe at School "Sex Education as Sexual Sabotage" meeting in Westminster, London. Accessed January 9, 2012, http://www.spuc-director.blogspot.com, Archives: Saturday, 10 December 2011.

Buth, Lenore. *How To Talk Confidently with Your Child about Sex*. Book 6 of the *Learning About Sex for the Christian Family* series. St. Louis, Missouri: Concordia Publishing House, 1998.

Calderone, Mary. "Fetal Erection and Its Message to Us." *SIECUS Report,* May-July 1983.

Calderone, Mary and James Ramey. *Talking with Your Child About Sex.* New York: Ballantine Books, 1982.

Colapinto, John. *As Nature Made Him: The Boy Who Was Raised as a Girl.* New York, NY: Harper Collins Publishers, 2000.

Center for Positive Sexuality, accessed September 21, 2013, http://www. positivesexuality.org/?p=468.

Chambers, Claire. *The SIECUS Circle: A Humanist Revolution.* Belmont, Massachusetts: Western Islands Press, 1977.

Colson, Charles and Nancy Pearcey. *The Problem of Evil.* Wheaton, IL: Tyndale House Publishers, 1999.

Coulson, William. "Values in the Classroom." Personal notes taken by author during Coulson presentation at St. Paul Lutheran Church in Ames, Iowa, April 13, 1991.

Coulson, William. "We Overcame Their Traditions, We Overcame Their Faith." Interview by William Marra, *The Latin Mass,* Vol. 3, No. 1 (January-February 1994), Accessed August 15, 2012, http://www.scribid. com/doc/3983186/Coulson.

Donovan, Charles and Robert Marshall. *Blessed Are the Barren: the Social Policy of Planned Parenthood.* San Francisco, CA: Ignatius Press, 1991.

Donovan, Charles. "The History of Sex Education in the U.S." Presentation to the Human Life International's National Sex Education

Conference in St. Louis, Missouri, October 21-23, 1994, Accessed November 12, 2012, http://www.vidahumana.org/english/family/sexed-history.html.

Feucht, Oscar E., Harry G. Coiner, Alfred von Rohr Sauer, and Paul G. Hansen. *Sex and the Church*. St. Louis, Missouri: Concordia Publishing House, 1961.

Franz, Wanda. "Sex and the American Teenager." *The World & I*, Vol. 4, No. 9. Washington, D.C: *The Washington Times* Corporation, September 1989.

Grossman, Miriam. *You're Teaching My Child What? A Physician Exposes the Lies of Sex Education and How They Harm Your Child*. Washington, D.C.: Regnery Publishing, 2009.

Grossman, Miriam. *Sense & Sexuality*. Herndon, VA: Clare Booth Luce Institute, 2009.

Grossman, Miriam. *Unprotected*. New York, NY: Penquin Group U.S.A., 2006.

Halley's Bible Handbook. Grand Rapids, MI: Zondervan Publishing House, 1965.

Heimbach, Daniel R. *True Sexual Morality: Recovering Biblical Standards for a Culture in Crisis*. Wheaton, IL: Crossway, 2004.

Hendershott, Anne. "The Postmodern Pedophile." *Public Discourse*, A Publication of The Witherspoon Institute, December 20, 2011. Accessed July 26, 2013, http://www.thepublicdiscourse.com/2011/12/4440/.

Institute for the Advanced Study of Human Sexuality (IASHS), http://www.iashs.edu/fags.html and http://www.iashs.edu/courses.html.

Jantz, Gregory L. and Michael Gurian. *Raising Boys by Design*. Colorado Springs, CO: Waterbrook Press, 2013.

Kasun, Jacqueline R. "Sex Education: The Hidden Agenda." *The World and I*, Vol. 4, No. 9, Washington D.C.: *The Washington Times* Corporation, September 1989.

Kinsey, Alfred J., Wardell Pomeroy, Clyde Martin. *Sexual Behavior in the Human Male*. Philadelphia, Pennsylvania: W.R. Saunders Co., 1948.

Kinsey's Paedophiles. A British Documentary. Accessed October 11, 2013, http://www.youtube.com/watch?v=uvc-1d5ib50.

Kirkendall, Lester. *Sex Education*, SIECUS Study Guide No. 1. New York: SIECUS Publications Office, January 1969.

Kolb, Erwin J. *Parents Guide to Christian Conversation About Sex*. St. Louis, MO: Concordia Publishing House, 1967.

Legato, Marianne J., founder of Partnership for Gender Specific Medicine at Columbia University. Accessed September 27, 2013, http://www.nlm. nih.gov/changingthefaceofmedicine/physicians/bibliography-197.html.

Lewis, C.S. *Mere Christianity*. New York, N.Y: Touchstone, Macmillian Publishing Co., 1952. Copyright renewed 1980 by Arthur Owen Barfield.

Love, Sex and God. Book 5 of the *Learning About Sex for the Christian Family* series. St. Louis, Missouri: Concordia Publishing House, 2008.

Luther's Small Catechism. St. Louis, MO: Concordia Publishing House, 1986.

Matthews, Timothy. "The Frankfurt School: Conspiracy to Corrupt." Catholic Insight, 2009. Accessed on-line publication November 20, 2011, http://www.CatholicInsight.com. Accessed Scribd publication August 5, 2013, http://www.scribd.com/doc/28282102/ The-Frankfurt-School-Conspiracy-to-Corrupt-by-T-Matthews.

Miller, Shirley. "Christian Family Life Education." Margaret Sanger Center International, 2001. Accessed July 9, 2013.

Mitchell, Christopher W. *The Song of Songs – Concordia Commentary*. St. Louis, MO: Concordia Publishing House, 2003.

Money, John. *PAIDIKA: The Journal of Paedophilia*, Vol. 2, No. 3, Spring 1991.

Money, John. "Pedophilia Opinions." Accessed June 20, 2013, http://www. wikipedia.orgwiki/John_Money.

Ney, Philip G. "Sex Education." Posted April 18, 2008, Accessed September 20, 2012, http://www.messengers2.com.

Reisman, Judith A. *Kinsey: Crimes and Consequences*. Crestwood, Kentucky: The Institute for Media Education, Inc., 2000.

Reisman, Judith A., Edward Eichel. Kinsey, Sex and Fraud: The Indoctrination of a People. Edited by John H. Court and J. Gordon Muir. Lafayette, Louisiana: Huntington House, 1990.

Reisman, Judith A. *Sexual Sabatoge*. Washington, D.C.: WorldNetDaily, 2010.

Reisman, Judith A. *Stolen Honor, Stolen Innocence* (formerly *Kinsey: Crimes and Consequences*) Orlando, FL.: Liberty Counsel, New Revolution Publishers, 2012.

Richards, Valerie. "Sex and Social Engineering." Family and Youth Concerns (The Responsible Society, 1986), Accessed May 20, 2012, http:// www.amen.ie/downloadsSEXANDSOCIAL-ENGINEERING.pdf.

SAR (Sexual Attitude Restructuring) technique explained by Martha Tara Lee. Accessed September 21, 2013, http://www.youtube.com/watch?v=bFg!75Cnly4.

Schmidt, Alvin J. *How Christianity Changed the World*. Grand Rapids, Michigan: Zondervan, 2004.

Sex Science, http://www.sexscience.org/resources and http://www.sexscience.or/continuing-education.

"Sexy Babies: How Sexualization Hurts Girls." Accessed December 20, 2013, http://www.aboutkidshealth.ca.

Sexuality. Accessed July 9, 2013, http://www.definitions.net/definition/sexuality.

Sexuality. Accessed July 9, 2013, http://www.wikipedia.org/wiki/Human_sexuality.

Sexuality. Accessed July 9, 2013, http://www.merriam-webster.com/dictionary/sexuality.

Sexuality. Accessed July 9, 2013, http://www.plannedparenthood.org/health-topics/sexuality-4323.htm.

Sexuality Information and Education Council of the U.S. (SIECUS), Guidelines for Comprehensive Sexuality Education, 2004. Accessed June 22, 2013, http://www.siecus.org/pubs/guidelines/guidelines.pdf.

Sonnenberg, Roger. "Sexuality: What Congregations, Parents, Pastors and Teachers Need to Teach." *Issues in Christian Education*, Vol. 46, No. 2, http://www.cune.edu/about/publications/issues-in-christian-education-issues-spring-2013.

Sonnenberg, Roger. "The Gift of Sexuality." *The Lutheran Witness*, October 2013.

Sowell, Thomas. "Indoctrinating the Children." *Forbes*, February 1, 1993.

Stonestreet, John. "The Power of Prudence: No Hindsight Needed." Accessed May 24, 2012, http://www.breakpoint.org.

The Children of Table 34: the True Story Behind Alfred Kinsey's Infamous Sex Research. A Documentary with companion booklet by Robert H. Knight. Washington, D.C: The Family Research Council, 1994.

The Humanist Manifesto I & II. Edited by Paul Kurtz. Amherst, N.Y: Prometheus Books, 1973.

Veith, Gene Edward. "Sex and the Evangelical Teen." http://www.world-mag.com/2007/08/sex-and-the-evangelical-teen, posted August 11, 2007.

Wessler, Martin. *Christian View of Sex Education*. St. Louis, MO: Concordia Publishing House, 1986.

Witt, Elmer. *Life Can Be Sexual*. St. Louis, MO: Concordia Publishing House, 1967.

Wood-Allen, Mary. *What A Young Woman Ought to Know* (Purity and Truth, Self and Sex Series). Philadelphia, PA: Vir Publishing Co., 1898 by Sylvanus Stall.

Yuan, Christopher and Angela. *Out of a Far Country*. Colorado Springs, CO: Waterbrook Press, 2011.

SOME ADDITIONAL RESOURCES

FOR PARENTS

ARTICLES

"Against Heterosexuality: The Idea of Sexual Orientation Is Artificial and Inhibits Christian Witness" by Michael W. Hannon, www.firstthings.com/article/2014/03/against-heterosexuality.

Articles about identity and behavior in *LifeDate*, the Quarterly Journal of Lutherans For Life, by Linda Bartlett: "From Father to Son" (Winter 2009), "Biblical Manhood and Womanhood" (Spring 2011), "Life in the Real World" (Spring 2012), "Purity Cannot Be Stolen" (Summer 2012), "Men and Their Identity" (Spring 2013), "What Makes Us Human?" (Summer 2013), "Cohabitating Seniors" (Summer 2013), "View Children the Way God Does" (Fall 2013), "Letter to a Friend Caught in Sexual Sin" (Winter 2013), and "Men and Women, Worship and Life" (Spring 2014). www.lutheransforlife.org

"Homosexuality & Child Sexual Abuse." The Family Research Council. www.frc.org

"The Top Ten Myths About Homosexuality" by Peter Sprigg. The Family Research Council. (A dispute of Kinsey's "science".) www.frc.org

"What's Behind Our Girl-Harming Culture?" by Dale O'Leary. MercatorNet. Wednesday, 20 June 2012. www.mercatornet.com (Search by title.)

BIBLE STUDIES

Dressing for Life: Secrets of the Great Cover-up by Linda Bartlett. (This ten-lesson study is for young women and the mothers who mentor them. It is available in reproducible PDF format.) www.cph.org #LFLDFLWEB.)

Men, Women and Relationships: Building a Culture of Life Across the Generations by Linda Bartlett. (This 12-lesson study with leader's guide is for college-age and older and is appropriate for individual use, men's groups, women's groups, or husbands and wives.) www.cph.org #LFL901BS.

BOOKS

And the Bride Wore White, Secret Keeper, and *Six Ways to Keep the Little in Your Girl* by Dannah Gresh, www.purefreedom.org

Boys Should Be Boys (7 Secrets to Raising Healthy Sons) by Meg Meeker, M.D. (Dr. Meeker explains how parents can influence, guard and help control what lies between the skull and heart of their son: his mind.) www.amazon.com

Christian Modesty and the Public Undressing of America by Jeff Pollard. (This historical and Scripturally-based discussion of clothing, most especially the swim suit, sheds light on modesty and its connection to purity.) www.amazon.com or www.christianbook.com

The Purity Principle by Randy Alcorn, www.amazon.com

BROCHURES

Fig Leaves Are Not Enough (Why do we wear clothes?) by Linda Bartlett. www.cph.org #LFL612B.

How to Mentor a Foolish Woman (Titus 2 for Life Satire) by Linda Bartlett. (This discussion-starter for discerning moms is based on the wisdom of Proverbs 14:1.) www.titus2-4life.org (Click on "Resources.")

Mystery of the Mixed Message by Linda Bartlett. (For high school students.) www.cph.org #LFL610T.

Purity, Mystery and Modesty by Linda Bartlett. (A discussion of holy living and God's design for parenting.) www.cph.org #LFL903T.

Real Love, Real Life. Lutherans For Life. (Facts about agape love, purity vs. "safe sex," sexually-transmitted diseases, fetal development and abortion statistics for parents to use with their children.) www.cph.org #LFL615T.

Why Not Just Live Together? by Linda Bartlett. (For college-age and older.) www.cph.org #LFL607T.

DVDs

The Agenda: Grinding America Down. (An award-winning film that connects the dots from the Frankfort School to present day and helps to explain what has happened to the family, church, education and American culture.) www.AgendaDocumentary.com

The Kinsey Syndrome: Uncovering the Truth Behind the Father of the Sexual Revolution. (Why has the truth about Kinsey been suppressed for so long? What can Americans do to make a difference?) www.thekinseysyndrome.com

WEBSITES

Kids Free 2 B Kids. (Committed to helping children develop their full potential without exposure to sexualized imagery before they are developmentally ready to process it.) www.kf2bk.com

Mercatornet - "Navigating modern complexities." (Mercatornet provides parents with lively news promoting human dignity and offers information on sex and society, marriage, family, bioethics, technology, and life issues consistent with the biblical worldview.) www.mercatornet.com

Society for the Protection of Unborn Children. (Information for parents concerned about the dignity and education of their children.) www.spuc.org.uk.

The Council on Biblical Manhood and Womanhood. www.cbmw.org

ABOUT THE AUTHOR

Linda Bartlett is the wife of Paul, mother of Jon (Angie) and Josh (Alison), and grandmother of six grandsons and two granddaughters.

Linda is the founder of Titus 2 for Life, a grassroots outreach that strives to mentor Biblical manhood and womanhood. She is the former national president of Lutherans For Life (LFL), co-founder of LFL of Iowa, and co-founder and president of The Lighthouse Center of Hope in Iowa Falls, IA. She is the author of the Bible studies *Men, Women & Relationships* and *Dressing for Life: Secrets of the Great Cover-up*; the devotionals *Into His Loving Care* for parents who have miscarried and *Not Alone* for single moms; *The Failure of Sex Education*, a resource for parents; and numerous articles and brochures on Biblical womanhood, modesty and purity (Lutherans For Life). She served as editor of Living magazine. Linda is the author of the Titus 2 for Life Study Guide and leads Titus 2 Retreats across the country (www.titus2-4life.org) She blogs at www.ezerwoman.wordpress.com and reminds women of Jesus' "Tender Mercies" at www.aftertheabortion.wordpress.com.

By vocation, Linda is a "helper." She is a listener, encourager and ally. Most of her learning adventures have been in the classroom of real life. It is there that she learned why our identity matters. During her sons' school years, Linda was an involved parent working to identify the source and consequences of sex education. She has spoken to middle and high school assemblies in both private and public schools and presented the message of biblical manhood and womanhood to mothers and daughters, fathers and sons. From home or locations across the country, Linda shares the hope and healing of Jesus Christ with women who grieve their abortion. She was instrumental in helping to launch the post-abortion ministry of Word of Hope (www.word-of-hope.org). With a desire to connect people who want to positively affect the culture, she has organized events for parents, pastors, single moms, pregnancy centers, young people, and grassroots volunteers. Linda served as chairman of the LCMS Sanctity of Life Task Force, on the board of Lutheran Family Service of Iowa, and as a high school youth leader. Traveling the country and working within the Church and community have given her opportunity to dialogue with biblical thinkers and contrast the world with God's Word. In all seasons and circumstances, Linda is encouraged to remember her Baptism which bestowed her true identity as a daughter of God in Jesus Christ.

Book website: www.ouridentitymatters.com
Blog: www.caseofmistakenidentity.wordpress.com

Made in the USA
Middletown, DE
03 August 2016